Pelican Books
Advisory Editor for Linguistics: David Crystal

Phonetics

J. D. O'Connor is Reader in Ph at
University College London. He was born in 1919
and was a pupil of the great phonetician, Daniel
Jones, at University College. His most recent
works are the revised second edition of
Intonation of Colloquial English (with G. F. Arnold)
and *Better English Pronunciation,* as well as two
associated phonetic readers. J. D. O'Connor's
main research interests are the intonation,
rhythm and syllabic structure of English and
other languages.

Phonetics

J. D. O'Connor

Penguin Books

741417

Penguin Books Ltd, Harmondsworth,
Middlesex, England
Penguin Books Inc., 7110 Ambassador Road,
Baltimore, Maryland 21207, U.S.A.
Penguin Books Australia Ltd, Ringwood,
Victoria, Australia

First published 1973

Made and printed in Great Britain by
Hazell Watson & Viney Ltd,
Aylesbury, Bucks
Set in Monotype Times

Contents

Foreword

The sounds of speech are all around us. We use them, we hear them, we enjoy and suffer from them, and in general we know remarkably little about them. Not from lack of interest or percipience, since we are in many ways fascinated by the sounds that we and others utter and immensely skilful at discriminating and interpreting them, but rather from the inherent difficulty of coming to grips with anything so transient. It seems worthwhile, therefore, to attempt to explain how speech sounds can to some extent be pinned down, so that we may have a firmer foundation for understanding how sounds contribute to the process of communication.

I have tried in this book to give a simple and practical introduction to the nature and use of sound in language. If I have succeeded it will be mainly due to the tradition of pragmatism which characterizes the Department of Phonetics at University College London. I have been associated with that department for more than thirty years as student and teacher; its tradition has largely shaped my attitudes, and I recognize very clearly the great debt I owe both to my predecessors and to my past and present colleagues. In so close-knit a community views are shaped by daily contact, so that a great deal of what this book contains is a product of their interest and expertise, and I thank them warmly for their contribution.

In phonetics, as in any other subject, there are various schools of thought whose views sometimes conflict and sometimes coincide. I have made occasional reference to these, but have not attempted to set out all possible current approaches to the theory of pronunciation because this book does not seem to me the place for that. Yet I do not mean to imply any inferiority in other views; I simply believe that the traditional approach which I have used provides the simplest introduction to the subject.

I have relied heavily upon published work in the field, and to all the authors cited in the list of publications consulted I make grateful acknowledgement for the information and enlightenment they have provided. It is customary to associate one's co-workers with any merit a book may have whilst assuming responsibility for its defects. I do this, too, but in no routine spirit: without them this book could not have been written.

1. The Role of Sound in Communication

When one person wants to convey a message to another he can use a variety of means. He may write it down on a piece of paper (parchment, wood, bone, clay, wax, stone) and hand it over; he may transmit it in sign language, as deaf mutes do; he may stand on one alp and wave or drape flags in a pre-arranged way to the recipient standing on another; or he may prefer to flash a mirror. All these are visual means. On the other hand the message may be passed by audible means, by fog-horn, morse-key or drum; or it may simply be spoken: transmitted by word of mouth.

In all ages, even the most literate, the vast majority of messages have been spoken: transmitted by means of sound generated by certain of the bodily organs available to every normal human being. The spoken word is, and is likely to remain, by far the most frequent medium of communication between man and his neighbour and it is, to this extent at least, the most important such medium. But since other media are also available – flags, drums, gestures, writing – and since the same message may be passed by any of these media, it would be wrong to argue that speech is at the centre of communication. Whilst the medium may vary, the message does not, and it is therefore the message itself, independent of the means of transmission, which is the heart of the matter. In this sense at least the medium is precisely *not* the message.

It is necessary to acknowledge the centrality of 'the message' in order to be able to place phonetics – the study of the sounds of spoken language – in the context of linguistic studies generally. Phonetics is concerned with the human noises by which 'the message' is actualized or given audible shape: the nature of those noises, their combinations, and their functions in relation to the message. Figure 1 may help to clarify our ideas about the domain of phonetics in the communication process; it is a simple model of a single act of communication, the passing of one message from a speaker to a listener.

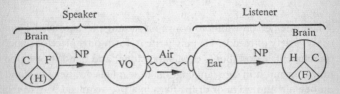

C – Creative Function
F – Forwarding Function
H – Hearing Function
NP – Nervous Pathways
VO – Vocal Organs

Figure 1: Stages in the passing of a spoken message

The act of communication starts in the brain of the speaker and we may think of the speaker's brain as having two distinct functions for our purposes: a creative function and a forwarding function.

Creative function. This is the central function and it is through it that the message is conceived and formed. Stored in the brain is a profound knowledge of the way in which the language operates, the rules of the game, as it were: this knowledge is of many kinds, all derived from our experience of operating the language as both speaker and listener from earliest childhood. We know the permissible grammatical patterns and the vocabulary items which can be used to fill out those patterns; we know what the voices of a man, a woman, a child sound like; we know what a good many individuals sound like; we have at least some knowledge of dialects other than our own; we know what the general probabilities are of one word or expression following another; and so on. This does not mean that each of us is capable of codifying all this stored information – that is the business of writers of grammars, dictionaries, etc. – but we are able to make use of it. Nor does it mean that each of us has exactly the same information stored away: almost certainly every individual's store is to a greater or lesser extent different from everyone else's. But if we are to communicate efficiently there must be a sufficient stock of common information at our disposal.

There are three distinguishable phases of the creative function. First, a need to communicate arises; this may be in response to some outside event or entirely to some inner thought process. Suppose that a wife sees her husband finish his first cup of tea at the tea-table. She may simply take his cup and refill it, or she may decide to initiate a message which will lead to that happening. If she decides on a message, she must then decide, secondly, what medium to use, speech, writing, sign language, etc.; this will often be determined by the circumstances of the case, but notice our frequent hesitation between telephone and letter. Thirdly, a decision must be made as to the form the message will take. Is it to be imperative (*Have another cup*)? Or interrogative (*Would you like another cup?*) If imperative, should it be: *Pass your cup*, or *Have some more*? And so on. We make these decisions of form very rapidly and indeed without consciously thinking of them at all in most cases, and the message is ready formed. The forwarding function of the brain now takes over.

Forwarding function. The part of the brain which is concerned with controlling muscular movement now sends out patterned instructions in the form of nervous impulses along the nervous pathways connecting the brain to the muscles of the organs responsible for speech sounds, the lungs, larynx, tongue, etc. These instructions call upon the muscles concerned to perform various delicate combinations and sequences of movement which will result in the 'right' sounds being emitted in the 'right' order.

Vocal organs. At this stage the neurological activity which has been taking place in the brain and along the nervous pathways is transformed into muscular activity: the lungs are contracted, the vocal cords vibrate, the tongue wags, the jaw goes up or down, the lips part or come together and so on. All these actions are most beautifully and accurately controlled – learning the coordination of movement required for the emission of speech is probably the most stupendous feat of muscular skill any one of us will ever perform. The result of these movements is to set air in motion, air from the lungs which is acted upon, impeded, obstructed, released by the vocal organs so that it comes out from the mouth in a sequence of complex waves of pressure. A second transformation has now taken place, from movement of muscles to movement of air. The movement of the lung air is now transferred in the same form to the outer air and the waves of varying air pressure spread out in every direction around us, gradually growing weaker as the distance increases and their original energy is absorbed. This moving air eventually impinges on the ear of the listener, if he is near enough.

The ear. The ear-drum is sufficiently sensitive for the air pressure waves to cause it to move in and out in a way closely related to the movement of the air itself. This further transformation – from air movement back to the organic movement of the ear-drum – is now followed by a final transformation, in the inner ear, of this organic movement back to neurological activity, which results in nerve impulses being sent along the nervous pathways connecting the ear to the listener's brain. The listener's brain may also be thought of as having two functions, a hearing function and again a creative function.

Hearing function. The impulses coming from the ear are accepted as sound sequences of constantly changing quality and characteristic length, pitch, loudness. The listener *hears* the message but does not yet *understand* it. This is what happens when we listen to a foreign language that we don't know: we hear the sounds but we do not receive the message. To understand the message the listener must interpret the sounds he hears in the light of the stored knowledge in his brain; he not only hears the sounds but recognizes them and matches them up with what he knows to be possible in the language at various levels, and finally selects the most likely meaning in all the circumstances; and this genuinely creative process is another part of the creative function of the brain discussed earlier.

The process of matching starts with the sounds themselves. If, at the stage of simple reception by the brain, I hear a sound or a combination of sounds which my stored knowledge tells me is not permitted in the language, I immediately reject the data and look around for something similar which is permitted. For example, if what I actually hear is this: *His name is Stveet*, I reject the *v* because I know from previous experience that *stv* is not a sequence used at the beginning of English words and I either replace it by something – probably *r* – which makes the sequence acceptable or I request a repetition. Until the brain has arrived at a satisfactory interpretation of the incoming sounds – satisfactory in the limited sense that they are at least English sounds in English sequences – no progress can be made, but since we are very ingenious at this game of matching and interpreting we very quickly go through the necessary processes, and allow the result to go forward to be matched at other levels. We may of course err in the match we make, but this will not be because we accept a non-English possibility; it will be because we select the wrong English one. There is a London pronunciation of the name Poole which makes it sound like what I would say in pronouncing the name Paul. If, because of this pronunciation, I wrongly accept the name as Paul, my error stems from using the wrong, but possible, dialectal frame of reference and not from accepting a non-permitted item. Exactly the same is true if an English pronunciation of *ballet dancer* is misinterpreted by an American listener as *belly dancer*; given an American pronunciation framework *belly dancer* is the more likely solution.

The accepted sound train must now be repeatedly matched with the possibilities at other levels. If what we hear (or what we think we hear) is: *The man are on strike*, we cannot accept it on the grammatical level: it is not a permitted form; and we therefore reconstruct it, probably as: *The men are on strike*, possibly as: *The man is on strike*, both being equally acceptable grammatically. It should be noticed that this is a grammatical decision and not a decision about sounds – the sound sequence represented by *man are* is perfectly acceptable: it is the grammar which is not. Equally, matching at the level of vocabulary is independent both of sound and grammar. If we hear: *He swallowed it hook, line and tinker*, we reject and reconstruct it because of our knowledge of what words are likely to go with what, not for grammatical or phonetic reasons.

Even when matching has been carried out satisfactorily at the different levels within the language itself, there is still more to be done. The utterance, which is now linguistically acceptable, must now be matched first against the situation in which it is functioning, and second against the general cultural background. The situation or context may be purely verbal or it may be a matter of surrounding things, people, events. There is nothing wrong linguistically with: *Come and see me at three o'clock*, but in the context: *I can't see you at three o'clock, so . . .* , there is a mismatch between the two parts, and the utterance must therefore be rejected. Similarly, if it is a question of an appointment the same day, and the time at the moment of speaking is 3.30, there is a lack of match between: *Come and see me at three o'clock* and the non-verbal situation. Finally, if the linguistically unexceptionable utterance, *My wives just told me about it*, occurs in a generally monogamous culture it will be rejected – or queried – because of failure to match cultural expectations.

The passing of a spoken message, then, involves a great deal of activity beyond the production, transmission and reception of sound. The sound is not the message, but it is what gives the message shape in spoken communication, and it is worth study simply for that reason; in speech we rely very heavily upon sound to make plain the significant distinctions of meaning which can be made by the more central operations of grammar and vocabulary. A word, when it is pronounced, must have a particular sound-shape if it is to be recognized, just as it must have a particular letter-shape when written. The spoken word *dog* must have a recognizable *d*-sound at the beginning, *o*-sound in the middle, and *g*-sound at the end, and if we use a different sound at any of these places the word will lose its shape and not be recognized; replace the *d*-sound by a *b*-sound and we hear *bog*, which is different in meaning, or replace the final *g*-sound by a *v*-sound and we hear *dov*, which we do not recognize at all. Furthermore, the constituent sounds must be in a particular order: *dog* is not *god* and still less *ogd* or *dgo*. In a language like English, stress too may help to give the word its individual shape: the word *forebear* is distinguished in pronunciation from *forbear* by the former having its first syllable stressed and the latter its second. Stress may also distinguish a word functioning as a noun, like *incense*, from an otherwise similar word functioning as a verb, like *incense* (anger).

Differences of pronunciation also allow us to distinguish longer forms such as *grey tape* from *great ape*; or *my tight shoes* from *might I choose*. And at the level of whole sentences, patterns of pitch (or intonation) permit distinctions which are not usually made in writing, such as: *I thought it was going to rain*, (but it didn't) and: *I thought it was going to rain*, (and it did).

It should be noticed at this point that not *all* the distinctions of grammar and vocabulary are reflected in sound: *taut* and *taught* (and for some people *tort*) are identical, as are *by*, *buy* and *bye*, and the noun *intent* and the adjective *intent*. Equally *a tack* and *attack* are rarely distinguished in pronunciation any more than ambiguous sentences such as *Buy me a present* (Buy it to give me or buy it as my agent). Yet by the nature of things *most* of the meaningful distinctions of the language must be capable of being given distinctive shape in sound, and it is this close dependence of sound and meaning which justifies the study of speech sounds, i.e. phonetics.

If we now return to Figure 1 (p. 10) we can delimit the areas of interest to the phonetician.

He is interested in the way in which the air is set in motion, in the movements of the speech organs and the coordination of these movements in the production of single sounds and trains of sounds. His interest at this point borders upon the study of anatomy and physiology, and his tools for investigating just what the speech organs do are tools which are used in these fields: direct observation, where possible, e.g. of lip-movement, jaw-movement and some tongue-movement; X-ray photography, either still or moving, for recording positions and movements of the tongue, soft palate and vocal cords; observation and/or photography through mirrors, as in the laryngoscopic investigation of vocal cord movement; and electromyography, or the detection and measurement of the small electrical potentials associated with muscle contraction at relevant points in the vocal tract. This whole area of interest is generally known as *articulatory phonetics* (see Chapter 2).

He is interested in the way in which the air vibrates between the mouth of the speaker and the ear of the listener. In this he is close to the physicist studying acoustics, and the tools he uses are such as will enable him to measure and analyse the movement of air in the terms of physics. This generally means introducing a microphone into the communication chain, converting the air movement into corresponding electrical activity and analysing the result in terms of frequency of vibration and amplitude of vibration in relation to time. This is the domain of *acoustic phonetics* (see Chapter 3).

He is interested in the hearing process; not so much in the physiological working of the ear, or the nervous activity between the ear and the brain, but more in the sensation of hearing, which is brain activity. Sounds may be characterized just as well in terms of hearing as by their articulatory or acoustic specifications. The means by which and the extent to which we discriminate sounds are relevant here, as well as the sensations of pitch, loudness, length and sound quality; and the methods by which we investigate these are the methods of experimental psychology. Particular interest is centred on the hearer's reaction to known physical stimuli fed into his ear. This is the domain of *auditory phonetics* (see Chapter 4).

The three facets of phonetic study mentioned so far are all general in scope; that is to say they may be applied impartially to the sounds of any and every language, and they may be used to describe and classify, in one all-embracing scheme, the sound features of all known languages, from Arabic to Zulu. But the phonetician is by no means content to act only as a taxonomist, a describer and classifier of sounds. He is interested, finally, in the way in which sounds function in a particular language, how many or how few of all the sounds of language are utilized in that language, and what part they play in manifesting the meaningful distinctions of the language. Because one knows what a sound *is* – how it is produced, what its physical characteristics are and what effect it has on the ear – one does not therefore know what it *does,* and the same sound may have quite different tasks to perform in different languages. That is to say, the difference in sound between *d* and *th* is used in English to differentiate between one word and another; *then/den, lather/ladder, breathe/breed*. In Spanish this is not so; the difference between *d* and *th* can never be used to differentiate one word from another because *th* occurs only between vowels, as in *todo* ('all'), and at the end of a word, as in *verdad* ('truth'), whereas the sound *d* never occurs in these positions. So in Spanish the two sounds can never be 'opposed' to each other in the same place in a word, and therefore they can never be 'distinctive'.

Similarly, variations of pitch play a part in all languages but the basic function of those variations may be quite different in different languages. In English, pitch changes are not a part of the shape of a word: that is to say, we can pronounce a word such as *No* with a variety of pitch patterns, level, rising, falling or combinations of these, so as to add overtones of doubt, certainty, apathy, interrogation and the like, but the word remains the same old basic negative. This is not the case, however, in a language such as Chinese where the pitch pattern is indeed a part of the basic shape of the word, which is not identifiable without it. There are four different words in the National Language of China all of which are pronounced rather like English *Ma*, and they are distinguished by their patterns of pitch. *Ma* with high, level pitch means *mother*; with a rise from medium to high pitch the meaning is *hemp*; a rise from low to medium gives *horse*; and a fall from high to low gives *scold*. In Chinese, then, pitch is an essential part of the shape or profile of the word, and is distinctive in the same way that stress is distinctive in the two forms of *incense*. In English pitch is not a part of word shape but rather a part of the shape of longer bits of speech. We can say single words like *No* with rising pitch to make them interrogative – *No?* But this is not a property of the word since we can also do the same thing with longer stretches, e.g. *You're not going?* In the two languages pitch has two quite different functions, just as the *d*- and *th*-sounds have different functions in English and Spanish. Such differences of function are the province of *linguistic phonetics* or *phonology*.

Types of sound difference

Having seen that the phonetician may look at speech sounds from different points of view it now remains to consider the wide variety of sounds and sound features which he has to look at. The richness of man's resources is not generally realized, and whilst I will make no attempt in this section to particularize, it is helpful to point out the main types of meaningful sound differences which occur in language.

There are perhaps 4,000 languages spoken in the world today. The sound resources of each of these languages are not necessarily entirely different from those of every other language, but on the other hand no two languages ever have exactly the same sound resources, so that this initial Babel provides a glimpse of the variety of sounds a phonetician must contemplate. Within each language there are dialects which have their different characteristic pronunciations or accents. We can tell an American accent from a Scottish or Welsh or English accent; we may, if we have a good auditory memory, be able to discriminate a great number of accents within our own language quite independently of any dialectal words or constructions used. And further, within each accent there are broader and less broad forms, differing again by the sounds which occur in them. Nor must we lose sight of the fact that not all accents are regional, there are also social accents which we recognize and label somewhat vaguely, e.g. 'County', 'Mayfair', 'BBC', 'Oxford', etc.; and occupational accents: compare the BBC news reader with, say, the politician (and obviously there are differences within these categories).

These large classes are made up of individuals and each of these has his own idiosyncratic differences. We can all recognize some hundreds of our relatives, friends, colleagues, acquaintances, notabilities by their pronunciation, that is, by the sound of their voices and the way they articulate sounds. But even that is not the end of it, for each of us has more than one *style* of pronouncing: we do not use exactly the same pronunciation in all circumstances. For instance, when we talk in a relaxed way to friends we do not do so as if we were addressing a public meeting (or if we do we are soon told about it), and at least part of the difference between the two is a matter of pronunciation. We do not speak to our beloved as we speak to the greengrocer or the boss, and again pronunciation is a part of the difference.

All these types of variety in pronunciation are there to be studied, and it is the phonetician's job to describe, classify and assess the function of all the speech sounds and sound attributes which come to his attention, whatever their source. The sounds of a generally despised local accent are no less interesting to him than the sounds of a widely used and prestigious one; the sound system of a language spoken by only a few hundred people must be investigated no less carefully and thoroughly than that of a language whose speakers number many millions: the Cabinet Minister has no phonetic priority over the cabinet maker. From this it will be inferred, rightly, that notions of 'correctness', of what is 'good' or 'bad' in pronunciation, are not uppermost in the phonetician's mind in his work of description, classification and assessment. He takes his data from his many sources and works on it without asking whether the pronunciations concerned are 'slovenly' or 'careful', 'beautiful' or 'ugly'. After his initial scientific analysis he may if he so wishes go on to ask the question: which of the features I have described are considered to be slovenly, careful, beautiful or ugly by speakers of the language or dialect? But if he does so he is taking off his phonetician's hat and putting on that of the sociologist; in Chapter 9 we shall mention some of the areas in which we need to know more about sound and society, but the bulk of the book will deal with sound in language: how it is described, classified and used.

You may find Chapters 2, 3 and 4 hard going; they deal with the three different aspects of speech sound: articulatory, acoustic and auditory, and are the technical basis of an understanding of what speech sounds are. Some people find technical matters like this rewarding in themselves – there can be great satisfaction in un- ravelling the delicate interplay of the different speech organs in producing a familiar or unfamiliar sound, for instance. Others, however, tend to get bogged down in the technicalities. If this happens, the best advice I can give is to try to get hold of the basic principles in each case, and not to worry too much about the detail, lists of phonetic symbols and the like – they can always be looked up if necessary. The rest of the book, in which I deal with the application of these principles to the study of language, should be intelligible to anyone who has got the gist of Chapters 2, 3 and 4.

2. Articulatory Phonetics:
How Speech Sounds are Produced

What we call 'the vocal organs' or 'the organs of speech' – lungs, vocal cords, tongue, lips, etc. – are not primarily organs of speech at all. Their first job is to make sure that the body survives, so that the lungs transfer oxygen to the blood and thence to the muscles, and remove impurities; the vocal cords help to prevent foreign bodies from getting into the airways of the lungs and also help us to cough up anything, such as food or phlegm, which the lungs reject; the tongue pushes food around in the mouth so that it gets chewed properly and then licks it into shape for swallowing; and so on. But we also use these same organs to produce very delicately and very accurately modulated chains of sound through which we communicate, so if we want to understand the speech process from the production side it is necessary to know at least enough about the functioning of these organs to enable us to describe how sounds and sequences of sounds are produced. The account of the vocal organs which follows will be as brief and as non-technical as possible, but it must contain all the information necessary for the description of how sounds are made and the classification of sounds on an articulatory basis.

The lungs

Most sounds of all languages are made with outgoing breath from the lungs. When we breathe in, air travels through the nose or mouth, down the windpipe or *trachea*, which branches into the two *bronchi* supplying the two lungs, and so down into the increasingly small airways of which the lungs consist. We may think of the lungs as large sponges being alternately filled with air and emptied of it. They are enclosed within the rib cage and are bounded at the bottom by the *diaphragm*, and it is the action of the ribs and the diaphragm which causes air to flow into and out of the lungs. Like sponges the lungs themselves are inert; in order to expel air they must be squeezed and in order to take in air they must be allowed to expand.

The ribs are capable of a certain amount of movement, and they are connected to the spine and to the breast bone in such a way that when muscles attached to them contract the ribs swing upwards and outwards, so increasing the distance between the corresponding ribs on either side. This has the effect of increasing the space within the rib-cage and allowing the lungs to expand. The upward and outward movement of the ribs can be clearly felt by placing the hands on the lower ribs on both sides and breathing deeply.

The diaphragm is a dome-shaped sheet of muscle immediately below the lungs, the dome pointing upwards. This dome can be flattened to some extent by muscular action and this again has the effect of increasing the volume of the space within which the lungs are contained and allowing them to expand in a downward direction (see Figure 2). The downward displacement of the dome

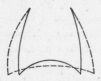

Figure 2: Schematic diagram of upward movement of ribs and downward movement of diaphragm in inhalation

also results in compressing the viscera below and bulging the abdomen. This too can be felt by touching the abdomen three or four inches below the breast bone and breathing in deeply.

The lungs expand outwards with the raising of the ribs and downwards with the lowering of the dome of the diaphragm, and this expansion, like the unsqueezing of a sponge, causes air to flow into the airways.

To expel air the process is reversed. In quiet breathing, when the muscles raising the ribs are relaxed the ribs will fall back to their lowered position and similarly when the diaphragm relaxes, the compressed viscera will push upward on it and return it to its former position. But in heavy breathing and in speech there are other muscles which actively pull the ribs downwards to decrease the volume, whilst muscles of the abdomen press inwards and, through the viscera, push the diaphragm upwards.

In quiet breathing, inspiration and expiration each take just about half of the time of the whole respiratory cycle, expiration being very slightly the longer. But in speech, inspiration is quickened up and expiration very considerably slowed down so that expiration may last eight or nine times as long as inspiration; yet most people do not breathe more air for normal speech than they do for quiet breathing. For loud speech air is pushed out more quickly, more forcefully, but again breathing is not necessarily deeper than for quiet speech. Our control of loudness is quite delicate and it is instructive to listen to a conversation and note how the volume of sound varies as between people and within the utterances of a single speaker.

The stream of expired air does not go out at an even pressure, the muscles pulling down the ribs do not pull evenly; the air comes out in patterns of greater and lesser pressure roughly corresponding to syllables, in such a way that the pressure is greater at the centre of a syllable and less at its borders, and greater on louder syllables and less on not so loud ones. The changing pressures on the word *eccentricity* may be represented as follows:

ec-cen-tri-ci-ty

Moving air is the first requisite for the production of speech sounds, but a great deal more is required besides. Air can be sent in and out of the lungs without making any noise at all. It is only by interfering with the stream of air in various ways that we achieve audible sound – let us look now at what the other speech organs can do to interfere with the air stream initiated by the lungs.

The larynx

The larynx is a fairly rigid box made up of cartilages, situated at the top of the trachea and continuous with it so that all air passing in and out of the lungs must pass through it. Inside the larynx are the first of the structures which can interfere with the air stream, the *vocal cords*. These are quite unlike cords or strings – they consist of two bands of muscle and connective tissue lying opposite to each other at the top of the trachea, fixed adjacent to each other at the front (the 'Adam's apple') end but horizontally moveable at the back, where they are attached to the *arytenoid* cartilages (see Figure 3). By muscular action the arytenoids can

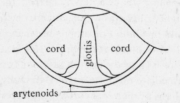

Figure 3: Vocal cords open

be drawn together or parted, causing the vocal cords to come together or part. They may come together very firmly and prevent air at very great pressures issuing from the lungs, as in very heavy lifting and defecation (see Figure 4). And they may be drawn wide apart at the arytenoid ends so that they allow air in and out of the lungs with no obstruction at all (Figure 3). They may therefore interfere totally or minimally with the air stream. An example of total interference in speech is the *glottal stop* (the *glottis* is the space between the vocal cords) which can be heard in various accents (e.g. Cockney, Glasgow, Birmingham) in pronouncing

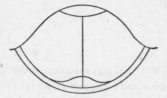

Figure 4: Vocal cords closed

words like *butter*, *water* (sometimes indicated by *bu'er*, *wa'er*). The air stream is completely blocked by the closed vocal cords, pressure builds up beneath them from the lungs, and is then released explosively when the vocal cords suddenly part. A very firm glottal stop is required for coughing, when considerable air pressure below the closed cords is released suddenly by opening them and so expelling whatever it may be from the lungs. A series of very, very light coughs will give you the feeling of the vocal cords closing and opening. For other sounds the vocal cords are wide apart and do not impede the breath, for example *Sh!*; what interference there is is in the mouth and not between the vocal cords. An intermediate position between the fully closed and the fully open positions of the vocal cords is found for the *h*-sound in *have* or *heart*, for which the breath causes slight friction as it passes between the half-open cords.

In many ways the vocal cords function like the lips (they are referred to by some writers as 'vocal lips'). In the glottal stop they obstruct the air completely, as the lips do for *p*; in *h* they cause friction, as the lips may do in coming close together for an *f*-like sound; or they may not interfere at all, in *Sh!*, like the lips in, say,

Ah! And there is yet another action that the lips can perform which may be useful in understanding what is perhaps the most important function of the vocal cords: the lips can be made to open and close rapidly in the air stream with a sort of rolling noise often used to indicate coldness and written *B'rrr*. The vocal cords too can be made to perform this rapid opening and closing in the air stream, though at rates very much higher and more capable of variation than the lips. So the lips may open and close ten times per second, but the vocal cords can do so at anything from about seventy times to more than a thousand times per second. The effect of this rapid opening and closing is to let air through the vocal cords in very short puffs, though we cannot perceive each of these puffs separately. What we perceive is a continuous vibration or note which we call *voice*. Squeeze the sides of the larynx lightly between finger and thumb, say *Ah*, and you will feel the vibration set up by the vocal cords. Voice is present in various speech sounds, for example, *ee* as in *see*, *oo* as in *too*, *m* as in *me*, and you can test for the presence or absence of voice by squeezing the larynx, as above, or by putting your hands over your ears and feeling the vibrations that way. Is there voice in *aw* as in *jaw*? In *l* as in *feel*? Make a long hissing sound, *sssss*; is there voice in it? No, there isn't. Make a long buzzing sound *zzzzz*; is there voice in that? Yes, there is. Now pass from *sssss* to *zzzzz* and back again continuously and you will be turning the voice on and off.

We can all vary the rate of vibration, and differences in rate correspond to differences in pitch; the slower the rate the lower the pitch and the higher the rate the higher the pitch. The rate of seventy vibrations per second mentioned above corresponds to a very low note in a male voice, and one thousand per second gives a high note in a female voice. The vocal cords are typically longer and heavier in the adult male than in the female and therefore vibrate at lower rates, though obviously there are variations of range for both males and females. The musculature of the vocal cords is such that they can be made longer or shorter and also thicker or thinner; length and thickness, as with harp strings, produce slower vibrations and lower pitches, shortness and thinness produce faster vibrations and higher pitches. Our control of rate of vibration and therefore of pitch is very sensitive and we make use of it very extensively in language; a brief example of the kind of use is the difference between *No!* said as an indignant reply to the question *Do you beat your wife?* and *No?* as a response to *I don't like caviar.* In *No!* the vocal cord vibration changes from rapid to slow and the pitch falls, whereas in *No?* the reverse takes place.

Voice, then, has two functions in speech. Its presence can characterize a particular sound, for example *zzzzz* as against *sssss*, and variations in the pitch of the voice can be used to make meaningful contrasts of other kinds, which will be discussed at length in Chapter 7.

We have spoken as if there were only one mode of vibration of the vocal cords in producing voice, but in fact it is worth noting three different modes. In the first, which we may call 'normal' voice, an average amount of breath escapes during each opening of the cords. In a second mode a great deal more air escapes than average, either because the cords do not close completely over their whole length or because the *open phase* is proportionately longer than in normal voice. This produces *breathy* voice, and an example of the use of this in English would be the pronunciation of *No!* in a shocked or awed way, or of *I love you* with breathy passion. This kind of voice is used in some languages quite regularly to contrast with normal voice in distinguishing one word from another (e.g. Hindustani). The third mode of vibration allows a much less than average amount of air to escape during the open phase of the cycle and gives rise to *creaky* voice. This is very often, though not necessarily, associated with low pitch and may be used in English in a scornful way of saying, e.g. *Silly old fool.* It is the sort of voice which we have to use when lifting a heavy weight and trying to talk at the same time; normally when lifting we close the vocal cords firmly to prevent our muscular efforts from simply expelling air, and if we *have* to talk, the less air we allow out the better for our lifting; hence the creaky voice. This is also the kind of voice which the ventriloquist uses in 'throwing the voice', i.e. making the voice sound more distant or more muffled than it should be. In other languages, again, this kind of voice is used to make regular distinctions between words (e.g. Danish).

Apart from the frequency of vibration (related to pitch) and the mode of vibration (giving rise to normal, creaky, breathy voice) the *amplitude* of vibration, i.e. the amount of horizontal opening of the cords, relates to loudness. The further the vocal cords move apart in the open phase the louder the resultant sound, and the smaller the gap the softer the sound. Loud sounds will have both extra pressure from the lungs and large amplitudes, soft sounds less pressure and smaller amplitudes.

Finally amongst the functions of the vocal cords we must mention whisper. For a very quiet whisper the vocal cords are close together in much the position for an *h*-sound, so that some friction is caused as breath passes between them. For louder whispers the vocal cords themselves are brought closer and closer together so that more and more friction is caused, until for the loudest one

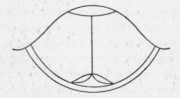

Figure 5: Whisper

there is only a narrow chink left open between the arytenoid cartilages (Figure 5) through which air is forced under great pressure causing maximum friction. Say the word *hat* in a loud whisper and notice that where the vocal cords themselves are parted more air passes for the *h*, than for the *a*, where only the arytenoids are apart.

To sum up, the vocal cords are responsible for the following, depending on the nature and extent of interference with the breath stream:

1. breath – unimpeded passage of air (*Sh!*).

2. friction – cords close together causing some turbulence of air (*h*).

3. whisper – as in 2, or for loud whisper, cords together and arytenoids apart.

4. voice
   a) normal, breathy, creaky depending on amount of air passing in open phase.
   b) loud/soft, depending on amplitude of cord vibration (and lung pressure).
   c) pitch, depending on frequency of vibration.

The pharynx

Figure 6 gives a general view of the vocal organs above the larynx. The general lay-out is of a single tube-like cavity, the *pharynx*, branching into two other cavities, the nasal above and the oral below. The pharynx stretches from the top of the larynx up to the back of the nasal cavity and serves mainly as the container of a volume of air which can be set into vibration in sympathy with vibrations coming from the vocal cords. Like the strings of a violin without the body of the instrument, the vocal cords, divorced from the upper cavities, would make very little noise. It is the sympathetic vibration (or *resonance*) of the air contained in the upper cavities (or in the body of the violin) which amplifies some of the characteristics of the vibrations produced in the larynx (or by the strings) and gives them strength, and therefore gives a particular quality to the resulting sound. The violin body is fixed

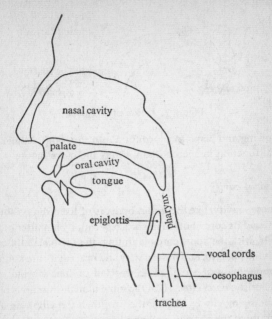

Figure 6: Supra-glottal speech organs

in shape and violin quality is therefore unchanging; the shape of the cavities above the larynx can be changed very considerably and therefore the quality of the resultant sounds changes accordingly.

The pharynx is not of itself very variable in shape but there are two ways in which its dimensions can be altered, by raising the larynx, which shortens the length of the tube and results in a less full sound, and by raising the *soft palate* (Figure 7), which again shortens the tube, this time from the top, but more importantly prevents the air from entering the *naso-pharynx* (that part of the pharynx behind the nasal cavity) and the nasal cavity proper.

The *epiglottis*, a flap of tissue which projects into the pharynx at the root of the tongue, folds over the top of the larynx during

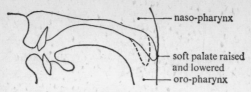

Figure 7: Action of soft palate

swallowing and helps to shoot food into the food-passage, but it has no function in speech and we may therefore ignore it.

The nasal cavity

The nasal cavity, like the violin body, is of fixed dimensions and shape, and its contribution to speech is entirely a matter of resonance. If, with the vocal cords vibrating, the soft palate is lowered so that the pharynx and nasal cavity and oral cavity are connected, the whole mass of air in the connected cavities vibrates with a characteristic *nasal* effect. If at the same time the mouth is blocked at some point, say by closing the lips, then the vibrating air will pass through the pharynx and nasal cavity and out of the nostrils, with a dull, humming effect. If on the other hand the mouth is open, as for *ah*, and the soft palate still lowered, then the vibrating air goes out of both mouth and nostrils and the result is a modification of a purely oral *ah*, which we recognize as *nasalization* (notice that the lowering of the soft palate does *not* of itself prevent air from entering the oral cavity). This nasalization is used in French, for example, to distinguish *banc* ('bench') from *bas* ('low') or *bon* ('good') from *beau* ('beautiful'), in which the distinction is purely between a nasalized and an oral vowel. There is a difference between a *nasal* sound, such as *m* or *n*, for which the mouth is blocked, forcing all the air to pass out through the nose, and a *nasalized* sound, for which air passes through both the nose and the mouth, as in the French examples above.

You can get the feeling of the raising and lowering of the soft palate in this way: say the word *top* and hold the final *p*, don't open the lips. Now try to shoot the air held in the mouth out through the nose *without opening your lips*. Do this several times and you will feel the downward and upward movement of the soft palate. You can also *see* the movement of the soft palate by using a mirror: turn your back to the light and reflect it into your mouth; say *ah* and the soft palate will rise; now relax, and the soft palate will lower to its normal breathing position. If you can keep it in this lowered position and say *ah* at the same time, you will be making the nasalized vowel in French *banc*. Make this nasalized vowel again (be sure the tongue stays flat and the soft palate lowered) and nip the nostrils. What happens? If you are making the sound correctly, there should be very little change. In other words, for nasalized sounds the important thing is that the air should pass *into* the nasal cavity, but not necessarily *out* of it through the nostrils. It is the coupling-in of the nasal cavity and the air vibrating within it which is crucial. Now hum a long *mmmmm*. All the air goes through the nose because the lips are blocking the mouth. Nip the nostrils again. What happens? The sound grinds to a halt because there is no longer any exit for the air through either the mouth or the nose.

If the passage through the nose is blocked at the *back* of the nasal cavity, say by adenoids, neither nasal nor nasalized sounds will be possible because air cannot enter (and, incidentally, breathing has to be by mouth, hence the typical adenoidal gape). If the passage is blocked at the nostrils, as with a cold, nasalized sounds will still be perfectly possible because air can resonate in the nasal cavity, but nasal sounds will be heavily impaired. The sounds *m* and *b* both require closed lips; *m*, as we know requires a lowered soft palate, *b* requires it raised so that air does not go through the nose. Notice that *m* said with nipped nostrils is *not* exactly the same as *b*. Say the word *baby* normally, then say the name *Mamie* with nipped nostrils. The reason for the difference is that for *baby* no air gets into the nasal cavity at all, whereas for

Mamie air does get into the nasal cavity even though it can't get out through the nostrils. Nevertheless the *m*-sounds are more *b*-like than they should be.

The particular quality of cleft-palate speech is due to the fact that the cleft in the palate or roof of the mouth, until it is repaired, allows air into the nasal cavity for *all* sounds, and those sounds which should be purely oral, with raised soft palate, come out nasal or nasalized. We have seen that oral *b* corresponds to nasal *m*; what corresponds to oral *d*? The nasal *n*. What happens to *s* if the soft palate is lowered? Most of the hiss, which is produced by air forcing its way through a very narrow passage in the mouth, disappears because the bulk of the air is lost through the nose. In cleft-palate speech many sounds are badly impaired and none is unaffected except sounds which are normally nasal, like *m* and *n*.

The oral cavity

The oral cavity is by far the most important of the three cavities because it is the most variable in dimensions and in shape. This is due partly to the mobility of the lower jaw, partly to that of the lips, but overwhelmingly to the tongue. The tongue is the organ of speech *par excellence*; in many languages 'tongue' is synonymous with 'language' itself and we can speak of 'the tongues of men and of angels', being 'tongue-tied' and 'having a silver tongue'. By the extent, the variety and the delicacy of its movements it far outstrips any other organ in its contribution to speech. Whilst the nasal cavity is invariable and the pharynx varies only a little, the mouth can vary enormously and it is here that most of the distinctions of articulate speech are fashioned.

The oral cavity (Figure 8) is bounded at the top by the *palate*. This is a dome-shaped structure whose front part is bony and fixed and whose back part, the soft palate, is moveable in the way we have already seen. It is useful to divide the palate into three main parts, the *soft palate*, the *hard palate* (the highest, concave, part) and the *alveolar ridge* (the convex ridge of the gums behind the upper incisor teeth). The function of the palate in speech (apart from the valvular action of the soft palate mentioned above) is to serve as a foil to the tongue in its articulatory movements. The *uvula*, the soft fleshy tip of the soft palate, needs to be identified separately from the soft palate; in a mirror it can be clearly seen hanging down at the back of the mouth.

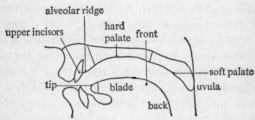

Figure 8: The oral cavity

The tongue may also articulate with the fixed upper incisors. The remaining teeth do not play any positive part in speech, though the loss of, for instance, the lower incisors may have an adverse effect on certain sounds, notably *s*.

The lower jaw, in moving up and down (its back/front and sideways movements are not relevant to speech) can decrease or increase the size of the cavity and so influence the quality of sound produced. Although this movement is not crucial, since we can speak intelligibly with a fixed jaw position, as when smoking a pipe, we nevertheless do move our jaw constantly in speech and it is not easy to inhibit the movement: ventriloquists try, but not always with complete success. Say *sssss* again, and as you do so lower your jaw gently and notice how a very slight increase in the distance between the teeth affects the hissing.

The tongue consists of a complex bunch of muscles, which make it enormously mobile; it is divided for convenience into three major parts according to their relation to the parts of the palate. When the tongue is at rest the *blade* lies below the alveolar ridge, the *front* below the hard palate and the *back* below the soft palate. The blade, and particularly its front-most extremity, the *tip*, is especially agile; it can be protruded between the lips and it can touch the whole of the palate as far back as the junction between the hard and soft palates; the tip is also elastic enough to trill against the alveolar ridge in the rolled *r*-sound characteristic of some forms of Scottish and also Italian and other languages. Most of us are conscious of the tip and blade of the tongue and its great variety of movement. Of the front and back of the tongue we are on the whole much less aware, but they too are capable of more or less independent movement: the front may assume any vertical position from flat on the floor of the mouth to a complete contact with the hard palate, whilst the blade and back remain relatively low, and similarly the back can be raised to any degree including contact with the soft palate whilst the front and blade remain relatively low. Use a mirror to see these movements: with the mouth wide open say the nonsense syllable *ahk*; for the *ah* the tongue is flat and for the *k* the back rises to make contact with the soft palate. Now say 'eye' and watch the front of the tongue rise from low to high. Hold the position at the end of the word and pull air inwards; you will feel the cold air passing between the front of the tongue and the hard palate. So the tongue can take up any position from complete contact with any part of the palate to complete non-interference with the air-stream by lying flat. It can also be drawn backwards so that the very back part of it comes close to the back wall of the pharynx.

The *sides* or *rims* of the tongue are also capable of making firm contact with the sides of the palate along the line of the teeth or of not making such contact. Say a long *lllll*, hold the position and breathe in through it. You will feel cold air on the sides of the tongue, which are not in contact with the palate. Now say *sssss* and again breathe in through the position. Cold air moves over the centre of the blade, but *not* over the sides which are now in firm contact with the sides of the palate.

The lips are capable of the same degrees of movement as the tongue – they come into firm contact as for *p* or *m*, they can be kept right out of the way so that they do not interfere with the passage of air at all, and they can take up any intermediate position. The lower lip can contact the upper incisors as in *f*, and

| close rounding | open rounding | spreading | neutral |

Figure 9: Lip positions

the two lips can assume various shapes (Figure 9), *close-rounded* as at the beginning of *wood*, *open-rounded* as in a vigorous pronunciation of *hot*, *spread* as in an equally vigorous pronunciation of *see*, and *neutral* as for *ah*. These different shapes have a strong influence on sound quality: say a vigorous *eeeee*, then, keeping everything else as still as possible, close-round the lips; the quality of the vowel sound will now be like that of the French vowel in *lune* ('moon'). For *eeeee* the front of the tongue needs

Figure 10: High front tongue position

to be raised close to the hard palate (Figure 10); in most kinds of English any such raising of the front of the tongue is invariably accompanied by a spread or neutral lip position and it is only when the back of the tongue is raised towards the soft palate that we get any lip-rounding, as for *ooooo* or the *w* in *wood* (Figure 11). That is why the French vowel of *lune* is difficult for

Figure 11: High back tongue position

most English speakers and why, for instance, the French *du* tends to be pronounced more like English *do* or *dew*. But there is no necessary connection between front tongue raising and spread lips, or back tongue raising and rounded lips: there are plenty of languages which have front tongue raising both with spread and rounded lips (French, German, Swedish, Danish, Norwegian, etc.) and others, though not so many, which have back tongue raising with both spread and rounded lips (Turkish, Vietnamese). However, the English are in good company: most languages have spread lips with front tongue raising and rounded lips with back tongue raising, and not the reverse.

Sound production

Differences of sound are produced by different actions on the part of the moveable organs of speech, from the abdomen to the lips and nostrils. In order to specify these differences from the production angle we have to state what each of the participating organs is doing at all relevant times. For *sssss* we need to state at least the following:

1. The lungs are pushing out air rather vigorously (as against *zzzzz*, where the pressure is less).

2. The vocal cords are not vibrating (as against *zzzzz*, where they are).

3. The soft palate is raised, shutting off the nasal cavity (as against *n*, where the soft palate is lowered).

4. The blade of the tongue is brought very close to the alveolar ridge (as against *t*, where it touches the alveolar ridge).

5. The sides of the tongue are clamped against the sides of the palate, funnelling the breath into the narrowing at the alveolar ridge (as against *l*, where the sides are not in contact with the sides of the palate).

6. The opening between the teeth is narrow (as against *ah*, where it is wider).

7. The lips are in a neutral or spread position (as against *w*, where they are rounded).

We must now examine at what *places* along the vocal tract differential movements are made, and what is the nature of those movements for the individual sounds of speech.

Lung action

In most speech sounds of most languages the lungs are pushing air outwards, but this is not necessarily so; for instance, when we make the clicking noise often written *Tut-tut* or *Tsk-tsk*, the lungs are not involved at all. This can be shown very simply by making a series of these sounds and breathing in and out quite normally through the nose at the same time. Therefore we must first state whether the lungs are actively engaged, whether the sound is being made with *lung air*. Then we must state the *direction* of air movement, since it is possible to make sounds on an *ingressive* stream of air as well as on an *egressive* one, though much rarer. We sometimes use a sound made with ingressive lung air to express pain, or sympathy with someone else's pain, and it is not unknown for people to articulate words or even phrases on an ingressive air stream, when they are out of breath for instance.

Also the lungs may push air out more vigorously or less vigorously for a particular sound. For example, at least part of the difference between the final sounds in *bus* and *buzz* is due to the fact that the lungs push harder for the *s* than for the *z*. Sounds with greater pressure are *fortis* sounds, and those with less are *lenis*.

Vocal cord action

Three main actions are distinguished: vibrating, for *voiced* sounds, e.g. *ah*, *zzzzz*; not vibrating, for *voiceless* sounds, e.g. *h*, or *sssss*; and stopped, in the *glottal stop*, as in *wa'er*, *bu'er*. In normal speech these three categories are usually sufficient, but it may be necessary to specify the *type* of voice (breathy, creaky, normal), and whether the glottis is wide open (*sssss*), narrow (*h*) or very narrow (whisper). Although whisper generally stretches over longer pieces of speech than the individual sound, there is no reason in principle why the distinction voiceless/whispered should not be used; generally, however, voiced/voiceless is sufficient.

Glottal stop occurs in *wa'er* where most educated speakers would look askance at it, but it quite often occurs much more respectably and less noticeably as, for example, a substitute for the *t* in *not much*. In both these cases closure of the vocal cords and their explosive opening constitute the primary articulation of the sound; this is true too of *h* where the vocal cords come close enough together to produce friction. The voiced/voiceless distinction, however, is almost always an accompaniment to some other articulation in the pharynx or mouth. In *s* voicelessness accompanies the main articulation by the blade of the tongue, and in *z* the same blade articulation is accompanied by voice.

Glottal stop often occurs, even more respectably, at the beginning of a word like *Idiot!* said vehemently. Here it serves simply as a hard beginning to the vowel sound for purposes of emphasis.

Complete closure of the vocal cords is essential too in producing a type of sound known as *ejective*, for which lung air is not used. For such sounds air is set in motion as follows: the vocal cords are firmly closed cutting off the lungs completely; the soft palate is raised; and the mouth is blocked at some point too, let us say by closing the lips. We now have a completely closed cavity stretching from the vocal cords to the lips. The air in this cavity is compressed by making the cavity smaller: the larynx is pushed upwards and so is the tongue (Figure 12). If the lips are now opened suddenly the compressed air pops out explosively and sounds a little like a cork coming out of a bottle.

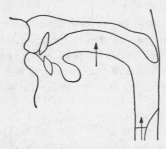

Figure 12: Pharynx-air mechanism: ejective *p*

Ejective sounds are not regularly used in English but they are in some other languages, e.g. Georgian, Zulu. The stop in the mouth need not be complete, and sounds such as *s* and *f* and various others, can be made in this way. This way of setting air in motion is known as the *pharynx-air mechanism*, and the direction of air flow may also be reversed, to draw air inwards: with the cavity enclosed as before the larynx is *lowered*, together with the tongue and jaw; this rarifies the air so that when the lips are parted air rushes inwards, again with a hollow explosion. Such sounds are known as *implosives*. Neither ejectives nor implosives should be confused with the clicking noises (like *Tut-tut*), whose production is explained on p. 43.

P.–3

Soft-palate action

As explained earlier, the soft palate is raised to prevent air going up into the nose and lowered to allow it to do so, producing oral, nasal or nasalized sounds. The raised position of the soft palate is usefully referred to as *velic closure* (in anatomical terminology the soft palate is the *velum palati*). The soft palate, including the uvula, has a second function, in common with the rest of the palate, namely to serve as a passive articulator, with the tongue as the active partner.

Tongue action

The very back of the tongue may, as we have seen, be pulled backward into the pharynx, thus modifying the latter's shape and affecting sound quality; this happens in some pronunciations of *ah*. Pulled further back still, the tongue may come so close to the back wall of the pharynx that air passing through causes friction

Figure 13: Pharyngal articulation

(Figure 13); two such sounds, one voiced, one voiceless, occur in Arabic. Sounds made in this way are known as *pharyngal* sounds; strictly speaking they should be referred to as *linguo-pharyngal*, but in all cases where the tongue is involved we generally omit 'linguo-' unless it is specially necessary.

The back of the tongue may touch or come close to the uvula for *uvular* sounds. Typically, Northern French and German *r*-sounds are uvular as in *rouge, rot* (red). The back may equally articulate with the soft palate proper, as it does for *k* or *g*. Such articulations are known as *velar* (note that velar closure is a closure made by the back of the tongue against the soft palate, whilst velic closure refers to the raising of the soft palate to the back wall of the pharynx, Figure 14).

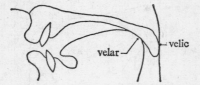

Figure 14: Velar and velic closure

We may need to distinguish the front part of the soft palate from the back part; for instance, for the first sound of *Kew* the contact is well forward on the soft palate whilst for *car* it is further back, and we may refer to them as *pre-velar* and *post-velar* sounds respectively.

A firm velar closure is used in producing the sounds known as *clicks* (e.g. *Tut-tut!*). Air is set in motion, not by the lung-air or pharynx-air mechanism, but by the *mouth-air mechanism*. The velar closure has a second closure at some point in front of it; for *Tut-tut!* the second closure is made by the tongue-tip at the alveolar ridge, and at the same time the sides of the tongue are clamped against the sides of the palate, so that there is a tiny cup of air enclosed between the tongue and the palate. This space is now enlarged by pulling the back of the tongue backwards whilst still in contact with the soft palate, and lowering the front of the tongue; this rarefies the enclosed air and when the tip is lowered air rushes in with a typical clicking noise (Figure 15). A kissing noise is made with the same mechanism but the forward closure is then at the lips. This is precisely the mechanism we use when sucking. The back of the tongue pulling backwards on the soft palate enlarges the cavity, decreases the pressure and causes liquid to flow into the mouth. Clicks are marginal to English – we have the *Tut-tut* one and the *Gee-up* one used meaningfully – but quite regular sounds of some languages. For instance Xhosa, in South Africa, has three different basic clicks and the X in Xhosa indicates the *Gee-up* click.

Figure 15: Mouth-air mechanism

The direction of air flow can be reversed with this mechanism too, so that the air in the enclosed cavity is compressed and forced outwards when the front closure is removed. Sounds made with egressive mouth air are commonly known as *reverse clicks*.

The front of the tongue can articulate with the hard palate in *palatal* sounds. The first sound in *Kew* may be made by a closure at this point rather than in a pre-velar position (Figure 16),

Figure 16: Palatal closure

and the sound at the beginning of *huge* is typically one in which air causes friction in a palatal narrowing. We may also, if we need to, distinguish pre- and post-palatal, but this is seldom necessary.

The tip of the tongue may also articulate with the hard palate, bending backwards to do so, hence the name *retroflex* for such sounds. Speakers of Indian languages often use retroflex sounds for *t* and *d* in English, and a retroflex *r*-sound is typical of many American, West Country and Irish speakers (Figure 17).

Figure 17: Retroflex *r*

The tip and/or blade of the tongue may articulate with the alveolar ridge in *alveolar* sounds. In English *t*, *d*, *s* and *n*, amongst others, are alveolar. Post-alveolar sounds also occur when the tip articulates with the back part of the alveolar ridge, as it does in most English pronunciations of the *tr* combination in *try!* We sometimes need to distinguish the tip from the blade as the active articulator and the terms apico-alveolar (apex = tip) and lamino-alveolar (lamina = blade) can be used for this purpose. *t* in English is usually apico-alveolar and *s* lamino-alveolar.

The tip can also articulate with the upper incisors for *dental* sounds. The *t*-sounds of French, Italian, Spanish and many others are typically dental rather than alveolar as in English, but we also find dental articulation in the *th*-sounds of English, as in *thin* and *then*. It may occasionally be necessary to distinguish between *post-dental*, where the tip articulates with the backs of the upper incisors, and *inter-dental* where it articulates with their cutting edge.

Lip action

The lower lip and the upper incisors are brought together in *labio-dental* sounds such as *f* or *v* and the two lips work together in *bilabial* sounds like *p*, *b* and *m*.

The terms we use for all these various places at which the air stream may be interfered with are: glottal, pharyngal, velic, uvular, velar (including pre- and post-velar), palatal (including pre- and post-palatal), retroflex, post-alveolar, alveolar (including lamino-alveolar and apico-alveolar), dental (including post-dental and inter-dental), labio-dental and bilabial. Figure 18 sums up the major place categories.

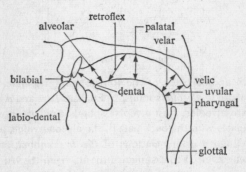

Figure 18: Major articulatory areas

Manners of interference

At all these various places there may be different types of interference. Basically there are three possibilities, complete *closure* of the air passage, *narrowing* of the passage so that air forced through the narrowing causes audible friction, and *opener* positions which do not result in friction.

Closure

There are three different types of closure: *stops*, *rolls* and *flaps*. Examples of stops are: bilabial *p*, *b*, and *m*; alveolar *t*, *d* and *n*; velar *k*, and *g*; glottal in the glottal stop. In principle stops may be made at any of the places mentioned above, but a pharyngal stop is not easy and is not found in language. When the closure is made within the oral cavity it may or may not be accompanied by velic closure. If not, the air-stream will go out entirely through the nose, giving nasal sounds like *m* and *n*. When there is velic closure the air-stream cannot get out through the nose, nor can it get out immediately through the mouth, which is blocked. Since the lungs are still pushing air upwards the air is compressed within the totally enclosed cavity, and then when the mouth closure is removed, this compressed air explodes out of the mouth, as in *pie, by, tie, die*, etc. This kind of sound, which has compression and explosion, is called *plosive*. Notice that plosion may take place as the result of the air being rarefied rather than compressed and does so in, for example, the *Tut-tut* click: such sounds also are plosives. Sometimes with these same sounds, instead of removing the mouth closure we remove the velic closure and the compressed air explodes up into the nose and out that way. This is called *nasal plosion* and it happens in English when a nasal sound immediately follows one of the other stops, as in *Agnes, Abner, Stepney, Edna, cabman*, etc. Say these words at normal speed and feel how the pent-up air explodes behind the soft palate and into the nose.

Rolls consist of several rapidly repeated closures and openings of the air passage, as in the rolled *r*-sounds of Scottish or Italian for which the tip of the tongue makes several quick taps against the alveolar ridge. The speed with which these closures and openings are made demand the participation of a particularly elastic organ, and this effectively restricts the places at which they can be made; the tongue tip obviously has the necessary elasticity so we can have alveolar, post-alveolar and retroflex rolls; the uvula too can roll against the back of the tongue, and this uvular roll is common in Dutch for *r* and may be heard in French and German too – the sound is reminiscent of a gargling noise. The lips can be made to roll in a similar way (as in the *B'rrr* noise mentioned on p. 27), but this is not found as a regular sound in language.

The speed of each closure and opening in a roll is clearly much greater than for the stops and it is this speed which characterizes *flaps,* which consist of a single fast closing and opening of the air passage. In a word like *mirror,* the *rr* may be made by an alveolar flap, one fast tap of the tongue-tip against the alveolar ridge; and uvular and bilabial flaps can be made in a similar way.

Narrowing

When two speech organs are brought very close together the air forcing its way through the resulting narrowing becomes turbulent, and this turbulence is heard as friction noise. Sounds having such friction are known as *fricatives* and fricatives can be – and are in language – made at every place from glottal to bilabial. Some fricatives are made with a rather high-pitched, hissy kind of friction, e.g. *s* and *sh*, and these are sometimes referred to as *sibilants*; others, the *non-sibilants*, have a less hissy, more diffuse kind of friction, like *f* or *th*.

Now make a long *s*-sound again, then draw the breath inwards and notice that the air flows in through a narrow groove along the median line of the blade. Do the same for *sh* and notice that the grooving is not nearly so narrow (this is not the only difference between them, by the way). Sounds with a narrow groove, like *s*, are called *grooved* fricatives. In English, the *th*-sound at the beginning of *thin* (notice that it is only one sound despite the two letters) is not grooved like *s* – try drawing air in through it and see. If you do groove it you will get a typical lisping *s*, which is not identical with the normal *th*. In German *s* is generally even more grooved than in English and this gives rise to a particularly sibilant sound very characteristic of much German speech.

Opener positions

If two organs are not so close together that they cause friction they may nevertheless be playing a major part in shaping the cavities through which the air flows. Say a long *vvvvv* and hear the friction coming from the labio-dental narrowing; now very gently lower the lip away from the teeth until the friction just disappears; you are left with a non-fricative sound, but one which is still labio-dental in effect since the lip-teeth approximation makes a difference of sound: lower the lip right away from the teeth and notice the difference. This frictionless *v*-sound can quite often be heard as a defective *r* in English: the word *ever* said with a frictionless *v* will sound like a defective version of the word *error*. The common non-rolled, non-flapped *r*-sound of *red* is similarly frictionless. Try making a frictionless *th* as in *this*; and a frictionless *z* as in *zoo*. Sounds of this kind are known as *frictionless continuants*.

So far we have considered only those sounds which are made just below the *friction limit*, i.e. the point at which the narrowing is just great enough to cause friction, but clearly the articulators may be much further apart than this and still be playing a major part in the production of a sound. This is true for the various lip-shapes shown in Figure 9 (p. 37); none of them gives rise to friction but they make important differences to otherwise similarly produced sounds, e.g. *ee* and the French vowel in *lune*. Similarly in pronouncing the vowel sound in the word *bat* the front of the tongue is highest (note, the *front*, not the blade) but not very high; for the vowel sound in *bet* the front of the tongue is also highest but this time it is raised higher than before. You can check on these positions in a mirror. Now neither of these sounds has any friction, so it is the different shapes of the oral cavity which make the difference between the sounds; these different shapes are mainly due to the position of the front of the tongue, in both cases well below the friction limit. Frictionless continuants, as we have seen, are made just below the friction limit. Sounds made with opener positions still are what we recognize as *vowel* sounds.

Vowel sounds

Notice, first of all, *sounds* not letters. There are only five (or six) vowel letters in our Roman alphabet, but there are far more distinguishable vowel sounds. The words, *seat, sit, set, sat, sot, soot, suit,* are distinguished in most kinds of English by the different vowel sounds which they contain. Now, to define the different shapes of the complex tract responsible for these and other vowel differences would be very difficult if we tackled it in one fell swoop, but fortunately we do not need to do that, we can break up the process into parts: the shape of the lips, the opening between the jaws, the position of the soft palate and, especially, the shape of the tongue. It so happens that the shape of the oral cavity in so far as the tongue is concerned can be roughly defined by locating the highest point of the tongue. Once that is located we have a very fair idea of how the rest of the tongue is behaving, and thus of the shape of the oral cavity.

In pronouncing normal vowel sounds we find that it is the front or the back or the centre of the tongue which is highest (the centre comprising the posterior part of the front and the anterior part of the back). The tongue can be raised rather *close* to the palate as it is in an educated southern-English pronunciation of the vowels in *beat* (front), *about* (the first, rather indistinct vowel) (central), and *boot* (back). It may be rather *open*, far from the palate, as for the vowels in *bat* (front), *but* (central) and *calm* (back); or it may be at some *intermediate* height, as for the vowels of *bet* (front), *learn* (central) and *bought* (back). So a two-dimensional scheme showing which part of the tongue is highest and to what height it is raised enables us to specify the tongue's contribution to vowel sounds. The nine vowels mentioned above can be classified as follows:

	front	central	back
close	beat	about	boot
intermediate	bet	learn	bought
open	bat	but	calm

We find when we examine X-ray photographs of tongue positions in vowel production that the high point of the tongue for various vowels describes an area in the mouth of the shape shown in Figure 19.

Figure 19: The vowel area

By abstracting this area from the mouth we can use it to show the high point of the tongue diagrammatically (Figure 20), and if we make it rectilinear (as in Figure 21) we can, with only a little loss

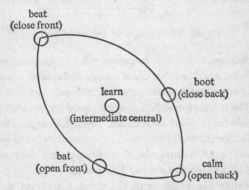

Figure 20: Tongue specification for vowels

of accuracy, get a very usable (and very widely used) tongue diagram for vowels.

The interior lines of Figure 21 need explanation: it is convenient to have two vertical reference levels between the uppermost and the lowest, and this accounts for the two additional horizontal lines; the central triangle is drawn in this way because the vowels whose high points fall within this area tend to be typically obscure-sounding, whereas other vowels have a more definite quality. The terms which we may need for reference to the lines of the vowel quadrilateral are shown on Figure 21 and are the ones most

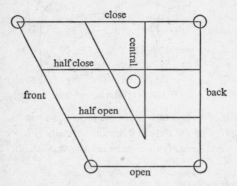

Figure 21: Regularized version of Figure 20

commonly used. We can therefore refer to the *beat* vowel as a close, front vowel, to that of *calm* as an open, back vowel, to that of *learn* as a central vowel between half-open and half-close and so on. The term *retracted* is sometimes used for vowels whose high point is between front and central, and the term *fronted* for high points between central and back; the vowel of *sit* is normally a retracted vowel a little above half-close, and that of *book* is fronted and also a little above half-close.

In dealing practically with the vowel sounds of this or that language or this or that accent we are not equipped with portable X-ray apparatus to determine the location of the high point of the tongue, nor is there any other good method of doing so, since our kinaesthetic sense is very unreliable where open positions of the back/front of the tongue are concerned, and direct observation is rarely possible. So that although vowel sounds *can* be classified in the way outlined above, it is much more useful in practice to deal with vowels as sounds, i.e. as something heard, and in Chapter 4 we shall discuss an auditory method of vowel classification.

Lateral sounds

One other method of interfering with the air stream should be noted. The passage of air through the mouth may be blocked along the median line but permitted laterally, so that air passes round the median obstruction on one or both sides. This is the case, as we have already seen (p. 36), for *l*-sounds, which have a firm alveolar closure but no contact of the sides of the tongue with the sides of the palate; the air passes out over the sides of the tongue and around the alveolar closure. The only other common places for laterals are palatal, where the front of the tongue is firmly against the hard palate, and retroflex. Palatal laterals are found in Italian in words like *oglio* ('oil') and in Spanish in, for example, *calle* ('street'); retroflex laterals occur in various Indian languages, e.g. Marathi.

Specifying sounds

In order to specify sounds from the production angle we need then to mention all of the following:

1. source of air movement: lung-air, pharynx-air or mouth-air mechanism
2. direction of air movement: ingressive or egressive
3. amount of air pressure: fortis or lenis
4. vocal-cord action: voiced (breathy, creaky, normal)
   voiceless
   whisper
   stop (where not accounted for in 1. under pharynx-air mechanism where glottal closure is essential, see p. 41)
5. state of soft palate: velic closure/opening
6. place of interference: glottal . . . bilabial
7. manner of interference: plosive . . . lateral

Let us specify a few sounds in this way, first the final sound of Scottish *loch*:

1. lung air
2. egressive
3. fortis (pressure higher than for equivalent voiced sounds)
4. voiceless
5. velic closure (air *must* pass only through mouth)
6. velar
7. fricative

Next the *Tut-tut* click:

1. mouth air (see Figure 15, p. 44)
2. ingressive (air is sucked inwards)
3. fortis
4. voiceless
5. immaterial (since the click, being made entirely within the oral cavity, is the same whether the soft palate is raised or lowered)
6. alveolar
7. plosive

Finally the *n*-sound of *tenth*:

1. lung air
2. egressive
3. lenis
4. voiced (normal)
5. velic opening (this is a nasal sound)
6. dental (in *no* the *n* is alveolar, but in *tenth* it is dental: try them)
7. stop (complete oral blockage at teeth)

In specifying vowel sounds we need to mention two places of interference, namely the tongue and the lips, since for every tongue position there is the possibility of having two or more lip positions. Here is a specification of the vowel of *day* in a Scottish accent:

1. lung air
2. egressive

3. lenis (normal vowels invariably are made with relatively small pressure)

4. voiced

5. velic closure

6. front (i.e. front of tongue raised highest) and neutral lip position

7. half-close (basically an 'opener position' but the degree of raising is more nearly specified)

And now the French nasalized vowel in *bon*:

1. lung air

2. egressive

3. lenis

4. voiced

5. velic opening (because air must pass into the nose)

6. back and with close lip-rounding

7. half-close

It is obvious from this formula for specification that various of the individual features contributing to sounds can and do combine together, for instance voicing can occur with a particular place of interference and both with a particular manner of interference. But it is also true that certain of the sub-categories within our larger categories 1–7 may also co-occur. We have already seen that in vowels we must specify two places, tongue and lips, and it is not uncommon to have to specify two places of interference in other cases.

Co-occurrent place features

Form a *p*-sound and hold it, with the lips closed; now put the tongue into position for a *k*-sound, i.e. a velar stop, and hold that. Now there are two places at which the air-stream is blocked and when both the stops are released simultaneously the resulting sound is different from both *p* and *k* separately and also from a sequence *pk* as in *upkeep*. This *co-articulation* is a labio-velar one, meaning that there is a bilabial interference and an equal velar interference going on at the same time (not that the lips articulate with the soft palate!). Sounds of this kind occur in Igbo; indeed the *gb* in Igbo stands for a co-articulation of the kind described, but voiced.

Such sounds are not commonly found in English but it is not difficult to make other co-articulations. Try *tk* co-articulated, and try to release both stops, alveolar and velar, at the same moment. Try *pt*, and *sf*. Be sure that you get them taking place at the same time, not successively. A co-articulation which you may hear in English is a glottal stop with a *p* or *t* or *k* stop in words like *supper*, *letter*, *lucky*. Try co-articulating those.

Co-articulation requires that the two strictures (i.e. stop, fricative or open position) shall be of equal rank – stop + stop (*kp*), fricative + fricative (*sf*), open + open (the nasalized vowel of *bon*). If the strictures are of unequal rank – stop + open and fricative + open – then we are dealing with subordinating articulations, one of which is primary and the other secondary. An obvious example of this is a *s*-sound said with close lip-rounding: the alveolar stricture is fricative and the lip position is open, therefore the alveolar stricture is primary and the lip stricture secondary, and we talk about a *labialized* alveolar fricative. So too with the *l*-sound at the end of *bottle* in most kinds of English, the so-called 'dark l'; the tongue-tip forms a complete closure at

Figure 22: 'Dark *l*' showing secondary velar articulation

the alveolar ridge (though the sides of the tongue are not touching the palate) and at the same time the back of the tongue is raised rather high towards the soft palate (Figure 22).

So the open velar articulation is secondary and the alveolar closure is primary, and we speak of a *velarized* alveolar lateral. In Russian there is a whole series of velarized sounds which is in opposition to a second series of *palatalized* sounds, with the front of the tongue raised high towards the hard palate: the use of, say, a palatalized *t*-sound instead of a velarized *t*-sound may be the only difference between two quite separate words. Figure 23

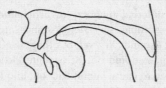

Figure 23: Palatalized *l*

shows a palatalized *l*-sound. In Russian these are usually referred to as 'hard' (velarized) and 'soft' (palatalized) consonants.

The English *sh*-sound has a primary articulation which is post-alveolar and fricative, and a secondary palatal articulation; we call this a *palato-alveolar* fricative. In Polish on the other hand the sound written *ś* has a primary palatal articulation and a secondary alveolar one, and is called an *alveolo-palatal* fricative. You can make this sound by first of all making the voiceless palatal fricative which occurs in English at the beginning of the word *huge* said rather energetically, and then gently closing the jaw, which has the effect of bringing the tongue-blade closer to the alveolar ridge and modifying the palatal friction.

Quite apart from these completely co-occurrent articulations we find a great deal of overlapping of articulations in the production of sound sequences. Generally speaking, we do not produce one sound, then rest, then produce the next sound. Whilst the first sound in a sequence is being formed the next is being prepared. So what happens during the *b* of *bought* is different from what happens in the *b* of *brought* to the extent that in *br* the tongue tip is brought into an open post-alveolar position *during* the lip-closure for *b*, so that when the lips are parted the tongue is ready for the *r*-sound. But whilst the articulations of *b* and *r* overlap they are not co-extensive since *r* continues its articulation after *b* is finished. Work out the sequence of events for the *pl* of *please*, the *ct* of *act*, the *sw* of *swim*.

Co-occurrent manner features

Certain of the different manners of articulation may also be combined. For example, the lateral sounds are generally non-fricative, e.g. the *l*-sounds in *level*, but there is no reason why the sides of the tongue should not be brought close enough to the sides of the palate to cause lateral friction, and this is what happens in the Welsh *ll*-sound in *Llanelli*; the tongue is in position for a *l*-sound and breath is blown strongly through to cause friction at the sides of the tongue. The manner categories fricative and lateral are then combined.

Roll and fricative can also be combined as in the Czech *ř*-sound of *Dvořak*. This is a post-alveolar roll in which a great deal of breath is pushed out each time the tongue leaves the palate, giving rise to friction whose sound reminds the English ear of the fricative consonant in the middle of *measure*, which is why we pronounce that consonant in *Dvořak*; but the Czech sound is a fricative post-alveolar roll.

Co-occurrent air mechanisms

The three air mechanisms mentioned earlier, the lung-air, pharynx-air (p. 41) and mouth-air (p. 43) mechanisms, may also combine together. For example, the implosive sounds made with ingressive pharynx air may be voiced by pushing up lung air and causing the vocal cords to vibrate at the same time as the pharynx-air mechanism is rarefying the air above the larynx. Since the air coming up through the vocal cords will eventually nullify the rarefaction above them such sounds can be of only brief duration. Stops made with this combination of air mechanisms can be heard in Swahili.

Since the click sounds made by the mouth-air mechanism are produced entirely within the oral cavity they may easily be accompanied by voice, produced by lung air. The voiced air-stream from the lungs can be allowed to pass freely through the nose by lowering the soft palate (you can do this by humming whilst making a series of *Tut-tut* clicks) or the soft palate can be raised in a velic closure, when the voiced air is compressed behind the back of the tongue in contact with the soft palate. Clicks made with simultaneous voice are known as *nasalized* clicks if the voiced air goes through the nose and as *voiced* clicks if it does not. Both of these, as well as the voiceless clicks, are found as regular sounds of Xhosa (see p. 44).

Notice here that both the voiced implosives and the voiced or nasalized clicks combine together an egressive and an ingressive air-stream. The lung air is egressive, whilst the pharynx air for the implosives is ingressive, as is the mouth air for the clicks. It is very difficult to combine a voiced egressive lung-air stream with an egressive pharynx-air stream and such sounds are not found in language, but it is easy to make reverse clicks (i.e. with egressive mouth air) in combination with egressive lung air. It is also quite possible to combine pharynx-air and mouth-air sounds together and even to combine all three air mechanisms to make a voiced (lung-air) click (mouth-air) implosive (pharynx-air) but such sounds are again not found in language.

Phonetic transcription

We are now in a position to characterize the sounds of language in accordance with the features of production so far discussed, but before doing so we must look at phonetic transcription. We have managed to do without it so far by using letters like *s* and *sh ad hoc*, but we do need an agreed way of designating sounds by means of letters, and that is what a phonetic transcription is.

Since we shall have to refer to a great many sounds we need more than the 26 letters of our Roman alphabet, and a stock of letter-shapes has been developed by the International Phonetic Association for this purpose. The alphabet of this Association is very widely known and used, and it will be used in this book. Any letter-symbol serves to sum up the way in which a given sound is produced and the association of the sound with the letter must be consistent. So whenever the symbol [p] occurs we may assume the following: 1. lung air, 2. egressive, 3. fortis, 4. voiceless, 5. velic closure, 6. bilabial, 7. stop, and whenever a sound with this specification crops up we must use [p] to designate it.

In order not to multiply the number of separate letter-shapes beyond bounds various diacritics are used; for example [m̥] designates a *voiceless* bilabial nasal, as opposed to voiced [m], and similarly [b̥, d̥, z̥] etc. indicate voiceless equivalents of voiced [b, d, z]. The symbols [ɫ, s̴, ɫ̴] indicate velarized sounds corresponding to non-velarized [l, s, t]. We use [t̪, n̪] to show *dental* place of articulation as opposed to alveolar [t, n]. And so on. The values of such diacritics will generally be obvious from their placing in the table which follows, but where necessary, explanation is provided.

The vowel sounds discussed on pp. 50–52 are not included at this point for the reason given on p. 52. Their specification will be dealt with in Chapter 4. Still we are left with a large number of consonant sounds, most of which appear in Table 1. This table assumes egressive lung air: the other air mechanisms will be treated separately.

Co-articulated sounds

Sounds which have double articulations (p. 55) are represented by two of the above symbols linked by a slur, e.g. [g͡b] = voiced, labio-velar plosive; [s͡f] = voiceless, alveolar + labio-dental fricative. The Czech fricative roll (p. 58) is represented by the single symbol [r̝] and the voiceless and voiced alveolar lateral fricatives

Table 1.

Phonetic symbols for sounds ordered in place and manner categories. The first symbol of a pair in any cell indicates the voiceless sound, the second the voiced.

	stop				fricative	lateral	frictionless continuant
	plosive	nasal	roll	flap			
glottal	ʔ				h	ɦ	
pharyngal					ħ	ʕ	
uvular	q G	ɴ N	ʀ R	ʀ̆ R	χ ʁ		ʁ
velar	k g	ŋ̊ ŋ			x ɣ		ɰ
palatal	c ɟ	ɲ̊ ɲ			ç ʝ	ʎ	j
retroflex	ʈ ɖ	ɳ̊ ɳ	r̝ ɽ̝	ʈ̆ ɽ	ʂ ʐ	ɭ̊ ɭ	ɻ
post-alveolar	t̠ d̠	n̠̊ n̠	r̠̝ ɾ̠̝	t̠̆ ɾ̠	ʃ ʒ	l̠̊ l̠	ɹ̠
alveolar	t d	n̥ n	r	ɾ̥ ɾ	s z	l̥ l	ɹ̝
dental	t̪ d̪	n̥̪ n̪			θ ð	l̥̪ l̪	ð̞
labio-dental	π b̪	m̥ ɱ			f v		ʋ
bilabial	p b	m̥ m			ɸ β		β̞

Notes

1. [ɦ] indicates breathy vibration of vocal cords (p. 28): this occurs between vowels for English *h* in e.g. *behind*.

2. For pre-velar and pre-palatal sounds the sign [+] may be placed above or below the appropriate letter, e.g. [k̟] as in English *key*. And the sign [−] may be used similarly to indicate post-velar and post-palatal sounds, e.g. [g̠] in English *got*.

3. [b̪] is a non-IPA symbol for the sound which may occur for *b* in English *obvious*.

4. The gaps in the table are due mainly to the impossibility of combining a particular manner and a particular place, e.g. glottal nasal and palatal roll, and sometimes to the non-occurrence of a possible sound, e.g. a bilabial lateral. If any such sound needed a symbol, one would be provided *ad hoc*. There are no voiceless frictionless continuants because this would imply silence; the voiceless counterpart of the frictionless continuant is the voiceless fricative.

(p. 58) by [ɬ] and [ʮ] respectively. [w] and [ʍ] denote the labio-velar frictionless continuant of *well* and the voiceless labio-velar fricative of Scots *why*.

Secondary articulations

Labialized sounds (p. 56) are indicated by [w] below or above the letter appropriate to the primary articulation, e.g. [s̫], [g̫] for the *s* of *swim* and the *g* of *Gwen*.

Nasalized sounds (p. 32) have [~] above the appropriate letter, e.g. [l̃] for the *l* of *channel nine*; also [ã] for the nasalized vowel of French *banc*.

Palatalized sounds (p. 57) usually have special letter shapes combining [j] with the appropriate letter, e.g. [ț], [d̦] for pala-talized [t] or [d]. If more convenient, a dot may be placed above the letter. The palatalized alveolar fricatives, initial in *shoe* and final in *rouge* have the single letter shapes [ʃ] and [ʒ]; the Polish alveolo-palatal fricatives (p. 57) are indicated by [ɕ] and [z].

Velarized sounds have special letter-shapes combining [~] with the appropriate letter, e.g. [ɫ], [ɖ] = velarized [l] and [d].

Pharynx-air sounds

Ejectives (i.e. egressive pharynx-air sounds, (see p. 41) have ['] following the appropriate letter, e.g. [t'], [ʃ'] = ejective [t] and [ʃ]. Ejectives are always voiceless; plosives and fricatives can be made in this way at all the places in Table 1 except glottal and pharyngal, whilst it is also possible to make rolls and flaps at all the places where these can be made with lung air. Only a few plosives and fricatives are found in language.

Implosives (i.e. ingressive pharynx-air sounds) are not very generously represented in the IPA alphabet. The symbols [ɓ], [ɗ] and [ɠ] are provided for the voiced implosive stops at the bilabial, alveolar and velar places of articulation, and other symbols could be created at need by means of the same hook, e.g. [ƥ] for the voiceless bilabial implosive stop. Alternatively [ʔ] can be linked to the appropriate letter, e.g. [t̪ʔ], [q̪ʔ] for the voiceless alveolar and uvular plosives made with ingressive pharynx air.

Mouth-air sounds

Three basic symbols are provided by the IPA alphabet for ingressive mouth-air sounds (clicks, p. 43); they are [ʇ] and [ʗ] for the voiceless clicks at the alveolar and retroflex places, and [ʖ], which represents the *Gee-up* click, i.e. an alveolar click in which air enters over one side of the tongue rather than over the tip: this is usually referred to as the lateral click. To indicate a click accompanied by voiced air issuing through the nose (p. 59) [ʇ̃ŋ], [ʗ̃ŋ] and [ʖ̃ŋ] are used, whilst for those accompanied by voiced air which does not go through the nose (p. 59) the symbols [ʇ͡g], [ʗ͡g] and [ʖ͡g] are used ([ŋ] and [g] refer to the velar stop which is an essential part of the mouth-air mechanism). No symbols are provided for the reverse clicks (with *egressive* mouth air) nor for various other ingressive sounds which can be made, e.g. a bilabial click plosive (a kissing noise), no doubt because they are marginal in language, but a feasible way of representing such sounds at need would be to use [k] in the same way as [ŋ] and [g] above linked to the appropriate letter, e.g. [p̰k] for the kissing sound mentioned above, or [f̰k] for a labio-dental fricative made with ingressive mouth air.

Sounds in sequence

Up to this point we have treated sounds as if they were 'given', but it is instructive to consider what we mean by 'a sound'. We have mostly been thinking of it as the product of a prescribed combination of activities on the part of the vocal organs and this is a result of considering sounds in isolation, but if we consider them in the stream of speech and then ask ourselves how we cut up the stream into single sounds, problems arise, because the movement of the vocal organs is continuous, they do not stand

still. To this extent our profile diagrams of single sounds are mis-
leading, though they are a part of the truth. We will now look at
the vocal organs in action. Figure 24 is a diagram of the movement
of some organs in the word *cleaned*.

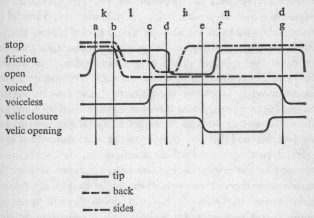

Figure 24: Movements of tongue-tip, back and sides; velic closure/
opening; and voicing, in *cleaned*

The back of the tongue starts in the stop position (for [k]);
while it is in this position the tongue-tip rises to a stop position on
the alveolar ridge for [l]; then when the back is lowered the tip
remains in contact. So the articulations of [k] and [l] overlap from
Time *a* to Time *b*. Since the tip is in contact (the back having
lowered) from Time *b* to Time *d* we might say that this is [l], but
notice that voicing does not start until Time *c*, and between
Time *b* and Time *c* breath passing between the sides of the tongue
and the sides of the palate ([l] being a lateral) causes friction,
which stops at Time *c* when voicing begins. So there is a clearly
audible voiceless fricative segment between Times *b* and *c*, and a
voiced non-fricative segment between Times *c* and *d*, both associated with [l]. Similarly, [n] requires both a tongue-tip stop and

velic opening, but the velic opening occurs at Time *e*, during the vowel, whereas the tongue-tip stop is not completed till Time *f*. This means that there is an oral part of the vowel (before Time *e*) and a nasalized part of it, Time *e* to *f*. Similarly again, [d] has tongue-tip stop, velic closure and voice, but the voicing is turned off at Time *g*, before the tongue tip is lowered for the final explosion of [d], giving a voiced and then a voiceless part of [d].

In all three cases there are two perceptually different segments produced by the different states of a particular organ of speech. If we define a sound in that way, as a perceptually distinct segment produced by a characteristic combination of organic actions, which seems a reasonable definition in view of our ability to distinguish, say, [l̥] and [l] both perceptually and organically, then what we have so far called [l] in *cleaned* is not a single sound but a succession of two different sounds, a voiceless fricative [l̥] and a voiced non-fricative [l]. Yet we are not complete idiots in the use of speech, so if we think that there is something unitary about [l] when we have proved that it is not unitary either in perception or production, there must be some other reason. The reason lies in the way in which sounds function in speech.

Sound function

Sounds function in language contrastively. In a series of words like *bat*, *rat*, *mat*, *hat*, *fat*, *that*, the initial consonants are *in contrast*, i.e. they are responsible for the meaningful differences between the words. For this to happen they must be able to occur in the same places in words, as they do here in initial position. If two different sounds never occur in the same place, they can never be in contrast. The *t*-sounds in *tea*, *tree*, *eighth* are all slightly different, the first alveolar [t], the second post-alveolar [t̠] and the third dental [t̪]. Try them and confirm this – it is true for most kinds of English. Now [t̠] only occurs before [r], never in other positions; [t̪] only occurs before [θ] or [ð], and [t] elsewhere. This state of affairs, when sounds which are clearly different never occur in exactly the same environment, is called *complementary distribution*, and [t], [t̪] and [t̠] are in complementary distribution in English. Such sounds can never distinguish one word from another, simply because they can never occur at the same place in words, whereas the initial consonants of *bat*, *rat*, *mat*, etc. can and do, because they are not in complementary distribution.

Not only are [t], [t̪] and [t̠] in complementary distribution, they also have common features of articulation which no other sounds in English share: they are all plosives, all with tongue-tip articulation, all voiceless. These two factors, complementary distribution and the exclusive sharing of phonetic features, account for our intuitive recognition that there is a single /t/ unit in English of which [t], [t̪] and [t̠] are the concrete manifestations or *realizations*.

There *is* a unity about /t/ which corresponds to our thinking, though it is not on the production or perception level, but rather on the functional level. The functional units of which sounds are realizations are known as *phonemes*.

In recognizing the phoneme as distinct from the sounds which realize it or give it a form at a particular place in the stream of speech, we have cleared the way to explaining why it is that we can have two successive segments of sound corresponding to /l/ in *cleaned*. There is no requirement that a single phoneme must be realized by a single sound, although it is often so (e.g. [s] in *seat* or [m] in *meat*). One phoneme may be realized by a succession of two sounds and that is exactly what happens in *cleaned*. /l/ is realized as [l̥l], /i/ as [ii̯] and /d/ as [d̪d̪].

Our thinking is tied so very much to phonemes rather than to sounds that it is easier to see the relationship between the two in foreign languages than in our own. In Spanish /d/ is realized between vowels and in final position as the voiced fricative [ð], like the English consonant in *other*, but in other positions it is realized as [d̪], a plosive. So *dos* ('two') is /dos/ = [d̪os], whilst *todo* ('all') is /todo/ = [toðo]. In Spanish [d̪] and [ð] are realizations of the same phoneme, but in English the equivalent sounds are realizations of two different phonemes, as witness *day*, *they*.

In French /pl/ before a pause is realized as [pl̥] where the [l̥] is completely voiceless and fricative, e.g. in *simple*. In other positions /l/ is realized by a voiced and non-fricative [l], e.g. in *seul* ('alone'). In Welsh on the other hand these two same sounds [l̥] and [l] realize two different phonemes, as in *dall* ('blind') and *tal* ('tall').

In German the [ts] sequence at the beginning of *Zimmer* ('room'), consisting of a stop segment followed by a fricative segment, is the realization of a single phoneme (as the German spelling suggests), whereas in English *cats* the [ts] must be regarded as a sequence of two phonemes /ts/. On the other hand the [tʃ] sequence at the beginning of *charm* in English is the realization of a single phoneme. Sequences of stop + fricative, e.g. [ts, tʃ] when they realize single phonemes, are generally called *affricates*.

Segmentation

Having established the difference between sound and phoneme we will now return to the possibility of cutting up the stream of speech into segments by considering the actions which produce them. (The term 'segment' is used in preference to 'sound' as being more neutral, less evocative.)

We can say that there are as many segments in a stretch of speech as there are changes in position on the part of the vocal organs, but this requires qualification. Firstly, the changes must lead to perceptible differences – any change which cannot be recognized by ear is irrelevant, it cannot be used for communication. For example, velic closure or opening is irrelevant to the voiceless clicks. Secondly, since the change of position of various organs is continuous and gradual rather than instantaneous it is the extremes of such movements which are important.

For instance, in passing from the vowel sound [ɒ] to [k] in *lock* the back of the tongue rises from a very open position to a velar stop, quite a wide movement. All the time the back is rising the shape of the oral cavity is changing and the resultant sound is being modified. This continuous modification may result in continuous perceptible difference, but we do not wish to reckon with several segments between the [ɒ] and [k] extremes, so we specify the ends of such a movement as the centres of the segments, and so long as the movement is direct and at an even pace we say that there are only two segments. If the movement is not direct, however, or if the pace is not even then we must reckon with additional segments: for example, in *Ike* we have three segments because in travelling from the first vowel position to [k] the tongue does not move directly but deviates through another vowel position, giving [aɪk]; and although the tongue-tip in *East* [iːst] travels in a direct line from an open position for [iː] to the alveolar stop position for [t] it does not do so at an even pace, slowing down in the fricative position, so again we must reckon three segments.

By taking into account extremes of articulatory movement, direction and pace, we can determine the number and nature of the segments in any stretch of speech, whether the language is native or foreign, and experienced analysts would expect to agree most of the time on the segmental analysis of a particular stretch. If we are studying a completely unknown language this is how we have to approach it: we cannot know at first how the segments function, we can only determine what they are and try to find out gradually what phonemes they represent. In dealing with a language we know, on the other hand, where we are aware of the phonemes, we can use them as a unifying factor and try to determine how each is realized in all the positions in which it occurs. Both these procedures are hampered by the fact that even the most experienced analyst is to some extent the prisoner of his native phoneme system and may miss important differences of sound simply because they are not used in his own system.

Phonetic training is a constant struggle for independence in sound perception.

When we say that it is extremes of articulatory movement which determine segments, that is not the same thing as saying that the extreme positions determine our *perception* of the segments. For example, take the words *lock* and *lot* /lɒk/ and /lɒt/. Suppose that they are both pronounced so that the final plosive sound is formed, but not released: say the words in that way and hold the final stop positions, do not allow the compressed air to escape. Both these final stops are voiceless, so when the stop position has been reached the result is silence in both cases, and the two segments cannot be differentiated at the stop position itself; yet we are able to recognize the difference between *lock* and *lot* said in this way and the reason is not far to seek. As I said before, the continuous movement of the tongue modifies the shape of the oral cavity continuously and we perceive this modification as a continuous change of sound quality; then, since the movement is different for [k] and [t] the cavity is being modified in a different way for each, and we are able to tell that in one case [k] movement is involved and in the other case [t] movement. In this case it is not what happens at the extreme position which governs our perception of [t] or [k], but what happens on the way.

A final word about the notation of segments and phonemes: when we use letters to represent actual segments of sound we enclose them in [ ], and when representing phonemes, in / /. The reason for this is that we use the same letters when talking about both, so /t/ refers to the unit that occurs three times in *tea*, *tree*, *eighth*, but [t] denotes the segment that occurs at the beginning of *tea* only; the notation [t̪] and [t̺] would be used for the other two words (see p. 65). In *phonemic transcription* we tend not to use the more complicated letter-shapes set out in Table 1 and subsequently, because we are not attempting to provide detailed articulatory information; the relationship of the phoneme to the segments which represent it in different environments must be stated for each language or variety of language concerned, in the shape of a series of rules, which make it possible to deduce the actual segment to be used from the occurrence of the phoneme in any environment. The use of /t/ in English implies underlying rules of the following kind:

1. Before /θ/ or /ð/ = [t̪], *eighth*
2. Before /r/ = [t̠], *tree*
3. Before lip-rounded sounds = [t̹], *twice*
4. Before other vowels = [t], *tea*
5. before /l/, [t] is laterally exploded, *bottle*
6. before /n, m/, [t] is nasally exploded, *bitten*
7. before other plosives, [t] is not exploded, *outpost*

We shall learn more about phonemes and their characteristics from Chapter 6 onwards.

3. Acoustic Phonetics:
Sound Between Mouth and Ear

The medium through which speech sound normally travels is air: it can travel through other media too, such as water or glass, but it is sufficient here to consider what happens when sound travels through air alone. Air is a mixture of gases, and an important property of a gas is that it can be compressed or rarefied; what this means is that the component molecules can be brought closer together or further apart. When we move our vocal organs in speech we disturb the air molecules nearest our mouth and thus displace them; they in turn displace other molecules in a similar way and so on in a chain reaction until the energy imparted by the vocal organs dies away at some distance from the speaker. When one molecule, as it were, collides with another it rebounds back to and beyond its starting point and continues to oscillate to and fro until eventually it stands still again. The sounds that we hear are closely related to characteristic oscillations or vibrations of the molecules about their place of rest, and as each molecule induces similar behaviour in the next one in the chain we can confine our attention to the behaviour of a single molecule. The detailed analysis of this molecular movement constitutes acoustic phonetics.

The patterns of air vibration in speech sounds are very complex and it is worth looking first at simpler forms of sound, i.e. sounds characterized by simpler forms of vibration, for example a tuning fork. When a tuning fork is struck it settles down to vibrate rather steadily. Each prong moves first in one direction by a certain amount then back through the place of rest and beyond that by a fractionally smaller amount, then reverses direction again and continues this inward and outward movement until eventually the vibration dies away altogether and the prongs are at rest again. The air molecules take on exactly the same back and forth movement, pushed and pulled by the prongs. We could illustrate this movement as in Figure 25, but this is not terribly revealing be-

Figure 25: The movement of an air molecule about its place of rest

cause it tells us nothing about the time the operation takes, and time is important. We can introduce time in a graph such as Figure 26, where the vertical axis represents time and the hori-

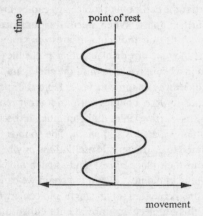

Figure 26: The movement of Figure 25 showing timing

zontal one movement. This is the sort of trace we would see if we could attach a pen to the moving molecule (or more practically to one prong of the tuning fork) and make it write on paper attached to a moving drum. Notice in particular that the molecule does not move vertically any more than the tuning fork does: it is the drum, representing time, which gives that effect in the graph. This is worth remembering because in normal practice the graph of Figure 26 is turned round so that time is always shown along the horizontal axis and movement along the vertical one. This is done in Figure 27.

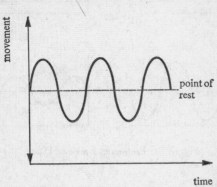

Figure 27: The usual orientation of Figure 26

There are two ways in which this movement can vary: if the molecule is given a good strong bump it will travel further from its place of rest than if it were bumped only lightly, like a child's swing pushed hard or gently; the maximum movement away from the place of rest is the *amplitude* of vibration. One complete cycle of operations – from the place of rest to the maximum amplitude in one direction, then back to the maximum amplitude in the other direction and finally back to the place of rest again – is known, appropriately, as one *cycle*. The second type of variation is in time; irrespective of amplitude a cycle may be completed in a longer or shorter period of time and the length of time is known as the cycle's *period*. If a vibration has a period of one hundredth of a second, then in one second there will be a hundred cycles. The number of cycles per second (cps) is known as the *frequency* of vibration. Figure 28 shows vibrations of different amplitudes and frequencies.

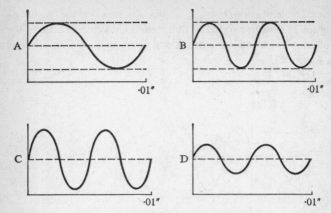

Figure 28: Frequency and amplitude

Periodic sounds

Sounds whose period remains the same for cycle after cycle are known as periodic sounds. Strike a note on the piano and the frequency of the vibration (therefore the period) will remain the same until the vibration finally dies away. Sounds where successive periods are different are *aperiodic*. Periodic sounds give rise to a clear sensation of pitch whose height is related to the frequency of vibration – the higher the frequency, the higher the pitch. But not all periodic sounds have the simple and elegant shape (*sinusoidal* shape) of the vibrations we have considered so far. A slightly more complex form is shown in Figure 29. This is obviously not sinusoidal in shape and yet the remarkable thing about it is that it can be analysed into a combination of two shapes which *are* sinusoidal, or, to put matters the other way round, the more complex shape is built up out of the two sinusoidal shapes shown in Figure 30. This is done by measuring the separate amplitudes at equal intervals of time along the horizontal axis and adding the amplitude values together whenever both are on the same side

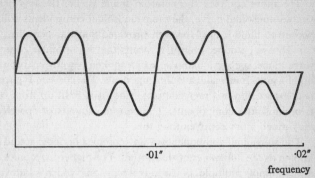

Figure 29: A more complex wave form (non-sinusoidal)

of the position of rest, or subtracting one from the other when they are on opposite sides, and then plotting the combined values: it is worth checking by measurement that the two curves of Figure 30 do in fact give the curve of Figure 29 (dotted on Figure 30).

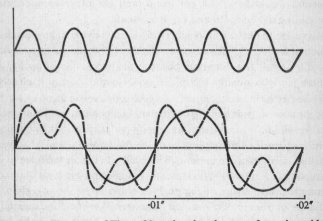

Figure 30: The curve of Figure 29 analysed as the sum of two sinusoidal curves

The more complex the periodic shape is, i.e. the less like a simple sinusoidal curve, the more sinusoidal components will be needed to build it up. However, provided that it *is* periodic, this can always be done, even if it means that a particular complex wave shape, such as a piano note or a spoken vowel, may be made up of a great many sinusoidal components. The curve in Figure 29 *is* complex, but not *very* complex, since it is built up from only two sinusoidal components. The periodic sounds of speech are very much more complex than this.

The sinusoidal components of any complex periodic sound are known as the *harmonics* of that sound. The higher harmonics are always simple multiples of the lowest harmonic which is known as the *fundamental frequency* or simply the *fundamental*. In Figure 30 the lower component, with a period of ·01″ and therefore a frequency of 100 cps, is the fundamental, and the higher component, at 300 cps, is its 3rd harmonic because its frequency is 3 times that of the fundamental. If a complex wave shape were built up of sinusoidal components at 100, 200, 400 and 600 cps, the fundamental would be at 100 cps again, and the other components would be the 2nd, 4th and 6th harmonics.

Two quite distinct sounds may obviously have the same fundamental frequency – for instance, the same note played by a violin and a piano. The difference between the two is one of *quality* – there is violin quality and piano quality, and quality is closely related to the harmonic structure of the sounds. The complex wave of the piano note is built up of different higher harmonics than that of the violin. We can therefore specify periodic sounds by stating the frequencies and amplitudes of the fundamental and whatever higher harmonics are present. We usually do this in the form of a graph as in Figure 31. This states in a simple graphic form that the complex wave shape of Figure 29 is made up of the two simple shapes of Figure 30. The first harmonic, i.e. the fundamental, has a frequency of 100 cps, and the higher harmonic is the 3rd since it has a frequency of 300 cps. Also, the fundamental has an amplitude which is 50 per cent greater than that of the 3rd harmonic. This type of specification of a sound is called the *spectrum* of that sound.

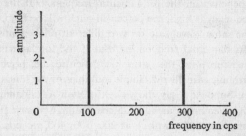

Figure 31: Frequency/amplitude specification of the complex wave of Figure 29

Strictly speaking, no speech sounds are absolutely periodic, that is, perfectly repetitive from one cycle to the next, but some are so nearly periodic (e.g. vowel sounds) that treating them as such will do very little harm. The wave forms of spoken vowels

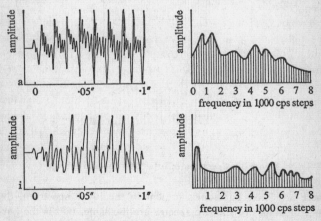

Figure 32: Wave forms and spectra of the vowels [i] and [ɑ]

are very complex – Figure 32 shows the wave forms and the corresponding spectra of the vowels [i] as in *see* and [ɑ] as in *half*.
The pitch of a note, i.e. our sensation of its being a high note or a
low one, depends on the fundamental frequency. If the fundamental frequency is high, the perceived pitch will be high, if low,
low. So the same vowel said on two different pitches must have
different fundamental frequencies. But if the fundamentals are
different, so too must the harmonic structures be, because the
higher harmonics are always simple multiples of the fundamental
(see p. 76). Suppose I say the vowel [ɑ] with a fundamental of
100 cps and then again at, say 175 cps. In the first case the 2nd,
3rd, 4th, etc. harmonics will be at 200, 300, 400, etc. cps. In the
second case, they will be at 350, 525, 700, etc. cps. Why is it, then,
if the harmonic structures are so different, that we recognize the
two vowels as the 'same'? Figure 33 supplies the clue: although

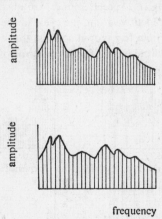

Figure 33: Spectrum of [ɑ] at 100 cps and 175 cps

there are fewer harmonics present in the lower spectrum, the
general shapes of the two spectra are the same, that is the harmonics with the greatest amplitude are at about the same fre-

quency in both, regardless of what number those harmonics have in the structure. It is therefore the general *shape* of the spectrum which characterizes a particular vowel, rather than the actual number and frequencies of the individual harmonics. That is why women and children, who have higher pitched voices than men, can still produce what are recognizably the 'same' vowels as men produce. More will be said about this later in this chapter.

Aperiodic sounds

Figure 34 shows the wave form of an aperiodic sound, one whose pattern does not repeat itself as do those of the periodic sounds discussed above: it is the wave form of [s]. Compare it with the

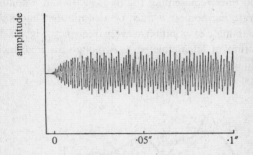

Figure 34: Aperiodic wave form of [s]

repetitive, periodic wave forms of Figure 32. Aperiodic sounds such as [s] can also be specified in terms of their spectra, but for them it is no longer a case of a tidy harmonic structure, with each harmonic being a simple multiple of the fundamental. For aperiodic sounds there is no fundamental, no harmonics; on the contrary, noise is going on at *every* frequency, which is why we do

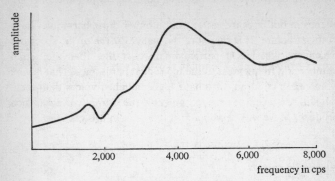

Figure 35: Spectrum of [s]

not perceive any clear pitch for such sounds as we do for periodic ones. The spectra of aperiodic sounds cannot therefore be a series of vertical lines representing the frequencies and amplitudes of the separate harmonics; it must be a continuous line representing the amplitude of vibration at every frequency. Figure 35 shows the spectrum of [s] in this way. Although all frequencies are

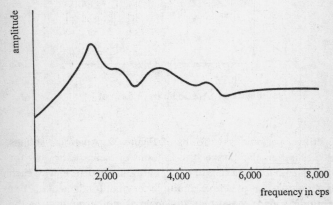

Figure 36: Spectrum of [ṣ]

present the amplitude is greater in some frequency regions than others and it is these differences in the amplitude profile over the frequency range which enables us to distinguish one aperiodic sound from another. Compare the spectrum of [ṣ] (the voiceless retroflex fricative) in Figure 36 with that of [s] in Figure 35.

Sound intensity

The *intensity* of a sound is the amount of energy being transmitted through the air at a particular point, say at the ear-drum or at a microphone within range of the sound. Intensity is related to amplitude of vibration in the following way. An air molecule vibrates back and forth about its place of rest at specifiable frequencies and amplitudes. Suppose that the molecule is vibrating at one particular frequency and the amplitude is suddenly doubled: it goes twice as far from its place of rest as before in each direction, but since the frequency has not altered it only has the same amount of time to do this, so it must move

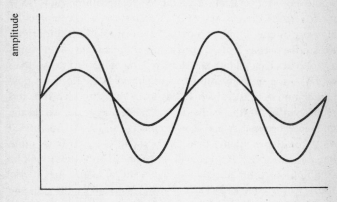

Figure 37: Velocity and energy of molecule movement increased by doubling amplitude

faster, twice as fast in fact; and the amount of energy expended in doing this is also increased. This is illustrated in Figure 37.

If the amplitude of a sound is doubled, the intensity will increase four times; if the amplitude is trebled, the intensity will increase nine times, so the intensity of a sound is proportional to the *square* of the amplitude.

Intensity is a physical measurement and is not to be directly equated with loudness; loudness is a perceptual matter, like pitch, a matter of hearing and judging what we hear. But there is a close relation between the physical dimension of intensity and the perceptual dimension of loudness, which we shall discuss in the next chapter, and because loudness is linguistically interesting, we are interested in its physical correlate, intensity.

The energies involved in speech waves are infinitesimally small compared with the energy applied in pushing a pen across paper, but the *range* of energy in the sounds we can hear is very large. The intensity of a very loud sound may be as much as a billion times as great as the quietest sound we can hear, so it would be inconveniently long-winded to use an absolute scale for referring to intensity. What we do instead is to compare the intensity of one sound with that of another and for this purpose we use the *decibel scale*. This is a logarithmic scale and it works as follows: if sound B is a hundred times more intense than sound A the intensity ratio between them is $10^2:1$; if we now take the power ^{2}, to which 10 has to be raised to give 100, and multiply it by 10 (this is the *deci* of the decibel scale) we get the difference between A and B in decibels (db), i.e. 20. So B is 20 db up on (more intense than) A. If sound C is 100 times more intense than sound B it too will be 20 db up on B, but it will be 40 db up on A, because the intensity ratio of C and A is $100 \times 100:1$ which equals $10,000:1$ which equals $10^4:1$. Taking the power 4 and again multiplying by 10 we arrive at 40 db. If one sound is a billion times more intense than another ($10^{12}:1$) it is 120 db up on it. In other words to get the intensity relation between two sounds in decibels, take the logarithm (to the base 10) of their ratio and multiply it by 10. Suppose that the ratio between two sounds is 3:1; the common logarithm of 3 (i.e. the power to which 10 must be raised to give 3) is 0·477, so the decibel difference equals 4·77. If the ratio is 1,200:1, the common logarithm of 1,200 is 3·08 and the db difference 30·8.

If, as we often do, we want to refer to the intensity of one sound we compare it to a standard reference intensity which has a fixed physical value close to the audible limit of sound. When we say that a sound is 20 db, what we mean is that it is physically one hundred times more intense (10^2) than the standard reference level.

Resonance

Vibrations can be transmitted from one body to another, often with increased amplitude. For example, if the prongs of a fork are set in vibration the amplitude is not very great and the associated sound is not very loud. But if the handle of the fork is placed on a table-top the loudness is increased because the large table-top is caused to vibrate in sympathy with the fork and the amplitudes it produces are greater. Similarly, if a violin string is set into vibration when it is not in contact with the body of the instrument the vibrations are weak, but when they are transmitted through the bridge to the body the resultant amplitude is greatly increased. This transmission of vibrations from one body to another is known as *resonance* and the body to which the vibrations are transmitted is called a *resonator*. The table-top and the violin body in our two examples are resonators.

Every resonator has a natural *resonant frequency*, that is, a particular frequency to which it will most readily respond. A tuning fork vibrating at 100 cps will cause a second fork set close by to resonate, provided that the second fork also has a natural frequency of 100 cps or something very close to it.

Resonators which respond to frequencies only very close to their own natural frequency also have the characteristic that their vibrations take some time to build up and die away. Other resonators react much more quickly in the building up and the dying away of their vibrations; for instance our table-top and violin body: resonance begins almost instantaneously when the fork contacts the table and ceases very quickly after contact is lost; so too the violin body resonates so long as the string is being bowed but stops when the bowing stops. Such resonators are said to be *damped*, and damped resonators have the characteristic (contrary to the undamped tuning fork resonator) of responding to a much wider range of outside frequencies. Whether a 100 cps or a 600 cps tuning fork is used, the table-top will resonate, and so too will the violin body whether the note played is high or low.

The extent to which a resonator responds to different frequencies can be shown in a *resonance curve*. Figure 38 shows the curves of two different resonators.

Both A and B have a natural resonant frequency of 100 cps, that is, their maximum amplitude is stimulated by an outside vibration with a frequency of 100 cps, but A's response falls off much more rapidly than B's, so that to an outside tone of 75 cps A's resonant response is greatly reduced, whereas B's is still high. The *output* of a resonator, namely, the way in which it vibrates in response to outside vibrations, is determined much more by its own characteristics than by the *input* (the vibrations causing resonance), and if the input consists of a large number of frequencies all of the same amplitude, the output will nevertheless be exactly as shown in Figure 38, since the resonator will react less and less powerfully to the frequencies further and further from its resonant frequency. If the output amplitudes from the resonator are very low compared with the maximum amplitude they will contribute very little to the sound which the resonator produces. Conventionally, it is reckoned that output from the resonator is ineffective if it is

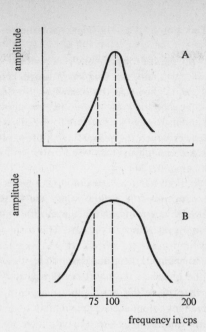

Figure 38: Resonance curves

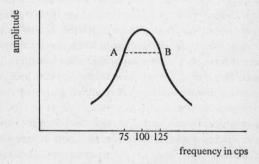

Figure 39: Bandwidth of a resonator

less than half as powerful as the maximum the resonator can produce.

In Figure 39 the part of the resonance curve above the line AB is the effective part, and the frequency range between these points, i.e. 50 cps, is known as the *bandwidth*. So the effect of a resonator can be specified by giving its resonant frequency (here 100 cps) and its bandwidth (50 cps), for by this we are saying that all frequencies which the resonator is putting out between 75 and 125 cps are making an effective contribution to the sound, the maximum being at 100 cps.

Not only solid bodies but volumes of air can be set resonating. This is what happens with a flute when the relatively weak vibrations caused by blowing across the mouth hole cause the column of air in the instrument to vibrate. This form of resonance is particularly important in speech. If we take the nasalized vowel [ã] in French *banc*, there are three distinct cavities which are relevant, the pharynx, the nasal cavity and the oral cavity. The vocal cords provide the input vibrations, rather weak but having a wide range of frequencies; the volumes of air in the three cavities are set resonating in accordance with their own character-istics, which are determined by the size and shape of the cavities. Each separate vowel sound has a different combination of two or three cavity shapes (the nasal cavity is not always included) and thus a characteristic pattern of resonance. It is this constant pattern of resonance that marks a vowel acoustically and enables us to recognize it each time it occurs, whatever the fundamental frequency of the input from the vocal cords. The vocal tract, being of a complicated shape, has not just one but many resonant frequencies, and therefore various of the com-ponent frequencies provided by the vocal cords will be picked out and amplified by resonance, so that for a given position of the speech organs above the vocal cords there corresponds an acoustic pattern consisting of particular sound intensities in particular frequency regions.

Acoustic characterization of sounds

Figure 40 shows the simplified acoustic pattern for the vowel [ɪ] of 'sit', pronounced by the author. The duration of the vowel is represented along the horizontal axis: it was continued for about a second. Intensity is shown by the darkness of the horizontal bands, and frequency is shown along the vertical axis. From this we can see that there are three areas where considerable energy is to be found, around 500 cps, 1,780 cps and 2,500

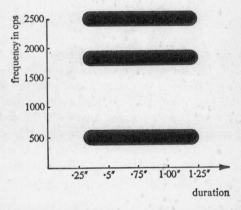

Figure 40: Simplified acoustic pattern of [ɪ] in *sit* (see also Plate 1)

cps. These banks of energy are typical of [ɪ] and are known as the *formants* of the vowel. The formants are numbered from low to high: formant 1 (F1) is centred on 500, F2 on 1,780 and F3 on 2,500 cps. F1 is not to be confused with the variable fundamental frequency, not shown in Figure 40. Vowels generally have more than three formants (F4, F5, etc.) but these higher formants do not seem to be needed for specifying vowels and are more connected with identifying the voice quality of a particular speaker.

This kind of analysis can be carried out quickly and accurately by means of the *acoustic spectrograph*, which produces traces like that shown in Figure 40. Photographs of the spectrograms of [ɪ] and other sounds are shown in Plates 1 to 13. The frequency and time aspects are well catered for in spectrograms of this kind, but the intensity is only very grossly represented by the relative darkness of the formants. However, the machine can also be used to give an accurate specification of the spectrum of the sound at a particular moment of time. This is known as an

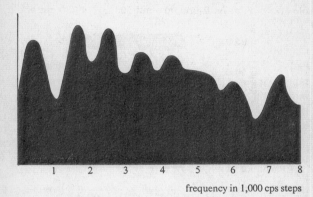

frequency in 1,000 cps steps

Figure 41: Amplitude section of [ɪ] (see also Plate 1)

amplitude section and is illustrated in Figure 41. We can see from this not only the three formant areas at 500, 1,780 and 2,500 cps, as in Figure 40, but also the relative amplitudes of the formants. One other factor which might be of importance is the bandwidth of the formants, but these do not seem to vary independently from vowel to vowel, so that in order to characterize vowels in acoustic terms all we need to do is to specify the frequencies and relative intensities of F1, F2 and F3. Sounds other than vowels may also display a clear formant structure, for instance [m, n, ɹ, l], etc. All sounds which are voiced and non-constrictive can be summed up acoustically in terms of their formants.

Fricative sounds give spectrograms which are rather messy-looking compared with those of vowels, etc. Plate 2 shows a spectrogram of [s] and it is clear from this that the energy is not neatly banded in well-defined formants, but spread over a rather wide area. We would expect this from the spectrum of [s] shown in Figure 35, and when we look at a section of [s] (Plate 3) we see that energy is distributed much more continuously over the wide frequency area, though with some variation of intensity at different frequencies. What is particularly important for fricative sounds is the frequency range over which energy is spread and the overall intensity of the sounds. Compare the sections of [s] and [f], Plates 3 and 4. Most of the energy for the [s] is in the range 3,000—8,000 cps whereas for [f] it is distributed much more evenly over the whole frequency range. On the other hand, the general level of amplitude is much greater for [s] than for [f], which corresponds to our perception of [s] as a noisier sound than [f]. Voiced fricatives are similar in their noise characteristics to voiceless ones, but they differ in that the vocal cord vibrations which accompany them cause resonance in the cavities *behind* the narrowing and one may therefore see more 'banding' of the energy in a formant-like way. Compare the spectrograms of [s] and [z] in Plates 2 and 5. A formant-type structure may also be quite characteristic of some voiceless fricatives: this is parti-cularly true for [h] sounds, since [h] is in effect simply a voiceless variety of a following vowel. Notice on Plate 6 how [h] before the vowels [i, ɑ, ɔ] in *he, hah, haw* has noise formants which corre-spond exactly in frequency to the formants of the following vowel. Similarly the voiceless velar fricative [x] of Scots *loch* (Plate 7) has a clear formant structure of its own.

Time is a factor which has to be taken into account in char-acterizing sounds in general, but it is crucial in the case of the plosives, and that in two ways: first, the explosion of the plosive corresponds to a burst of noise, similar to the noise present in fricatives, but of very short duration. This burst is visible in the spectrogram of the syllable [dɔː] *daw* on Plate 8 as a thin vertical line right at the beginning of the trace. Because the burst is very short we hear it as an explosion; if the duration of the burst were extended, it would be heard as more and more like a fricative as the duration increased. Then secondly, the time between the burst and the onset of a following sound is important. It is clear from Plate 8 that after the burst and before the vowel is fully established a change is taking place – the vowel formants bend upwards, that is, they increase in frequency, before they reach their steady positions, which is only after a certain time: this corresponds to the movement of the speech organs from the stop position of the plosive to the open position of the vowel. Changes of this kind in vowel formants are known as *transitions* and their duration is important because if it is above about a tenth of a second, the sound will again tend to lose its plosive character. So the duration of the burst and the duration of the transitions are both very characteristic of plosives in general. But there is more to both than merely duration.

The bursts of different plosives have different noise characteristics; the main energy, as with the fricatives, is distributed differently according to the different places of articulation. The explosion of [p] does not sound like that of [t] and it is acoustically different in that, like the fricative [f], its energy is distributed fairly evenly over all frequencies, whereas [t] has most energy either between 2,000 and 4,000 cps if the following vowel is rounded, or between 3,500 and 6,000 cps if it is not rounded. But more than this, the transition of F2 is directly related to the place of articulation of the various plosive consonants: for [d], for instance, this transition will always be related to a frequency of about 1,800 cps, so if the F2 of the adjacent vowel is high, as for [i] (about 2,800 cps) the transition will rise from a preceding plosive or fall to a following one; if the F2 of the vowel is low, as for [u] (about 600 cps), then the transition will fall from a preceding plosive and rise to a following one. This is illustrated

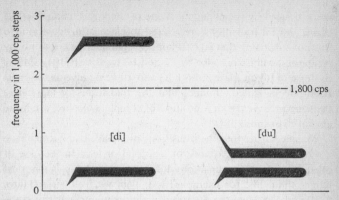

Figure 42: F2 transitions of [d] before [i] and [u]. Locus 1800 cps

in Figure 42. Notice in particular that the F2 transitions do not necessarily originate *at* 1,800 cps but merely point *towards* it. For [b] this *locus* frequency is lower, at about 800 cps; this is shown in Figure 43.

Whilst other consonant sounds do not have bursts like the plosives, they do naturally enough have transitions, since these

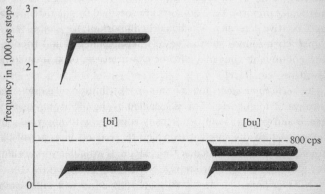

Figure 43: F2 transitions of [b] before [i] and [u]. Locus 800 cps

are produced by the changing shape of the vocal tract. The loci of F2 and F3 transitions are related to place of articulation, so it is not surprising that [s] on Plate 2 is characterized not only by its aperiodic noise but also by F2 and F3 transitions very similar to those of [d] on Plate 8, both [s] and [d] being alveolar sounds. It should be noted, though, that the transitions of [d], where the tongue moves from a position of complete closure, are more abrupt than those of [s].

We said earlier that the transitions of plosive consonants have a duration of about a tenth of a second or less. In the case of other sounds, the transition durations may be a good deal longer than this, for example [w, j, ɹ] in *we*, *you*, *reed* (Plates 9, 10 and 11). Here the durations are clearly longer than for the plosives. Furthermore, the duration of one formant may be less than that of others: this is the case, for example, in [l] (Plate 12), where F1 changes abruptly as the tongue-tip contact is lost, whereas F2 and F3 change a good deal more slowly.

To sum up, the following factors must be taken into account when describing sounds in acoustic terms:

1. *Formant structure:* the concentration of energy into well-defined bands at different frequencies, F1, F2 and F3 being of particular importance. Formants are specified by their frequency and relative intensity. (Particularly important for voiced non-constrictive sounds such as vowels, nasals, laterals and frictionless continuants, but may also be characteristic of at least some fricatives, e.g. [h, x].)

2. *Noise component:* the continuous distribution of energy over a range of frequencies. This is specified by the effective frequency range and general level of intensity together with any peaks of intensity, also the speed with which the general intensity of the sound builds up at particular frequencies. (Particularly important for all fricatives and for the burst of plosives, flaps, rolls.)

3. *Transitions:* the characteristic changes of formant frequency associated with changes in the shape of the vocal cavities in

passing from one articulatory configuration to another. These are specifiable in terms of

(a) initial and terminal frequencies of transition

(b) initial and terminal intensity of transition

(c) duration of transition, including differential durations of F1, F2, F3 where this applies

(Not important for vowels but crucial for most consonants, especially with regard to place of articulation (frequency, intensity) and manner of articulation (duration).)

Acoustic complexity

The spectrograms discussed hitherto have been either of isolated sounds or of very simple syllables, yet even in these latter we have noticed considerable acoustic changes taking place. If we look at Plate 13 which is the spectrogram of the spoken phrase *Penguin linguistics* we see that there is a good deal more change than steady-state. It would be perfectly possible, by adopting the criterion of 'extreme position' which we used in articulatory segmentation (p. 67f.), to divide up the acoustic picture along the time-line into a number of segments, though it would not always be easy to establish the exact boundary between segments. So, in the simple example of [sɔ] *saw* on Plate 2, we see first of all a block of high-frequency noise (corresponding to the friction of [s]), which we could call segment 1 (although notice that at the end of this noise there is some change going on corresponding to the progressive rounding of the lips for the vowel). Then there is a very short gap where nothing much is going on at all before a clear formant structure appears. Call the gap segment 2. And then we have the transition period where F2 and F3 are quite clearly moving from a higher to a lower frequency – segment 3 – and finally there is the steady-state of the vowel, segment 4. As far as articulation goes we have 2 segments [s] and [ɔ]; acoustically we have four. We can fairly easily identify segment 1 as part of [s] and segment 4 as part of [ɔ], but how about segments 2 and 3? Presumably both correspond to the articulatory movement from the extreme fricative position of [s] to the extreme open position of [ɔ], that is to the boundary area between the articulatory segments. It would not, therefore, be sensible to ask whether segments 2 and 3 belong to [s] or to [ɔ]: one method of segmentation produces one result, the other another. What we can sensibly ask, however, is: what happens acoustically in the syllable [sɔ], and this is what we do. Acoustic segmentation should not be carried out for its own sake, but rather in relation to articulatory segmentation and to our perception of sounds when we listen to them. We simply note that in a particular sequence of articulatory or perceptual segments such and such acoustic segments occur in a certain order.

We must be particularly careful not to draw premature conclusions about which acoustic features are particularly important for sounds and sound sequences, for two main reasons. In the first place the acoustic information present in speech is enormously abundant and detailed and we need to find out how much of it is in fact relevant to speech. And secondly, human beings are, from an acoustic point of view, very variable in their performance: if I say [sɔ] twice, in apparently identical ways, the machine will show acoustic differences, and if we compared the acoustic records of me saying [sɔ] and you saying it, the differences would be very considerable. Bearing these two considerations in mind we must ask and answer various questions before we can have real insight into the acoustic basis of speech. For instance, how much of the acoustic data can we perceive? There may be acoustic energy present which our ear simply will not react to because it is too high or too weak or too short-lived, in which case it is useless to us and may be jettisoned. Or again, if we can perceive it, how much, if anything, does it contribute? We have seen that the upper vowel formants are not essential for recognizing vowels, but apparently tell us something about the quality of an individual's voice. They contribute to speech, but in a less central way than the lower formants, which can distinguish one vowel from another even when no upper formants are present. And then, if there are differences in the acoustic record as between you and me, which of them are vital and which not?

Until we can answer such questions as these it is impossible to see the linguistic wood for the acoustic trees and a very great deal of work has been and is being done towards providing answers. One method of tackling the problem is by filtering, that is by mechanically removing certain of the frequencies which normal speech contains. If we get rid of all frequencies above 3,000 cps we find that the friction of [s] becomes unrecognizable but that of [f] remains recognizable, and we may conclude that energy below 3,000 cps is not relevant to [s], but that it is relevant to [f]. Another powerful tool for answering such questions is synthetic speech; most people by now have heard examples of artificial speech produced entirely by electronic means. Its importance for research is that it enables us to perform experiments with artificial acoustic patterns very much simpler than normal speech could possibly produce, and by ignoring more and more of the total acoustic record one can gradually find what is essential in a particular sound sequence and what is not.

But all such experiments depend for their success on the human ear; acoustics alone cannot give the answers. It is only by submitting the filtered speech or the artificial speech to people's judgement that we can find out what is relevant and what is not. If I get a machine to produce an acoustic pattern which I believe represents [sɔ] and the subject to whom I play it consistently fails to *hear* [sɔ], there is no appeal. I shall just have to go back and back and back until I produce something which he does recognize as [sɔ]. This interplay between the acoustic record and what people hear is of extreme importance not only in research but in general for the understanding of the communication process, and the following chapter will examine it more closely.

4. Auditory Phonetics: Ear and Brain

Despite a great deal of important and intricate research work, we cannot yet relate what goes on in the ear proper to, say, the acoustic features of sounds, in at all as detailed a way as we can relate together articulatory and acoustic features. It is the brain – or perhaps we should say our perception as mediated by the brain – rather than the ear itself which is of major importance in the chain of events which constitutes oral communication. Because of this there is no need to give here a very detailed account of the ear's anatomy and physiology. It will be sufficient to say in quite general terms what the ear does.

The ear has three major functions, to collect stimuli, to transmit them and, to some extent at least, to analyse them. The *outer ear* consists of what we can see plus the canal which leads to the *ear-drum*. Sound waves are channelled down the canal and cause the ear-drum, a sensitive diaphragm, to vibrate very much as the adjacent molecules of air vibrate; but the canal itself, a short tube full of air, acts as a resonator and causes some amplification of frequencies near its resonant frequency. So the sound wave at the ear-drum does not have exactly the same form as it does at a microphone outside the ear. Also, the ear-drum is not capable of vibrating at all the frequencies which may be present in the sound wave. The upper limit of frequency which we can perceive is at most 20,000 cps and in most people, depending a good deal on age, quite a lot less. Television sets with 605 lines emit a high-pitched whistle at 15,000 cps, but many people cannot hear it. Similarly a sensitive microphone can pick up sounds whose intensity is too weak for the ear to register. In the outer ear, then, there is both an amplification of some frequencies and a rejection of some frequencies and intensities.

The *middle ear*, behind the ear-drum, is a small air-filled cavity in the skull which contains a chain of three tiny bones connected to the ear-drum at one end and the *inner ear* at the other. These transmit the vibrations of the drum and, because of the way they are articulated together, they amplify the vibrations a little before they pass them to the inner ear. The middle ear is connected to the nose by the *Eustachian tube*, which ensures that the air pressure in the normally enclosed middle ear can be equalized with outside air pressure quickly and easily if they become very different, as when an aircraft gains height.

The main part of the inner ear is the *cochlea*, a completely enclosed gallery with rigid walls and filled with fluid, coiled round itself like a snail-shell and becoming narrower as it does so. If we could uncoil the cochlea it would look somewhat as in Figure 44. The broad end of the cochlea connects with the middle

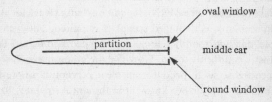

Figure 44: Diagram of the cochlea

ear. Along almost the whole of its length the cochlea is divided into two by a membranous partition which runs from the broad end almost as far as the narrow end. There are two openings from the middle ear into the cochlea, one on each side of this partition. The first of these, the *oval window*, is filled by the innermost of the three little bones of the middle ear, whose vibrations are therefore transmitted to the fluid of the cochlea. The second opening, the *round window*, is covered with elastic membrane which takes up the pressure changes in the fluid. When the vibrations are passed to the fluid they cause the dividing membrane to vibrate also, but because of its structure different points on the membrane respond more actively to different frequencies, so that the complex wave is as it were analysed into its component frequencies by cochlear action. This information is then transmitted to the brain via the auditory nerve.

The information going from the cochlea to the brain differs from the information arriving at the outer ear in five ways: one, the ear canal amplifies some frequencies; two, the ear-drum rejects some frequencies and intensities; three, the middle-ear bones amplify slightly the vibrations of the ear-drum; four, the difference in size between the ear-drum and the oval window (about 25:1) makes the pressure at the latter very much greater than at the former; and five, the cochlea analyses the component frequencies of the complex wave.

What happens when the signals from the ear reach the brain is largely a mystery still. It is clear that the activity in the brain which is connected with speech is, to some extent at least, localized. If the speech area is damaged speech is impaired, but even considerable damage to other areas leaves speech intact. Further than this it is difficult to go. How the incoming nervous signals are processed so as to produce our clear perceptual impressions is not known. Nor do we know how the brain operates to give effect to an intention to speak, to produce the nervous impulses necessary to make the speech organs move in their delicate, complicated dance. Direct investigation of the brain is hampered, ironically, by man's unique capacity for speech; since animals cannot talk, experiments with their brains can tell us nothing about speech function, and direct experimental investigation of the human brain is largely, and rightly, ruled out by moral considerations. Yet we do perceive sound, we can hear high and low pitch, loudness and softness, changing sound qualities, and it is this perceptual, psychological aspect on which we shall concentrate.

The perception of sound

I have already pointed out that the hearing system cannot react to all of the features present in a sound wave, and since anything which cannot be perceived is useless for communication purposes, the essential thing is to determine what we perceive (as opposed to *how* we perceive it), what different sorts of perception we have, and what are the limits of our capabilities in perception. At the same time we are interested in how these perceptions of ours relate to the acoustic information present in sound waves and to the production of the pressure changes initiated by the vocal organs, in order to be able to observe and categorize the transformations which take place at the different stages of speech.

We hear speech sounds in terms of the four perceptual categories of pitch, loudness, quality and length. These are subjective categories and must not be equated exactly with the related physiological or physical categories of vocal-cord vibration/ fundamental frequency, breath effort/intensity, cavity shape/ spectral structure, and physical duration. It is perfectly true that if we double the rate of vibration of the vocal cords or the fundamental frequency we hear a note of higher pitch, but we cannot assume that the second note will be heard as exactly double the height of the first note, nor that a doubling of intensity will result in a doubling of loudness. We must therefore keep the perceptual dimensions and terms separate in our minds from the dimensions and terms of physiology and physics. In the following pages we will look at the perceptual categories and try to relate them to the others.

Pitch

Whether we hear the pitch of a note as high or low is related to frequency, but not in a simple way. In the lower regions of frequency, below about 1,000 cps, the relation is more or less direct: that is to say, a change of, say, 150 cps of frequency will lead to a comparable change of pitch whether the frequencies are 350–500 cps or 850–1,000 cps. But above 1,000 cps a given frequency interval makes less and less difference of pitch, so that to double the perceived pitch of a note in the higher regions we may have to multiply the frequency by four. The amplitude of vibration may also affect the perceived pitch: if in listening to the ringing or engaged tone of a telephone you hold the earpiece tightly against your ear you will hear a particular pitch; if you then take it a little away from your ear, which reduces the amplitude, you will hear that the pitch is slightly higher. But this effect of amplitude is slight and we can disregard it for practical purposes.

Our hearing is most sensitive in the region below 1,000 cps. In this region, if listening conditions are perfect, we can perceive a difference of pitch between two notes which are as little as 3 cps apart. This region includes the range of fundamental frequencies corresponding to the vibrations of the vocal cords and we are indeed very sensitive to small changes of pitch in speech, but it would be wrong to think that a 3 cps difference which is perceptible in ideal conditions could possibly be used for communication in the hurly-burly of speech, or that our control of the vocal cords is as delicate as that would require. It seems that any difference of pitch less than about a semitone would not be usable in speech even though we are capable of detecting differences of about one-twentieth of a semitone.

We ought to distinguish at this point between our perception of pitch as related to vocal-cord vibration or the fundamental frequency of periodic sounds, and our perception of both the higher harmonics of such sounds and the aperiodic vibrations of other sounds. When there is no fundamental frequency, as for instance in [s], we cannot easily hear a definite pitch. It would not be true to say that we have no idea of pitch for [s] – if we compare [s] with [ʃ] as in *Shush* we are quite clear that [s] is in some sense the higher pitched. For such sounds it seems that we average the component frequencies to arrive at our impression: but the impression is by no means so clear cut as that which we have of the pitch of voiced sounds. In periodic sounds, such as vowels, we are certainly affected by the higher harmonics; as we have seen, the formant pattern is related to our perception of their different qualities. But we do not perceive these higher harmonics as identifiable pitches: instead we perceive them as differences of sound quality. This kind of perception will be discussed below.

We do not use a very great range of vocal pitch in speech. It varies quite widely from person to person but probably does not exceed about two-and-a-half octaves even in wide-ranging voices, and it may cover as little as one octave. Clearly, the exact musical limits of the pitch range of an individual's voice is of little interest to us because men, women and children must be able to make use of the conventional pitch patterns of their language even though their voices have very different pitch ranges. However, relative pitch is of great importance within one individual's voice; the use that we make of it will be discussed in Chapters 6 and 7.

Loudness

Loudness – another perceptual dimension – is primarily related to sound intensity but as with pitch and frequency the relation is not simple. In the middle of the ear's frequency range we can perceive tones which have relatively little intensity. Tones of very low and very high frequency, however, need to be of very much greater intensity to be perceived. So a tone of 4,000 cps may be just audible very close to the reference level (0 db) but one of 50 cps will need its intensity raised by as much as 50 db before it becomes audible, and a tone of 10,000 cps will need 40 db more intensity than the 4,000 cps tone before it is heard. When we bear in mind that 40 db means a ratio of 10,000:1 our variability in reacting to intensity in relation to frequency becomes very clear.

In the most sensitive middle-frequency areas the range of intensities we can respond to is very great: it is not until we reach a level of about 140 db that pain begins to be felt in the ear. But the sort of intensities we encounter in normal speech are only between about 25 and 85 db which correspond to a soft whisper and a loud shout measured about a yard from the speaker's mouth. Furthermore we are a good deal less sensitive to differences of loudness than we are to changes of pitch; experiments have shown that at a given frequency we can, in ideal conditions, distinguish some 250 or more degrees of loudness of a pure tone, whereas at a fixed loudness we may be able to hear more than 1,000 differences of pitch. Whether this is the reason or not, we use loudness in language in a very much grosser way than pitch. The complexity of pitch patterns used in language and the delicacy of our reaction to them are in no way matched by the patterns of loudness found in language, as we shall see later in Chapters 6 and 7.

Here we must mention again the fact that, as with frequency, we certainly react to differences of intensity at the different frequencies of the spectra of sounds; however, we do not perceive these differences as differences of loudness in the sense in which we hear one syllable or utterance as louder than another. Rather we perceive them as differences of sound quality; if the intensity of the second formant of a vowel is weakened we do not react by saying that the second formant is less loud or even that the whole vowel is less loud. Our reaction is to say that the vowel has changed its quality, its colour. And parallel to this, although it has been shown that there is an order of average intensity amongst the sounds of language – the open vowels being most intense, then the close vowels, then voiced continuants and so on down to the voiceless fricatives such as [f] and [θ] – our immediate reaction is not to say, for instance, that the [ɑ] of *half* is louder than the [i] of *see* or the [θ] of *thin*, but rather that they are of a different quality or a different nature. So our perception of intensity, like our perception of frequency, is on two levels; in one area we relate to it loudness and in another to sound quality.

Sound quality

Our perception of the quality of sounds is, as we have seen, related to their spectral pattern and to the actions of the vocal organs which produce them. We are much better at discriminating differences of quality than at stating the productive mechanisms or the acoustic patterns. To take one example, if you and I both say the word *see* [si], we may well hear, if we listen very closely, that your [s] is not quite the same as mine and that my [i] is different from yours, but I would be hard put to it to capture the differences in either articulatory or acoustic terms. I might be able to do it if the differences were great enough, but minute differences, which are none the less clearly perceptible, are not easy to tie down in acoustic or articulatory terms. However, much more important than these minutiæ, it would be perfectly obvious that when you said *see* it was *you* saying it – it would have your individual voice quality – and when I said it it would have mine. Differences of voice quality may be very great and we are well aware of them – we can all recognize some hundreds of individuals by the sound of their voice – yet very little work has been done to relate such differences to articulatory or acoustic facts. It seems likely that differences in size and shape of the individual's vocal cavities, structure of vocal cords and control of their vibration, and air-flow characteristics all have an effect on voice quality; on the other hand it seems that voice quality is also related to the higher formants of voiced sounds. However, we really know very little about the causes of the differences, and the reason no doubt is that so much effort has been put into elucidating the basic differences of sound which we rely upon to distinguish one word from another that little has been left over for those aspects which we disregard when we speak of two people pronouncing the 'same' sound.

With these provisos, we can nevertheless relate our perception of sounds and sound classes to the way in which they are produced and their acoustic properties, and we can notice that in some cases our 'articulatory' categories are at least labelled in auditory terms.

Plosives

Two things must be present for us to hear a plosive: the phase of complete closure when air is being compressed; this corresponds acoustically to a 'silent' segment where there is either no energy at all, in voiceless stops, or energy at only very low frequencies, in voiced stops. And secondly, the rapid movement of the speech organs to or from the place of articulation, corresponding to the fast formant transitions. The explosion of air, corresponding to the acoustic burst, does not have to be present: if you say the word *up* without an explosion at the end of [p], by keeping the lips together, it is still recognizably [p] and nothing else, though the explosive burst makes identification easier. Characteristic formant transitions and different burst spectra, corresponding to stops and releases at different places of articulation, govern our ability to discriminate [p, b] from [t, d] etc. Notice here, as we shall throughout this section, that we have no developed system for a purely auditory labelling of a [p] as opposed to a [t]. What terms would you use to express the clear difference in sound between them without referring to their places of articulation or their burst/transition features but only to the sort of noise they make? On the other hand 'plosive' as a generic term would seem to be auditorily based.

Nasals

Nasals like [m] and [n] are similar to stops in their transitions but differ from them in having a vowel-like formant structure, which corresponds to the free passage of voice through the nose, though the formants are weaker than vowel formants because of the blocked mouth. There is no burst/explosion. All nasals sound much alike – a kind of humming sound – when they are held continuously, and we differentiate one from another by transitions corresponding to the closing/opening of the mouth at different places. 'Nasal' as a term is articulatory; we might refer to these sounds by means of an auditory label such as 'humming' sounds, but this is not generally done.

Rolls

Our perception of rolled sounds is related to several rapid interruptions of the air-stream, i.e. complete closures, compressions and releases made much faster than for plosives but otherwise with the same acoustic features. In addition a clear vowel-like formant structure is visible between the short 'silent' segments of closure. 'Roll' is an auditory label, c.f. drum-roll.

Flap

As for roll, but with only one rapid movement.

Fricatives

This is very much an auditory term since it is our ear alone which tells us that friction is present. Our perception of friction relates to turbulent air-flow through a narrow channel and to aperiodic vibration. It is sometimes useful to divide this category auditorily into sibilants ([s]-like sounds) and fricatives; and the sibilants may also be divided, again auditorily, into hissing ([s]-type) and hushing ([ʃ]-type). The differences relate to place of articulation and nature of narrowing, and to the frequency areas in which the noise is present and the intensity of the energy.

Laterals

This is clearly an articulatory label; it would be difficult to agree an auditory one. Perception relates to blockage along the mid-line of the mouth and lateral air-flow. Acoustically, laterals have a vowel-like formant structure but with weaker formants, and a sudden upward shift of F1 when tongue contact is broken.

Frictionless continuants

Being voiced, oral and non-fricative these have very vowel-like formant structures but somewhat reduced in intensity and with slow transitions. This corresponds to their open articulation and gliding nature.

Vowels

Our perception of different vowel qualities is related articulatorily to lack of obstruction of the vocal tract and the different shapes of the oral, nasal and pharyngal cavities, shapes determined by the tongue, lips and soft palate. Acoustic energy is clearly banded into powerful formants. In practical language work, where quick decisions have to be made about similarities and differences of vowel quality, neither the articulatory nor the acoustic level are of immediate help, so a method of mainly auditory comparison has been developed, known as the *cardinal vowel* system. To establish this system a number of reference vowels distributed more or less evenly over the whole auditory field were selected and recorded; the vowels found in language can then be compared with the cardinal vowels and described by reference to them. This is rather like having a number of cardinal colours, distributed over the whole visual colour continuum, to which all other colours can be related.

These chosen vowels are generally displayed on the diagram illustrated in Figure 21 (p. 52). The fact that this diagram is derived from tongue positions tends to obscure the basically auditory nature of the cardinal vowel system, but it has a certain practical utility in enabling us to roughly deduce the tongue positions related to the vowel qualities we hear. Initially, eight cardinal vowels were selected; the symbols for these vowels and their placing on the diagram are shown in Figure 45. The vowels [i] and [ɑ] were chosen first as representing the closest front and the openest back vowel respectively. Then, [e, ɛ, a] were determined in such a way that the quality intervals [i–e], [e–ɛ], [ɛ–a] and [a–ɑ] were judged *auditorily* to be equal. This same interval was then continued in the back-vowel line [ɔ, o, u]. We now have eight equally spaced vowels of fixed quality to which, simply by listening, we can compare a new vowel, and it is remarkable how readily one can say, for example, that the new vowel is 'halfway between [e] and [ɛ]' or 'one-third of the way from [a] to [ɑ]'.

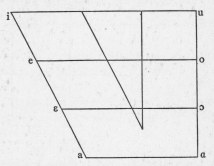

Figure 45: The primary cardinal vowels

Eight vowels were found to be insufficient to cover the whole vowel field, so eight more were added by applying changes of lip position to the original vowels. Cardinal [i] is made with the lips spread and cardinal [u] with the lips close-rounded. If we hold everything still in the position taken up for one vowel, then reverse just the lip positions and try to say the vowel for which the original position was taken up, we get two new vowels, a rounded front vowel (symbol [y]) which has the tongue position of [i] and the lip-rounding of [u], and an unrounded back vowel (symbol [ɯ]) with the tongue position of [u] but the lip spreading of [i]. Similarly, the lip positions of [e] (spread) and [o] (close-rounded) are reversed to give the new vowels [ø] and [ɤ], and those of [ɛ] (neutral) and [ɔ] (open-rounded) to give [œ] and [ʌ]. Then open lip-rounding is added to both [a] and [ɑ] to give [Œ] and [ɒ]. To these sixteen cardinal vowels were finally added two more close central vowels [ɨ] and [ʉ] which have a tongue position midway between [i] and [u] and with spread and rounded lips respectively. Figure 46 shows all eighteen cardinal vowels in relation to the vowel diagram.

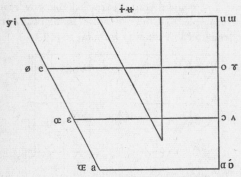

Figure 46: The eighteen cardinal vowels

The cardinal vowel system was devised partly on an auditory and partly on an articulatory basis but our use of it in pinning down the qualities of real-life vowels is entirely auditory, in that we 'place' the new vowel by relying on our ear's capacity to relate it accurately to the known qualities of the cardinal vowels. This requires a good deal of practice both in learning and remembering the cardinal vowel qualities and in relating the new vowels to them, but with practice there is quite good agreement between trained observers as to the location of any given vowel.

The diagrammatic presentation of the cardinal vowels could no doubt be made more logical. There is no compelling reason why its shape should be as it is. The auditory vowel field might be represented as square or circular; perhaps it ought to be three-dimensional, though this would be inconvenient for practical

purposes. In any case, it ought to be possible to place, say, [i] and
[y] at different points on a diagram to correspond to their difference in quality, rather than having them at the same point as at
present, which makes it necessary to refer to lip position in order
to differentiate them. Such a possible rearrangement is given in
Figure 47. It is clear from this, and even clearer from Figure 46,

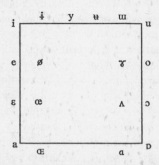

Figure 47: Possible auditory rearrangement of the cardinal vowels

that the central area is rather poorly served by the cardinal vowel
system. It would be helpful to have some agreed vowel qualities,
fixed and recorded like the others, which would let us locate more
accurately central vowels such as that in *bird*, and in practice we
do have vowels in this area to which we refer, but until they are
generally agreed, our reference will be less accurate here than it is
in the more peripheral areas.

The time is ripe for a thorough-going investigation into the
auditory similarities and differences amongst the cardinal vowels.
In Figure 47 [i ɨ y ʉ ɯ u] are spaced equally, as though the
auditory intervals between them were equal; but this is by no
means certain, and even the order in which they are shown might
be disputed. Such an investigation might reveal just how the vowel
field is shaped: at present there is no auditory reason to suppose
that a square represents it better than any other regular or

irregular shape. Also, the trained observer recognizes that his ability to discriminate vowel qualities is not equal over the whole vowel range – experience shows that we have more difficulty in locating vowels within the 'low back' area than elsewhere – and this is no doubt connected with the auditory shape of the vowel field. As things stand, however, the cardinal vowel system, as summed up in Figure 46, is extraordinarily resistant and extremely useful, and no other system of vowel classification, of which a good many have been put forward, is as widely used and as useful.

There are two particular aspects of vowel quality which fall outside the scope of the cardinal vowel system: nasalization and retroflexion. In articulatory terms nasalization refers to the coupling-in of the nasal cavity by lowering the soft palate, but we recognize nasalized vowels by the characteristic sound which this produces, and since the nasality is caused by the same means whatever the shape of the mouth cavity, it is not surprising that we recognize it as something superimposed on vowels and account for it separately rather than integrating it into the cardinal-vowel system. The same is true of retroflexion (often referred to as 'r-colouring') which is typified by an Irish or Somerset or Mid-Western pronunciation of the vowel in bird. This is produced by raising and pulling back the tip of the tongue and contracting the whole tongue laterally, and, like nasalization, it can be superimposed upon a wide variety of vowel qualities. It is not certain, though, that we can discriminate as many nasalized or retroflexed vowels as we can purely oral vowels and we cannot therefore say that we can double and double again by these two features the number of vowel qualities we can discriminate. Nonetheless our ear is capable of distinguishing large numbers of distinct vowel qualities, even though only a small fraction of them are used to distinguish meaning in any one language, and we are able to characterize these vowels with a fair degree of accuracy.

Listening

We hear whether we want to or not, in the sense that any sound within range arrives at our ear and is passed on. But we do not have to *listen*, we do not have to attend to all the sounds that come at us, and we might define listening as hearing attentively. At a party there may be several different conversations going on, all of comparable loudness, but we can to a large extent decide which we will listen to; those we ignore are still present as sound but in the background, not attended to. We are able to switch our attention quite quickly back and forth, and often in such circumstances we mostly listen to one conversation whilst monitoring another or others for brief periods; then if our monitoring turns up an interesting remark we can decide to listen to that conversation rather than the one we started with. In a similar way we can 'listen for' potential noises: a mother can engage in a loud and lively conversation, and yet not miss a comparatively weak cry from her baby, because she is geared up to detect a noise of a particular kind which is important to her.

Listening is highly selective, then, and means paying attention. But when we listen to our own language we do not have to listen with undivided attention every split second of the time. We do not hear the exact nature of every single sound uttered in sentence after sentence. Because we know the rules of our language and of our society we have a pretty good idea of what may be said, and so long as we listen enough to get the general shape of what is actually said, we can devote a good part of our attention to other things, such as what we are going to say in reply when we can get a word in, or what a delicious dimple the speaker has. Furthermore, we can listen to some degree retrospectively; everyone must have had the experience of hearing an utterance without attending to it, and then as it were, hauling it back from memory to give it full attention, to 'listen' to it after the event.

Even when we say that we are listening very carefully we may not always mean exactly the same thing. When I say that I listened very carefully to a lecture I generally mean that I was keenly concerned to get the lecturer's meaning clear and that I did not allow myself to go off into daydreams. My attention was certainly focussed, but mainly on the intellectual or factual content. On the other hand when a phonetician says he listened carefully to someone's speech he means that he was paying particular attention to the *sound* of it. He may have got very little of the meaning behind the sounds, but he will have a clearer idea of the sounds themselves than anyone listening mainly for the meaning. It is this kind of listening, concentrated attention on sound features, that we are mainly interested in here.

There was a time, not so long ago, when 'ear phonetician' was a term of scorn. It was felt that the truth about the sounds of speech would ultimately be revealed by the machine, in the physiology or acoustics laboratory. This is no longer the case, for two reasons: first, the development of cheap, easy and faithful sound-recording equipment, and second, a fundamental reappraisal of the ear's role.

Since the advent of the tape-recorder it has been possible to make good permanent recordings of natural speech which linguists of all interests can use as their raw material. The phonetician in particular blesses it because he can now listen over and over again to features of sound until he is sure of his analysis. Before sound-recording, once an utterance was out it was gone; it might be possible, if the utterance was a one-word affair, to capture its salient sound elements by means of detailed phonetic transcription, and this was indeed done, but the span of attention of the concentrated kind needed is short and it is not possible to carry in one's head for even a very restricted time all the interesting distinctions of sound present in an utterance of quite modest length. Repetitions could be elicited, certainly, but these were new events, the original was gone beyond recall, and there was no guarantee that a repetition would be the same – indeed there was virtual certainty that it would not be. So the picture of a Professor Higgins standing on the steps in Covent Garden and taking down verbatim the detailed sound patterns of Cockney back-chat is a figment of Shaw's imagination. Yet much good and important work was in fact done by Henry Sweet, the model for Higgins, and many other dedicated ear-phoneticians, despite the difficulties. It should be mentioned here that the ability to recognize shades of sound previously heard and to use this recognition to place the geographical or social background of the speaker – as Higgins so spectacularly did – is one that certainly exists. Anyone dealing with the sounds of speech needs a good auditory memory and some of them have a mental classification system which enables them to make the necessary connection between the sounds and the speaker's background, as learned in previous experience. Not all phoneticians are particularly good at this, and some people who are good at it are not phoneticians. A good auditory memory of this kind is only one of the attributes necessary for the analysis of sounds.

Feedback

It is now clearly recognized, as I mentioned earlier, that the results of machine analysis of sound cannot, without the check of the ear, tell us anything particularly helpful about speech sounds. The amount of machine information is so vast as to be overwhelming and it is only by sieving it through the ear, as it were, that we can get any idea of what is relevant or irrelevant, crucial or dispensable. And if the ear is dominant in this way it is also dominant in a much more vital way, as a monitor of what we ourselves are saying. When we speak, the sound waves strike the listener's ear, but they strike our own ear, too, and this feedback mechanism, whereby we continuously monitor our own utterances, is extremely important. If a child does not have this feedback, that is to say if he is born deaf, he will not learn speech in the normal way at all. Deaf-mutism begins with deafness. And although teachers of the deaf are able to give such children *some* speech, the result does not usually reflect the enormous amount of patient and expert work which these dedicated people put in. Knowledge of how sounds are made and their acoustic structure is no substitute for hearing them, so far as learning to speak is concerned. We notice too that if a person goes really deaf his speech gradually deteriorates: lacking the sensitive monitor of hearing, he can no longer control with the same delicacy the movements of his speech organs, even though he has been making them for years.

The effect of interference with this mouth-to-ear feedback can be strikingly demonstrated by *delayed feedback*. The speaker wears sound-proof earphones and speaks into a microphone; his speech is recorded and fed back to him through the earphones with a slight delay, so that it arrives at his ears a little later than he would normally expect it. If the delay is just right (about one-third of a second) the speaker is immediately overtaken by a sometimes devastating stammer. He starts to speak and nothing reaches his ear at the expected time, so he assumes some fault of pronunciation and starts again; the first attempt arrives at his ear, but the second one doesn't, so he starts again; and so on. Immediately the delay is removed (or if it is made longer than the critical value) the stammer disappears. It must not be assumed that stammering is due entirely to faulty feedback, but it has long been known that some stammerers perform better if they rub brown paper over their ears as they speak; the noise produced by this in the speaker's ears has the effect of breaking the feedback link. Why some people's feedback should be defective, as this suggests, and at what point along the chain from ear to brain the defect occurs remains obscure.

Ear training

Some people have a natural talent for making delicate discriminations of sound, for hearing in this concentrated and attentive way which we have called 'listening'. Others are very much less gifted. The first group, when they listen to a foreign language, are more conscious of the foreignness of the sounds, that is to say they listen to them as sounds and, if the sounds are unfamiliar, they recognize the unfamiliarity. The second group tends to hear everything in terms of their own language, interpreting even grossly different sounds as being the same as some sound or sound sequence which they hear every day. For example, the first group will hear the vowel [y] of the French word *rue* ('street') as different from any common English vowel; they may not be able to reproduce it correctly (though they will have a good chance of doing so) but at least they will recognize its Frenchness. The second group, on the other hand, will identify this sound with the [u] vowel of English *too* [tu] or the [ju] sequence of English *you*. Similarly, some people can make quick and accurate judgements of changes in pitch, whilst others are so bad at this that they are called 'tone-deaf'; however, even if they are incapable of telling *God Save the Weasel* from *Pop Goes the King* they do not appear to be any less sensitive to the changes of pitch which are significant in their own language; they may not be able to tell up from down in an analytical way, but they have nevertheless learnt to react correctly to the significant differences of tune which their language uses. The talent for singing and the talent for speech are strangely different in this respect.

No matter how great or how little a person's natural talent for sound discrimination, it can always be improved, and the basic factor in improving it is the belief that two sounds really are different. Once he can be convinced that [y] and [u] and [ju] are all different, even if at first it is only an act of faith, then he will concentrate his listening and eventually succeed in separating each from the others, and retaining the distinctions. This is done in practice by alternating the sounds to be discriminated and drawing the person's attention to the relevant auditory *and* articulatory factors until he thinks he can hear the difference; then he is given one of the sounds to identify and corrected when necessary until his performance becomes reliable. A great deal of this ear-training is done by dictating nonsense words, made up of sequences of the sounds we are trying to discriminate between. Nonsense words are used rather than words from a particular language for two reasons. Suppose that we are teaching the pronunciation of German and we want the learner to be able to discriminate one, between the different German sounds and two, between the German sounds and similar, but incorrect, English sounds. We could fulfil the first aim to some extent by dictating only German words, but if the learner has any knowledge of the language he may recognize the words and therefore have some idea of their phonetic shape without careful listening. Nonsense forces him to listen closely all the time, since there is no help to be had from recognizing the word. Also, to fulfil the second aim, we need to be able to combine both German and English sounds in our dictation, sometimes to put the German [y] amongst English sounds and sometimes the English [ju] amongst German, so as to force the learner to distinguish between them, and this can only be done in made-up words. A third advantage of nonsense is that it enables us to present many or few difficulties within a small compass and therefore to suit the material to the learner's needs in an economical way. In a nonsense word such as [tybon] the learner need concentrate only on the vowels since the three consonant sounds would not be materially different for English or German; in [ʃvɔyʁə] a decision would be needed at each segment since none is pronounced in the same way in the two languages.

Articulation and hearing

As soon as one does any work of this kind it becomes clear, if it was not so before, that there is an intimate link between listening and pronouncing. The better we hear the differences, the better we are able to make them, and we would certainly expect this from what was said above about the importance of feedback in controlling accurate articulation. What is perhaps less expected is the reverse: the more capable we are of making differences of sound, the better we can hear them, so that training in actually making different sounds improves our ability to distinguish them by ear. In fact what usually happens when an analyst comes across a sound which he finds difficult to place is that he immediately imitates it, and when he has imitated it to his ear's satisfaction he can draw conclusions about its nature from the combined operations of mouth and ear. This is easily understandable in relation to a single speaker: the association between his own articulation and what he hears is naturally and necessarily close: a single brain is dealing with both. It has been suggested, however, that we somehow 'hear' other people in articulatory terms. Now obviously we cannot have any direct perception of the articulations they are making, as we can of our own, so this suggestion must be taken to mean that we interpret the sounds that we hear as having been produced by articulations similar to those we would use ourselves in producing the same sounds. That is certainly what the analyst does consciously when he tries a sound himself before he specifies it in whatever terms he finds appropriate, but can this be extended to our way of perceiving all sounds? If it could it would be helpful in explaining certain apparent discrepancies between what we hear and the acoustic record.

For example, we saw in the previous chapter that [d] sounds in English have a locus at about 1,800 cps (p. 90). Figure 48 shows this position. If we produce artificial speech based on these F2 transitions, all of them are clearly audible as [d] + vowel, though the point of actual origin of each transition is different, the locus at 1,800 cps being no more than an idealized point. Yet we hear [d] in each case. How does this happen unless in some way we deduce from what we hear that for all these [d]'s the tongue-tip is making contact with the alveolar ridge for the stop of [d], so bringing unity to diversity? Even more serious than the [d] situation is the [g] situation. For [g] it appears that there is not one

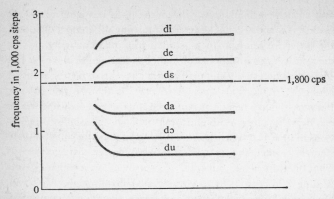

Figure 48: Schematization of F2 transitions for [d] before various vowels

locus but two: one at about 3,000 cps when [g] occurs before front vowels like [i, e, ɛ, a] and a second at around 1,200 cps before back vowels such as [ɔ, o, u]. This is shown in Figure 49. There seems to be a big discontinuity here on the acoustic plane. How do we recognize that each of these different transitions represents

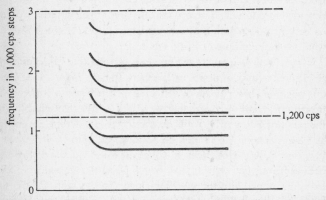

Figure 49: Schematization of F2 transitions for [g] before various vowels, showing loci at 3,000 and 1,200 cps

[g] unless we somehow perceive that the back of the tongue is involved in the *articulation* each time? That would again provide a unifying factor.

The first thing to be noticed in clarifying this problem is that the different transitions do *not* correspond to a single [d]-sound or a single [g]-sound. Take [d]: to be sure, the tongue-tip touches the alveolar ridge whatever the following vowel, but the remainder of the tongue takes up the position required for articulating the following vowel and therefore the cavity shape is different for every combination of [d] with different vowels; so the transitions must be different too. The same, *mutatis mutandis*, is true for [g], with the addition that the actual place of contact of the back of the tongue with the soft palate varies slightly according to what vowel is following; try the [g]-sounds of *geese*, *guard*, *goose*, and you will feel this. The articulatory unity is only approximate, therefore, yet still it is clearly the tongue-tip in the case of [d] and the tongue-back in the case of [g] which is making the stop, and equally clearly there is no discontinuity in our perception of the different [g]-sounds such as the acoustic record shows. We might still maintain that there is a closer relation between hearing and articulation than between hearing and the acoustic facts.

And consider the case of a man and a child talking to each other. The child's vocal organs are so much smaller than the man's that it is virtually impossible for them to produce the same sounds, and the acoustic record shows much larger differences between man and child than between man and man. It is again tempting to suppose that in some way each hears the other's very different sounds as being the product of similar articulations. Before committing ourselves to this 'articulatory' theory of hearing, we must take note of the fact that there are also discontinuities of articulation which the ear does not notice. For instance it is well known that the [ɹ] at the beginning of *red* can be made with the tongue-tip raised close to the hard palate or at rest behind the bottom teeth without any apparent difference of sound, that [s] is made by some people with the tongue-tip raised and by others with it lowered, that [θ] as in *thaw* can be made just as well at the alveolar ridge as at the upper incisors. If articulation can vary to this extent without any corresponding change in perception, it is difficult to argue that perception must be based *only* on articulation, and certainly in these cases we rely for our judgement upon the fact that the incoming acoustic signal does not show any significant difference whether the sound is produced in one way or the other.

Against this it may be argued that identical incoming signals are not always interpreted identically; one experiment with synthetic speech has shown that a plosive-type burst of noise centred on a particular frequency may be interpreted as [k] before [ɑ] but as [p] before [i] and [u]. But this is too narrow a view; what is important in identifying [p] or [k] in this experiment is not the fact that the burst is the same in both cases but that the frequency relation between the burst and the vowel formants is different, and therefore there is a difference in the incoming signal, if it is viewed widely enough, which accounts for the identification of either [p] or [k].

Undoubtedly the prime factor in our recognition of speech sounds must be the operations which our ear and brain perform on the incoming sound wave. It has not so far been shown that we make use of our experience of our own articulatory movements to help us in recognizing the sounds of speech but, as we have seen, there are one or two pointers which might lead us in that direction, and it may be that a connection of this sort will be proved in the future. For the present there is no reason to doubt the capacity of our brain to group together in the same perceptual category sounds which are physically different.

Listening and language

The sort of careful listening we have been considering is by no means the sort of listening that we do in everyday life. When we listen in a quite ordinary way to our own language we accept as being 'the same' a great many things which are clearly different whether they are considered from an articulatory, acoustic or perceptual point of view. As we have seen, we ignore differences of individual voice quality and of absolute voice pitch as between men, women and children; we certainly notice them and act upon them, but we are able to go beyond the differences to a sameness which is essential to communication as a social activity. In a similar way we can discount differences of accent: if they are gross differences we certainly notice them, and in Britain, where accent has, rightly or wrongly, connotations of social class, we probably take more notice of small differences of accent than most other nations do. Nonetheless, even though the difference between a Cockney and a Scottish pronunciation of the vowel in *mate* is very great, we recognize that they represent in some way the same underlying unit of the language. Even within one accent there are noticeable differences of pronunciation: one Cockney does not have exactly the same pronunciation of *mate* as his neighbour. And each one of us has several different styles of pronunciation depending on whether we are giving a public speech, chatting to our family, appeasing a policeman, talking to a baby, etc.

We can hear all of these differences more or less clearly. There is another type of difference, perfectly perceptible in terms of 'careful listening', which we do not ordinarily notice at all. In the word *clearly* there are two occurrences of the phoneme /l/ (for 'phoneme' see p. 66); but in most English pronunciations the sounds which represent the phoneme are by no means the same, whether in articulatory, acoustic or auditory terms. The first one is [l̥], that is, it has little or no vocal cord vibration and therefore has clearly perceptible friction; but the second is [l], with voice the whole way through the articulation and no sign of friction. Once our attention is drawn to the difference we can hear it all right, and if the sounds were produced in isolation we would not think that they even sounded very similar. The point is, of course, that in English speech they are *not* produced in isolation but in particular sequences, and so long as they keep to these sequences and our attention is not particularly drawn to them we do not notice that they are different in sound; indeed most people are surprised when they realize that sounds like this really are different and can be heard to be so. In our own language we hear in phonemes and not in sounds; that is, we hear /l/ as distinct from /m, n, p, h/ etc. but we do not pay attention to any differences amongst the *allophones* of a particular phoneme, i.e. the actual sounds which represent the phoneme in particular sequences. In the case of [ɬ] and [l], allophones of the phoneme /l/ in English, the difference in articulation is not great: the tongue, lips, soft palate, etc. perform the same actions for both – it is only the absence or presence of voicing which is different; because of the friction of [ɬ] the acoustic and auditory differences are greater. But there are also cases where the articulatory difference is considerable, for example the case mentioned on p. 40 where [t] and [ʔ] (glottal stop) represent the same phoneme /t/: in saying *tight corner* with this type of pronunciation /t/ occurs twice, once at the beginning and once at the end of *tight*; the first occurrence of /t/ is realized as [t], a plosive made with the tongue-tip on the alveolar ridge; the second /t/, however, is represented by [ʔ], i.e. a complete closure of the vocal cords. The difference in place of articulation – alveolar *v.* glottal – is very great, yet this is a difference which regularly goes unnoticed *in these sequences*.

If a particular allophone occurs *outside* the sequences where it is customarily found, we will notice it. If glottal stop, for example, occurs between vowels, as in Cockney *butter* [baʔə], those who do not themselves use it in this position will notice it very clearly. And if [ɬ] and [l] were reversed in *clearly* we would perhaps be puzzled to know what the word was. So this is not a matter of pure perception – we can hear that the sounds are different even in their appropriate sequences provided that our attention is drawn to the difference, and the difference leaps to the ear at once if the sounds are used in contexts where they do not usually occur.

There are at least some exceptions to this general failure to notice allophonic differences. In Cockney and in many other varieties of London pronunciation the two sounds which represent the vowel in the words *go* and *gold* are distinctly different, and if they are allophones of the same phoneme, which is the usual interpretation, one would not expect the difference to be noticed. In fact, however, students with this kind of pronunciation often refuse to equate the two, identifying the vowel in *gold* with that in *God*, which is a different phoneme from that in *go*. Such exceptions are rare and far outnumbered by the cases where allophonic differences are not noticed at all.

Since different languages have different numbers of phonemes and different allophones representing them, it follows that in a foreign language we do not hear the sounds in the same way that a native speaker does. He is accustomed to making the distinctions which separate the phonemes but not able to distinguish allophones; we may not be able to distinguish clearly the phonemically significant features because they are not significant in our own language. On the other hand, differences which in our language are significant may only be allophonic in the foreign language. In Polish the difference between [ɕ] and [ʂ] is significant: [ɕ] (the voiceless alveolo-palatal fricative) occurs in the word *prosie* ('pig') and [ʂ] (the voiceless retroflex fricative) in *prosze* ('please'). To an English ear these both sound like [ʃ] as in *shoe* (the voiceless palato-alveolar fricative) and a good deal of practice is needed before they can be consistently separated either by ear or by mouth. Conversely, [d̪] and [ð] in Spanish (p. 66), are allophones of the same phoneme, yet because in English these sounds represent different phonemes we hear the differences in Spanish quite clearly, whereas a Spaniard does not.

The conditioning of our hearing by the typical phoneme/allophone arrangements of our own language means that there is no such thing as neutral hearing, no possibility of listening to sounds without being affected by lifelong habits of hearing and speaking one's own language. No one is equally good at discriminating all the types of sound that occur in all languages, and whilst long practice gives the 'ear-phonetician' an approximation to this neutrality it is no more than an approximation and he must always guard against the possibility that he may fail to notice important differences of sound simply because they are not used in his native language.

5. The Description and Classification of Sounds

In Chapters 2, 3 and 4 we have looked at three different aspects of speech sounds: how they are produced, how they are analysed physically, and what they sound like. We will now apply what we have seen in those chapters to the description and classification of some of the sounds we hear in English. We cannot deal with all the English sounds because, as we have seen, there is a vast variety within English, but we can look at most of the major types of sound and see how they can be described in terms of the three aspects mentioned above.

Before doing so we should clarify the difference between classification and description: in describing sounds we try to set down as many as possible of the features which are present in them; in reality, complete description is beyond our powers since it would mean mentioning an infinite number of features, e.g. in order to specify the exact dimensions of the vocal tract along the whole of its length. So our descriptions are bound to be partial, and on the whole we restrict ourselves to mentioning those features which seem to contribute substantially to the sound in question. The following might, for example, be such a description, in articulatory terms, of the [d] of *do*: 'the lips are somewhat rounded (ready for the following vowel); the teeth are close together; the soft palate is raised; the tongue-tip is firmly in contact with the alveolar ridge and the sides of the tongue are in continuous contact with the sides of the palate; the back of the tongue is raised to approximately the close vowel position (again ready for the vowel); air under pressure from the lungs is compressed within the completely stopped mouth cavity and pharynx; the tongue-tip (but not the sides or the back) then lowers suddenly allowing the compressed air to escape with a slight explosion; just before the explosion the vocal cords start to vibrate in normal voice and continue to do so into the vowel'. You may think that this is a reasonably comprehensive description and there are probably things included in it which you would not have thought of or which seem irrelevant. But it is actually very incomplete: what is the exact lip aperture? just how far apart are the teeth? what is the front of the tongue doing? how firm is the contact of the soft palate and the posterior wall of the pharynx? what is the shape of the pharynx? how much pressure are the lungs exerting and what is the exact duration of voicing before the explosion? and so on. We could go on adding detail after detail to the description above, and still be left with others unspecified. In practice this description is generally quite satisfactory for our needs: if we find that for a particular purpose we need to specify an extra feature we can certainly do so, but however much we add the description would never be totally exhaustive.

In classifying sounds, on the other hand, as in classifying items in any other group, all we need to do is to mention those features by which they differ and leave it at that. If all I have to do is to classify [s] and [d], without considering any other sounds, I need only mention one feature, for instance that [s] is fricative and [d] is not, or that [d] is a stop and [s] is not, or that [d] has voice in it and [s] has none. Any one of these features is sufficient to separate the two sounds and it is not necessary to quote all three. But if I have to classify [s], [d] and [t], one feature is no longer enough: [s] is a fricative but both [d] and [t] are not; [d] and [t] are both stops, whilst [s] is not; [d] has voice in it, but both [s] and [t] have none. So we need two features to classify them: presence or absence of voice and presence or absence of stop or friction. If we want to classify the sounds of a particular dialect we shall need more than these two features; all the sounds of English will need more features again, and if we attempt to classify all sounds of all languages, still more features will be needed, since no single language makes use of all the possibilities of the human vocal tract.

But there is a certain economy in the use to which features of this kind are put in making distinctions of sound; we do not necessarily have to look for a new feature every time we have to separate one sound from another. To specify the difference between [t] and [d] in *too* and *do* we may select the feature of voicing, [t] being voiceless and [d] voiced. Then when we come to [p] versus [b] and to [k] versus [g] we find the same feature operating, [p] and [k] voiceless, [b] and [g] voiced. To separate all six we need only add the three different places of articulation, labial for [p, b], apical (tongue-tip articulation) for [t, d], and dorsal (tongue-back articulation) for [k, g]. This use of a single feature to separate more than one pair of sounds is known as a *correlation*, and we say that the pairs [p] and [b], [t] and [d], [k] and [g], are differentiated by the voice correlation.

The selection of one particular feature to set up a correlation of this kind for the purposes of classification must not be taken to imply that this is the sole feature by which we *recognize* the sounds as being different. Any pair of sounds is generally distinguished by more than one feature – there are several cues to their recognition. For example, [t] and [d], as in *too* and *do*, are indeed different in their voicing characteristics, but this is not the whole story: they are also different in that [t] is more strongly articulated than [d], that is, there is also a fortis/lenis difference (p. 40). And in most types of English there is also an *aspiration* difference; when the tongue-tip leaves the alveolar ridge to release [t] the vocal cords do not start to vibrate immediately, there is a short period when breath is flowing out of the mouth more or less unimpeded – this we call aspiration. For [d] on the other hand there is no aspiration since the vocal cords start vibrating either before the release or immediately it takes place. All three of these features – voiceless/voiced, fortis/lenis and aspirated/

unaspirated – help us to distinguish *too* from *do*, and the fact that we select one of them to use in our classification system is a matter of logical economy and must not make us think that it is the only or even the major differentiating factor.

The sounds of English

Because of the large number of different and distinguishable sounds in English it is useful in dealing with them to start with the English phonemes (p. 66) rather than the concrete sounds themselves. The phonemes are limited in number and will serve as useful focuses for describing the variety of sounds by which they are realized. The actual sounds which stand for /p/ in *paper*, *ape*, *apt*, *halfpenny*, are all different, but all of them represent one occurrence of the phoneme /p/, and since, as we have seen, we all tend to operate at the phoneme level rather than the sound level, the English phonemes are useful centres for the description of the sounds.

Not every form of English has the same number of phonemes: an accent without /h/ is one phoneme short vis-à-vis one which has /h/; a Cockney who pronounces both *fin* and *thin* as [fɪn] has one phoneme less than those who distinguish the two words; anyone who distinguishes the words *rain* and *reign* has one more phoneme than those (like me) who do not. So there is no single list of phonemes which will do for all of the speakers of the language: the list used here is that typical of the kind of English called Received Pronunciation, RP for short. This is a pronunciation of English which gives little or no clue to the speaker's regional affiliations; it has been known by various names, Queen's (or King's) English, BBC English, Public School English, Educated Southern English, and other more opprobrious labels attached to it by non-lovers of this particular accent. It is perhaps more often heard in London and the South-east than elsewhere, but it is by no means a local accent of that area as

Cockney or Berkshire are. It covers a multitude of sins in the sense that there are various varieties of it, but most of its speakers use the same list of phonemes, it has been very thoroughly described, it is still an accent of considerable prestige (though this is diminishing amongst younger speakers), and it will serve as a base for describing English sounds.

Consonants

The consonant phonemes of RP are symbolized below, with key-words to help with their identification:

/p/	pop	/f/	fife	/m/	mime
/b/	bib	/v/	verve	/n/	nine
/t/	tot	/θ/	thigh	/ŋ/	singing
/d/	did	/ð/	they	/l/	loyal
/k/	kick	/s/	cease	/r/	rarer
/g/	gag	/z/	zoos	/j/	yo-yo
/tʃ/	church	/ʃ/	shush	/w/	wayward
/dʒ/	judge	/ʒ/	azure		
		/h/	how		

Fortis/lenis

The pairs /p, b/, /t, d/, /k, g/, /tʃ, dʒ/, /f, v/, /θ, ð/, /s, z/, /ʃ, ʒ/ are all distinguished by the correlation mentioned above which we shall now call the fortis/lenis correlation. The reason for this is that though the aspiration difference may distinguish the plosive pairs it does not distinguish the remainder, and similarly whilst there may be a voicing difference between /p/ and /b/ etc., voice may be lacking in both. This leaves the energy difference, fortis/lenis, as a constant. Auditorily this corresponds to strong versus weak sounds, with the addition that the lenis sounds are regularly shorter than the fortis ones. Acoustically the intensity of the burst of the fortis plosives /p, t, k/ is greater than that of /b, d, g/ and the intensity of the noise of the fricative sounds (including /tʃ, dʒ/ which have a fricative segment after the stop) is greater for the fortis sounds than for the lenis. The duration of both stops and fricatives is greater for the fortis than for the lenis ones.

Stops

These can be immediately divided into /p, t, k, b, d, g/ on the one hand and /tʃ dʒ/ on the other. /p, t, k, b, d, g/ are almost always realized in both RP and most other accents as plosive consonants, with a rapid release of compressed air leading to a short, sharp explosion. This corresponds to the very brief, spiky burst of energy on spectrograms. /tʃ, dʒ/ on the other hand are always realized as *affricates*, that is stops with a notice-ably fricative release, caused by removing the tongue-tip slowly. On a spectrogram this shows a segment of noise very much longer than the burst of the plosives, though shorter than the corre-sponding purely fricative sound: compare /tʃ/ and /ʃ/ in *chip* and *ship*.

/p, t, k/ versus /b, d, g/

There are various general remarks which can usefully be made about the correlated pairs /p, b/, /t, d/ and /k, g/ before going on to consider each separately. All six phonemes are most often realized in all accents of English as plosive consonants. Sometimes, however, we find cases where the stop of the con-sonants is not completely formed, so that air is never completely stopped from flowing and a very short fricative sound is heard rather than a true plosive. This happens most often medially, between vowels, and the medial consonants of *supper*, *oboe*, *pretty*, *ready*, *lacking* and *bigger* may be heard, not as [p, b, t, d, k, g] but as the corresponding fricatives [Φ, β, s, z, x, ɣ]. Mostly in RP these realizations would in fact be plosive, but in many accents of Ireland the fricatives are quite regularly found, especially representing /p, t, k/ in medial and final positions.

In RP allophones of /p, t, k/ are invariably voiceless, those of /b, d, g/ may be and often are voiced but they do not generally have full voicing (i.e. from closure right through to release) unless they are surrounded by other voiced sounds. In *oboe*, *table*, *under*, *tidy*, *anger* and *ago* [b, d, g] are fully voiced, but in *abscess, bedsore, bagpipe*, where they are in contact with a voiceless sound, or when they occur immediately before or after a pause, as in the isolated word *dog*, voicing does not go right through. Indeed it may not be present at all. Figure 50 shows

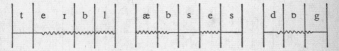

Figure 50: Differences of voicing in the /b, d, g/ of *table, abscess* and *dog*

that in these cases voicing either stops before the release or starts after the closure, whereas in *table* it continues throughout.

The voiced/voiceless distinction is much the same in most other accents, but one exception is the voiced allophones of /t/ in many accents of America and South-west England. Because of the voicing /t/ tends to resemble /d/ more than in other accents, so that *betting* may be confused with *bedding*. (The *New Yorker* had an anecdote years ago about an architect who was commissioned to design a waiting-room in a children's hospital and turned up with plans for a room where they could wade.) Even so, /t/ and /d/ are not usually identical in such accents: /t/ is represented by a shorter and more flap-like plosive which, although voiced, is still fortis, reminding an English ear of a kind of /r/. This tendency is on the increase in England, no doubt due to American influence. In acoustic terms voicing corresponds to very low frequency periodic vibration, generated by the vocal cords, and the F1 of the preceding or following vowel also has a marked negative transition, i.e. it moves upward to a following vowel or downward from a preceding vowel; this transition does not take place with the voiceless consonants.

/b, d, g/ never have aspirated allophones, but /p, t, k/ commonly do, in RP and many other accents, notably before a stressed vowel in the same word. In *pip*, *tot* and *kick* the first plosive is quite heavily aspirated whilst the second, before a pause, is less so; in *pepper*, *totter*, *kicker*, the second plosive in each word has little or no aspiration because it is followed by an unstressed vowel, whereas the first is heavily aspirated. After /s/ none of them has aspiration. Figure 51 shows various aspiration dif-

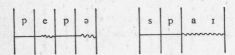

Figure 51: Aspiration differences for /p/ in *pepper* and *spy*

ferences. In other accents of English, aspiration may be heavier than in RP; for example, in Cockney initial /p, t, k/ are very heavily aspirated, and /t/ in particular may be realized as an affricate: that is, instead of the explosion being followed by more or less unimpeded breath, it is followed by a clear fricative segment like [s]. If RP *tar*, with an aspirated [t], is represented as [thɑː], then the Cockney pronunciation can be shown as [tsɑː]. On the other hand, in some accents of Lancashire and Scotland, aspiration may be totally lacking. Then the difference between /p, t, k/ and /b, d, g/ is an almost pure fortis/lenis distinction, and for people who are accustomed to rely on aspiration as the chief difference between the pairs, the unaspirated /p, t, k/ tend to resemble /b, d, g/ rather closely, so that *pull* might sound to them like *bull*, and so on.

Aspiration corresponds acoustically to aperiodic energy in at least part of the formant transition between the consonant burst and the following vowel. In unaspirated consonants these transitions have periodic energy (since the vocal cords vibrate immediately on explosion).

It is interesting to notice that different features play different parts in distinguishing between these pairs of consonants according to the position they occupy in the utterance. Taking the RP case, aspiration is of great importance in contrasts such as *pie/by* and voice much less important since /b/ in this position may have little or none. In *sacking/sagging* the voicing contrast is much more important for distinguishing /k/ from /g/ since /k/ has little or no aspiration but it is voiceless whereas the /g/ is fully voiced. Before a pause, as in *site/side*, voicing is again relatively unimportant since the /t/ has none and /d/ may well have none either; the aspiration difference is minimal since /t/ has little in this position, and the weight is therefore on the fortis/lenis feature, /t/ being more strongly and /d/ more weakly articulated. But in this position there is often help to be had in making the distinction from quite another quarter: the vowel is of noticeably different length before /t/ and /d/. In *site* it is considerably shorter, in *side* considerably longer, and this is regularly so before fortis/lenis consonants in final position; so there may be clues to a particular distinction that are located right outside the segment with which the distinction is usually associated. This, even more than the importance of vowel-formant transitions for the recognition of consonants, should make us wary of taking too narrow a view of the features distinguishing one phoneme from another.

Incomplete plosives

When one plosive consonant follows another in English only one explosion is generally heard; for example, in *apt* the [p] has a normal closure followed by compression of air, but before the lips are parted to release the air a second closure is made for [t], so that when the lips do part there is no corresponding explosion, the air being held back by the [t] closure. This is illustrated in Figure 52. Other examples are /bd/ in *rubbed*, /kt/ in *act*, /db/ in *good boy*, /gt/ in *ragtime*, etc., etc. Try these sequences in both ways, with the normal incomplete plosive and then with that plosive released audibly as well as the second. Some people do regularly make two explosions, but in English this is relatively rare; in other languages, such as German, two explosions are the general rule, e.g. in *Akt* ('act').

Figure 52: Double closure in *apt* showing the [t] stop formed before the [p] stop is broken

Auditorily, we hear the change in quality of the preceding vowel due to the movement towards closure for the first plosive, then a prolonged compression stage, then the noise of the explosion of the second plosive. Acoustically, the formant transitions of the first vowel are appropriate to the first plosive, the 'silent' interval is double the duration of a single stop, and the burst and following transitions correspond to the different second plosive.

Incomplete single plosives may also occur in English in final position in an utterance. For example the /t/ of *good night* is often not exploded. The closure and compression stages are made, but the lung pressure then ceases and we go into normal breathing without any explosion.

Nasal plosion

When any of the plosives is followed by any nasal consonant the explosion takes place nasally: the soft palate is lowered sharply so that the compressed air bursts out through the nose. For the /dn/ of *goodness* the tongue simply retains its alveolar closure for [d], the soft palate lowers and nasal air-flow immediately produces [n] which has the same tongue position as [d]. The same applies, *mutatis mutandis*, for any case in which the plosive and the nasal have homorganic articulation, i.e. the same primary place of articulation, e.g. /pm/ in *Upminster*, /tn/ in *chutney*, and /bm/ in *cub-master*. When the plosive and the nasal are not homorganic, two changes are needed: the lowering of the soft palate, as described above, and also a change in the place of the mouth-closure, e.g. in /tm/ of *atmosphere*, /dm/ in *admit*, /kn/ in *acne*, /bn/ in *glibness*, etc. Occasionally one hears the plosives in these sequences exploded orally, by removing the mouth-closure before the soft palate lowers, but this is usually in ultra-careful speech. In other languages, e.g. German, French, the plosive is generally exploded orally rather than nasally, particularly when the following nasal is not homorganic, e.g. /kn/ in German *Knabe* ('boy'). It is no doubt due to nasal plosion in past centuries that we have lost /k/ in this position in English, c.f. *knave*, because nasal plosion leaves a much less clear impression of the plosive than does oral plosion.

/p, b/

These are most often realized as bilabial plosives, with the fortis/ lenis, voicing, aspiration, and release characteristics mentioned above. Occasionally the place of articulation is labio-dental when either /p/ or /b/ is immediately followed by /f/ or /v/, for example in *hopeful* and *subversive*, where the sequences /pf/ and /bv/ may be realized as labio-dental throughout. Labio- dental plosives may also occur for /p,b/ if the speaker is smiling broadly as he speaks, when it is easier to make a lip-teeth contact than a lip-lip one. The lips may be more or less pro- truded during the bilabial stop if a following vowel requires lip- rounding; compare the /p/'s in *pea* and *paw*. The tongue is not directly involved in the closure of /p/ or /b/ and therefore adopts the position needed for the sound immediately following: in *pea* the front of the tongue during the stop of /p/ is high for the following /iː/; in *pray* the tongue-tip is close to the rear of the alveolar ridge; in *play* it is in contact with the alveolar ridge, and so on. These various preparatory movements make differences in the shape of the mouth cavity, with consequent differences in the exact nature of the explosion when the lips part.

The glottal stop [ʔ] often figures in the realization of /p/ (never of /b/) in RP and other accents. In RP [ʔ] is added before the bilabial plosive, and this occurs frequently before a pause. For example, in *What a hope!* the vowel of *hope* is cut off by closure of the vocal cords; the [p] is then formed, the glottal stop released and the [p] exploded normally. The same sequence of events is even more common in RP and many other accents before consonants, e.g. in *apse*, *apt*, *hopeful*, etc., where again [ʔ] precedes [p]. This does not occur between vowels in RP but it does in, for instance, Cockney and Tyneside, in both of which the bilabial plosive following the glottal stop is lenis rather than fortis though without voice. *Happy* pronounced in this way in Tyneside could be transcribed [haʔb̥i]. Cockney speakers occasionally use [ʔ] alone in this position to represent /p/, e.g. [wɒʔɪn] for *Wapping*. Before consonants, however, [ʔ] alone is fairly common for /p/ in Cockney, e.g. *I hope so* [ɑɪ aʊʔ saʊ], where there is no bilabial closure. In other accents [ʔ] alone for /p/ is restricted to positions where /p/ is followed by a bilabial, e.g. in *cap-badge* or *shopman*.

/t, d/

These are generally apical (tongue-tip) stops with the fortis/lenis, etc. characteristics mentioned earlier. In English the place of articulation is most often alveolar but it may be dental when a dental fricative follows, as in *width* or *at this*. In RP and most other accents the place of articulation is post-alveolar when /r/ follows, as in *true*, but in Irish and Scottish accents /t/ has dental articulation before /r/. There will be lip-rounding during /t/ if a rounded vowel or /w/ follows, and the body of the tongue will move into position for whatever articulation follows while the tip is in the alveolar stop position. Both /t/ and /d/ are laterally released when /l/ follows, as in *bottle*, *middle*; that is, instead of the tongue-tip lowering to release the compressed air, the sides of the tongue lower and the air bursts over them, the tip remaining in position for the alveolar lateral [l].

The sequence [ʔt] for /t/ follows the same pattern as in /p/; that is, it occurs fairly commonly before pause and more commonly before consonants. Before consonants it is not uncommon in RP to find [ʔ] alone for /t/, particularly if the following consonant is a stop, e.g. in *whiteness* or *that bus*, and this is very common in many other accents. Between vowels [ʔ] for /t/ occurs in Cockney and Glasgow speech, amongst others, in words such as *water* and *better*.

/k, g/

These are generally velar stops, made with the back of the tongue in contact with the soft palate, but the actual centre of contact varies according to the surrounding sounds; so the /k/ of *car* is made slightly further back than that of *cur* and the /k/ of *key* or *cue* is noticeably further forward still and may be post-palatal rather than velar. /k/ and /g/ have the same fortis/lenis, etc. characteristics as /p, b/ and /t, d/. Lip position is influenced by following sounds – spread in *key*, rounded in *Gwen*, for instance, and the tip of the tongue, being without primary responsibility for the stop, takes up whatever position is needed for the following articulation. Compare the /kr/ of *crowd*, the /kl/ of *clean* and the /k/ of *key*: for /kr/ the tongue-tip is raised close to the back of the alveolar ridge ready for [ɹ] during the stop of the [k], in /kl/ the tongue-tip is placed actually on the alveolar ridge ready for [l] before [k] is exploded, and for /kiː/ the tip of the tongue is at rest behind the lower incisors during the whole syllable. Check these positions for yourself.

In Jamaican English /k,g/ are realized as pure palatal plosives [c,ɟ] in words such as *cat* and *gas*; and the same is true of some Irish accents in words like *car*, *garden*. Glottalization of /k/ is frequent in RP and other accents before pause and before consonants, e.g. in *back* [bæʔk] and *axe* [æʔks], and glottal stop alone is sometimes heard for /k/ in Cockney, e.g. *back door* [bæʔdɔə]. In other accents glottal stop for /k/ is restricted to positions immediately before velar stops, e.g. *back gate* [bæʔ geɪt] and *black car* [blæʔ kɑː].

/tʃ, dʒ/

These are invariably realized as palato-alveolar affricates: the tongue-tip is against the back of the alveolar ridge, the front of the tongue rather high in a secondary palatal articulation, and after air has been compressed by lung action the tip is removed slowly, allowing homorganic friction to be heard. The fortis/ lenis and voicing characteristics of these affricates are as for the plosives, and /tʃ/ may have a little aspiration after the friction segment before vowels. Neither is ever incomplete in the way that the plosives may be; compare the fully formed [tʃ] of *watched* with the incomplete [k] of *act*. Lip position will certainly vary with neighbouring vowels, but some speakers regularly have lip-rounding in all contexts. Notice the difference in realization between the single phoneme /tʃ/ in *watch out* and the sequence of /t + ʃ/ in *what shout?* where the fricative segment of /tʃ/ is shorter than that of /ʃ/. Similarly notice /tʃ/ in *orchard* as against /t + ʃ/ in *courtship*.

/tʃ/ is frequently glottalized, like the plosives, before pause and before consonants, e.g. *watch* [ʔtʃ] and *watched* [ʔtʃt], but unlike the plosives it is frequently glottalized before vowels: compare *watching* [wɒʔtʃɪŋ] and *getting* [getɪŋ]. In some accents, e.g. of Yorkshire, the alveolar stop is lost and only the glottal stop remains, so *watch* = [wɒʔʃ].

Some occurrences of /tʃ/ and /dʒ/ have developed from earlier sequences of /t + j/ and /d + j/, e.g. *venture* /ventʃə/, from /ventjur/, and /tj/ may still be heard in such cases in, e.g. North Wales. In some words there is fluctuation, e.g. *statue* may be heard as /stætʃuː/ or /stætjuː/. Substitution of /tʃ/ for /tj/ and

/dʒ/ for /dj/ in words such as *tune* and *due* is frowned on by many but is increasingly common, just as it is in juxtapositions such as *what you want* ... /wɒtʃu wɒnt/.

Fricatives

The phonemes /f v, θ ð, s z, ʃ ʒ, h/ are all commonly realized as friction sounds. They can be divided into the four correlated pairs /f v/, /θ ð/, /s z/ and /ʃ ʒ/ on the one hand, and /h/, with no correlate, on the other. /f, v, θ, ð/ are distinguished by their relatively weak fricative noise from /s, z, ʃ, ʒ/ whose fricative noise is generally stronger. This corresponds acoustically to low general intensity for realizations of /f, v, θ, ð/ as compared with higher intensity for those of /s, z, ʃ, ʒ/.

/f, θ, s, ʃ/ *v.* /v, ð, z, ʒ/

The fortis/lenis correlation applies to these groups in much the same way as to /p, t, k, tʃ/ *v.* /b, d, g, dʒ/. Greater energy is given to /f, θ, s, ʃ/ than to /v, ð, z, ʒ/ and differences of voicing are present to the same extent as with the stops; but there is no aspiration difference as there is for the plosives. Vocal vibration is never present with /f, θ, s, ʃ/ but may be, to a greater or lesser extent, for /v, ð, z, ʒ/; the amount of voicing in the latter depends, as for the stops, on the surrounding sounds – full voicing throughout the articulation occurs only when the neighbouring sounds are also voiced, e.g. [v] in *ivy*, where the vowels on either side are voiced. Otherwise, voicing may be partial or completely lacking: in *visions* /vɪʒnz/, said between pauses, the initial [v] will typically have some voice, the medial [ʒ] will be fully voiced, and the final [z] little or none. Figure 53 illustrates this.

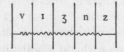

Figure 53: Different degrees of voicing in the /v, ʒ, z/ of *visions*

The fortis/lenis correlation implies that, no matter whether the sounds are fully voiced, partially voiced or completely without voice, there will always be a difference between them on an energy basis. [f, θ, s, ʃ] are always stronger sounds, with more obvious friction, than [v, ð, z, ʒ]. Amongst the latter group, /v/ and /ð/, which are, as we have noticed, of relatively smaller intensity than /z/ and /ʒ/, are quite often, as a result, realized as non-friction sounds, and are therefore recognized not by the type of friction, but by the way in which the vocal organs move to the following or from the preceding sound, which corresponds acoustically to formant transitions rather than to the nature of any aperiodic noise associated with them. Even when perceptible friction is present for [v] and [ð] it is the articulatory movements (or formant transitions) which provide the main cues for distinguishing between them. In the case of /z/ and /ʒ/ on the other hand, it is mainly the nature of the aperiodic noise which differentiates them, their different formant transitions being of less importance in this respect. It is perfectly clear that when [v] and [ð] are pronounced in isolation they are a good deal more similar as sounds than [z] and [ʒ] are.

The fortis consonants /f, θ, s, ʃ/ are typically longer in all contexts than the lenis /v, ð, z, ʒ/ and this is an additional cue for their identification. Compare /s/ and /z/ in *said* and *Zed* and the difference in length is noticeable; compare *loose* and *lose* and the length difference is clear not only in the [s] or [z] segment, but also, as with the stops (p. 133), in the preceding vowel segment, the vowel in *loose* being a good deal shorter than that in *lose*.

/f, v/

These are generally realized as labio-dental fricative sounds, the friction being less pronounced than for /s, z, ʃ, ʒ/. In the case of the lenis /v/, there may quite often be no audible friction at all, particularly between vowels, in which case the sound is the frictionless continuant [ʋ]. Lip position varies a little in their articulation according to the neighbouring sounds: in *fool, roof* there is some lip-rounding and protrusion, in *feel, leaf* the lips are flat and spread; this affects the exact place on the lip of the fricative narrowing. As with /p, b/ the tongue is wholly free to take up whatever position is next needed, so in *feel* the tongue is in the close-front position for the vowel [iː] during [f], and in *farm* it is in the open-back position; in the word *selfless* the tongue-tip is in contact with the alveolar ridge throughout the [f].

/θ, ð/

These are usually dental fricatives, with the tongue-tip close to either the edge or the back of the upper incisors; the exact place of articulation is not very important, and perfectly recognizable [θ] and [ð] sounds can be made with the tongue-tip quite well back on the alveolar ridge. The main point is that the resultant friction shall be much less strong than for /s/ and /z/. The sides of the tongue are in close contact with the sides of the palate from back to front, ensuring that the air-stream is funnelled to the point of maximum narrowing; we are not usually aware of this lateral contact, but it can be appreciated if the breath is drawn inwards through the [θ] position in contrast with the [l] position (for which the sides are not in contact); in the latter case cold air can be felt on the sides of the tongue, whereas for [θ] and [ð] this is not so. Like /v/, /ð/ is quite often realized intervocalically as a frictionless sound rather than a fricative, but after /t/ or /d/ and followed by a vowel, /ð/ may be realized as a dental plosive; so in *wait there* or *hold this* the sequences /tð/ and /dð/ are realized as dental throughout, i.e. [t̪d̪] and [d̪d̪].

The phonemes /θ/ and /ð/ do not exist in all accents of English. This is true of broad Cockney, where the gap is filled by using /f/ for /θ/, as in *thirty* [fɜːʔi], and either /v/ or /d/ for /ð/, so that *father* = [fɑːvə] and *this* = [dɪs]. In some accents of Irish /θ/ and /ð/ exist but are realized as dental plosives [t̪, d̪] rather than fricatives, whilst in other accents (e.g. Cork) they have no separate existence and their place is filled by /t, d/; in the first case *tin* and *thin* are distinguished as [tɪn], [t̪ɪn], and in the second case no distinction is made, and both are pronounced [tɪn].

/s, z/

These are always realized as alveolar sibilants (p. 48), formed by the blade of the tongue making almost complete contact with the alveolar ridge but leaving a narrow groove along its median line. This groove is considerably narrower than the narrowing made for the non-sibilant /f, v, θ, ð/ sounds. As with /θ/ and /ð/ the sides of the tongue are in close contact with the sides of the palate so that the breath is channelled through the groove and does not escape laterally. The teeth are always close together for /s/ and /z/ and it is noticeable that separating the teeth to any extent immediately reduces the necessary sibilance; generally speaking, /θ/ and /ð/ also have the teeth close together but they can be made with the teeth quite wide apart with little change of sound quality. Differences in realization of /s/ and /z/ are due to more or less grooving of the tongue-blade, leading to greater or less sibilance, and to the conformation of the incisor teeth. When children lose these teeth their /s/ and /z/ sounds are temporarily altered, becoming less sibilant; ill-made false teeth may have a similar effect, either because of the different relation of the sharp biting edges, onto which the breath is directed, or to the bulk of the false palate over the alveolar ridge, which interferes with the tongue grooving. Such differences are individual and idiosyncratic, and there are no regular differences as between different accents of English. This is a little surprising since /s/ and /z/ appear to give a good deal of trouble in speech development, and various different lisps (i.e. /s/ and /z/ defects) occur, e.g. [ɫ] and [ɬ], the alveolar lateral fricatives, and [s̪] and [z̪], the grooved dental fricatives, which are by no means rare. One might have expected that some such difference would have been generally used in one accent or another, but this does not seem to be the case.

/ʃ, ʒ/

These are also sibilants but, like /tʃ/ and /dʒ/, their realizations are palato-alveolar: the tongue-blade is close to the back of the alveolar ridge and there is grooving similar to that of /s/ and /z/ though not so narrow: confirm this by pulling air in through the [s] and [ʃ] positions. The front of the tongue is raised rather high in the secondary palatal articulation. Some speakers have a degree of lip-rounding for these sounds in all positions; for others lip position is dictated by neighbouring sounds. The difference between /s/ and /ʃ/ and between /z/ and /ʒ/ lies, as we said earlier, mainly in the nature of the friction noise: for /s/ and /z/ sounds it is typically more hissy and less hushy, that is, there is very little acoustic energy below about 3,000 cps, whereas for /ʃ/ and /ʒ/ it reaches down to about 1,500 cps. Again there are no regular differences as between one accent and another, though the friction noise may vary on an individual basis depending on the exact positioning of the tongue and lips.

Some of our /ʃ/ occurrences and most of our /ʒ/ ones have developed from earlier sequences of /sj/ and /zj/, e.g. *sure* from /sjur/ and *measure* from /mezjur/. In some words there is fluctuation, so that *issue* may have /ʃ/ or /sj/, and *casual* /ʒ/ or /zj/. In some words, too, there is fluctuation between /ʃ/ and /tʃ/, e.g. *French* may be /frenʃ/ or /frentʃ/, and between /ʒ/ and /dʒ/, e.g. *orange* may be /ɒrɪnʒ/ or /ɒrɪndʒ/, and *garage* may be /gærɑːʒ/ or /gærɑːdʒ/.

/h/

/h/ is different in two respects from the phonemes discussed above: it does not participate in the fortis/lenis correlation and the friction associated with its realization is not necessarily localized so narrowly as theirs is. The turbulence of air which produces the friction noise of /s, z/ etc. is caused by air squeezing through a narrowing at a particular point in the mouth. /h/ sounds, on the other hand, are simply strong voiceless versions of a following vowel and therefore do not generally have a close enough tongue position to produce that kind of local friction. There may be a little local friction between the vocal cords, but mostly what we hear is a more generalized friction of breath passing through a relatively open vocal tract: this is known as *cavity friction*, and it is what we hear initially in *heart*, *hurt*, *hat*, for example. It is only as it were by chance that we get local friction for /h/, as when the following sound needs a high tongue position, for example in *heat* or *huge*; then there is often local friction between the front of the tongue and the hard palate, giving the voiceless palatal fricative [ç]. There are as many allophones of /h/ as there are vowel sounds which can follow it.

Also /h/ can and does have voiced allophones when it occurs between voiced sounds, as in *rehearse*, *alcohol*, *manhood*, etc. For these the vocal cords vibrate in a breathy way, allowing more air to escape between them than they do in normal voice (p. 28). The voiceless allophones of /h/, whatever their exact quality, can economically be symbolized by [h] and the voiced ones by [ɦ], but these symbols refer to the classes of sounds mentioned above and if it is at any time necessary to symbolize a single sound it is more accurate to use, e.g. [ɑ] or [æ] as in *heart* [ɑɑːt] and *hat* [ææt], etc. Generally, however, [hɑːt] is sufficient indication.

Most accents of England are naturally /h/-less, that is, /h/ is missing in the broadest forms of those accents. Exceptions to this are RP and Northumbrian speech; and accents of Scotland, Ireland and North America (but not Wales) all naturally have /h/. Since /h/ is a powerful shibboleth it is one of the first things to be tackled when the need is felt to modify a naturally /h/-less accent, and this attempted modification quite often results in the insertion of /h/ where it is not generally approved, e.g. *modern heart* for *modern art*. These extra /h/'s and those that are missing when they should be present often give rise to the belief that this or that accent 'reverses its /h/'s', leading to stories of deliberate topsyturvydom like *the 'air of the 'ead, not the hair of the hatmosphere*, but this is never true and any difficulty that may arise in locating /h/ in accordance with normal /h/ practice is a sign of awareness. The difficulty is quite severe for the /h/-less speaker: out of a large mass of words which for him naturally begin with a vowel he must select those and only those which are appropriate for the addition of /h/ and it is small wonder if his selection is sometimes at fault one way or the other.

There is accepted fluctuation in the use of /h/ in a few words, mostly borrowings from French, e.g. *hotel*, *historical* (but not *history*) where the addition of /h/ in these forms, which originally lacked it – as *hour*, *heir* still do – is the result of *spelling pronunciation*, i.e. bringing the pronunciation into line with the orthography. The word *home* is sometimes /h/-less in the pronunciation of some old-fashioned RP speakers in the phrase *at home* which is then identical with *a tome*; this applies only to that particular phrase – the word *home* in all other contexts has /h/ for such speakers as well.

In the well-known Scottish pronunciation of *bright*, *light*, etc. there occurs before the final /t/ a voiceless palatal fricative [ç], which can be regarded as an allophone of /h/ surviving in a position where in most accents it has long ceased to exist. Then *light*, for example, would be represented phonemically as /lɪht/; the alternative of considering this [ç] sound as an independent phoneme /ç/ is not a good solution because it would be very restricted in its places of occurrence, and since [h] does not occur before /t/, [ç] complements it very tidily, since that is its only place of occurrence.

Nasals

The phonemes /m, n, ŋ/ are generally realized as nasal sounds, with a complete stop in the mouth and lowered soft palate, so that the air-flow is through the nose. Like /h/ they do not participate in the fortis/lenis correlation, and mostly the allophones are fully voiced; after voiceless plosives the nasal consonants may lose some voice, but never all or even most of it. Examples are *utmost*, *Putney*, and Figure 54 shows how this voicing may occur. Occasionally, as with the plosives (p. 130), the stop in the mouth may not be quite completed, in which case a nasalized frictionless continuant results; in *coming*, for example, the lips may not completely close for /m/ and instead of all the air going through the nose some continues between the almost closed lips, the remainder issuing nasally. This is relatively rare.

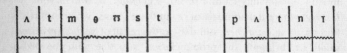

Figure 54: Devoicing of [m] and [n] following voiceless plosives

/n/ is often syllabic, i.e. forms a syllable by itself, as the vowels do; this happens in *button*, *garden* when no vowel intervenes between /t/ or /d/ and /n̩/. /m/ is less often syllabic but may be so in, for example, *happen* when it is pronounced /hæpm̩/, with the [p] nasally exploded and the lips remaining closed throughout /pm̩/. /ŋ/ is rarely syllabic but again may be so when surrounded by velar plosives as in *bacon cutter* if it is pronounced /beɪkŋ̩ kʌtə/.

/m/

The allophones of /m/ are bilabial unless /f/ or /v/ follows, in which case the labio-dental nasal [ɱ] is common, e.g. in *nymph*. Generally the lips are flat in shape but may be protruded if a neighbouring sound is rounded, compare *rumour* and *Lima*. The tongue is free to take up its position for whatever articulation is to follow – in *me* it will be in place for the close front vowel [iː], in *more* for the back vowel, in *elm-like* the tongue is in the /l/ position throughout /m/, and in *hymnal* the tongue takes up the alveolar stop position for /n/ before the lips are parted after /m/, so that no oral segment intervenes between the two nasals. There are no regional differences in the production of /m/.

/n/

Allophones of /n/ are all made with the tongue-tip on or near the alveolar ridge. Most allophones are indeed alveolar, with the sides of the tongue in contact with the sides of the palate preventing lateral escape, but when /n/ is followed by the dental fricatives /θ/ or /ð/, as in *tenth* or *clean them*, the allophone may be dental, with the tongue-tip against the upper incisors. Similarly, when /n/ is followed by post-alveolar [ɹ] as in *Henry*, the /n/ allophone will also be post-alveolar, with the tongue-tip placed further back than usual. In the sequence /nm/ as in *inmate*, the lips will be closed for /m/ before the tip is removed from the /n/ position, so that no oral segment intervenes. Before /l/ as in *only* the tongue-tip remains on the alveolar ridge during both /n/ and /l/. As with /m/ there are no regional variations of /n/.

/ŋ/

Allophones of /ŋ/ are velar or post-palatal: the back of the tongue, or a part slightly forward of that, makes a complete stop against the soft palate or the back of the hard palate: adjacent front vowels encourage a post-palatal contact, back vowels a velar one; compare *sing* and *song*. Before /m/ or /n/, as in *hangman* or *hangnail*, the stop of /ŋ/ is retained until the following stop has been established, and no oral segment intervenes.

In RP and many other accents *banger* is simply /bæŋə/, whereas *anger* is /æŋgə/, with the sequence /ŋg/. In some other accents of the Midlands and North of England these words are exact rhymes, both having /ŋg/. If in addition words such as *song*, *hang* always have the sequence [ŋg], even in final position (which is rather rare), then [ŋ] must be reckoned an allophone of /n/ rather than an independent phoneme, since there are then no cases of direct contrast between [n] and [ŋ], as there is in RP *sin v. sing*

/sɪn/ v. /sɪŋ/. What is often called 'dropping one's g's' – as in *goin'* for *going* – is a substitution of /n/ for /ŋ/ in unstressed *-ing* syllables, but this does not extend to stressed syllables like *sing*, etc. /ŋ/ never occurs initially in English words.

Lateral

Most of the allophones of /l/ in all accents of English are alveolar lateral sounds; dental laterals may occur before /θ/ and /ð/ as in *health* or *tell them*, and post-alveolar laterals before a post-alveolar as in *bell-rope*, but mostly the tongue-tip is on the alveolar ridge. The sides of the tongue are not in contact with the sides of the palate along all their length and air is therefore free to pass over the sides of the tongue, round the alveolar obstruction and so out.

Most allophones of /l/ are voiced throughout, but if /l/ follows one of the voiceless plosives, as in *play, neatly, clean*, part or all of the lateral articulation may have no voice. This is the equivalent of aspiration when a vowel follows the voiceless plosives (p. 132). When this happens the breath passing between the sides of the tongue and the palate may and often does cause lateral friction; otherwise /l/ allophones are non-fricative.

Whilst the tongue-tip is on the alveolar ridge the main body of the tongue is free to take up any position, and what generally happens in English is that it takes up either a fairly high front position ('clear l') or a fairly high back position ('dark l'), see Figure 55. Both of these are found in RP, the clear [l] before all

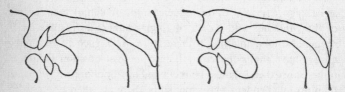

Figure 55: Clear [l] and dark [l]

vowels and the dark [ɫ] elsewhere, that is, before consonants as in *help*, or before pause as in *feel*. Other accents may have the same distribution or they may have clear [l] in all positions, e.g. Irish, S. Welsh and Highland Scottish accents, or dark [ɫ] in all positions, many American, Australian and S. Scottish accents. In some accents, e.g. Cockney, Birmingham, /l/ before consonants or pause, as in *well*, *help*, may be realized by a vowel-type articulation, in which, whilst the back of the tongue is raised as for dark [ɫ] the tongue tip is *not* in contact with the alveolar ridge and there is central rather than lateral escape of air, giving [wɛo, hɛop].

/l/ is often syllabic following consonants in words such as *total*, *middle*, *vessel*, *raffle*, etc. This is true when /l/ is word-final whatever follows, pause, vowel or consonant, but word-medially, when a vowel follows, /l/ may or may not be syllabic, e.g. *settling* may have two syllables or three, and this depends on the relative lengths of /l/ and the other vowels; when /l/ is syllabic it is of much the same length as the vowels, when non-syllabic it is shorter.

Frictionless continuants

The phonemes /r, j, w/ mostly have allophones which are frictionless continuants, i.e. sounds which are vowel-like in their voicing, lack of friction, and non-lateral oral air-stream, but which function consonantally. However, when they are preceded by the voiceless plosives /p, t, k/ they are often partly or wholly voiceless, and the voiceless segment is then fricative because all these allophones have a tongue position rather close to the palate and the voiceless air-stream is strong enough to cause local friction. This happens in *prove*, *cue*, *twice*, in most accents and is equivalent to the aspiration of /p, t, k/ before vowels (p. 132).

/r/

In RP *red* the initial consonant is a post-alveolar frictionless continuant [ɹ]; the tongue-tip is fairly close to the back of the alveolar ridge, the sides of the tongue are in contact with the sides of the palate and there is lateral bunching of the tongue, which seems to be an important feature of the consonant, since the correct effect can be given without raising the tongue-tip, provided that the bunching is present. It is still commonly believed that /r/ 'ought' to be rolled in English, a belief no doubt stemming from the Italianate tradition in the teaching of singing, but this is certainly not what happens in most accents. It may do so in Scottish though more often it is an alveolar flap [ɾ] (p. 48) or, particularly before pause, a post-alveolar fricative [ɹ]. The flap may occur in RP and other accents in words such as *marry*, *borrow*, where /r/ is preceded by a short, stressed vowel and followed by an unstressed one, but this is not very common.

The tongue-tip may be drawn back further, to the true retroflex position (p. 45) in accents such as Somerset, S. Ireland, N. Lancashire and the Mid-West and West of America, but what is most noticeable about such accents is not so much the different quality for /r/, but the fact of its occurrence before pause or before consonants. In RP and other accents of the East and South-east of England /r/ does not occur in such contexts, so that *bird* is /bɜːd/, with no /r/ in the pronunciation, and the pronunciation /bɜːrd/, with whatever quality of /r/, stands out, just as the omission of /r/ in these contexts does for those accustomed to using and hearing it.

In the county of Northumberland and parts of Durham (though no longer on Tyneside) a uvular fricative [ʁ] is found for /r/. This [ʁ] is also heard in other areas as a defective /r/ though perhaps not so frequently as labio-dental or dental frictionless continuants.

/j/

This consists of a vocalic glide from a close or half-close front vowel position to whatever position the following vowel requires; if the vowel is lengthened it gives rise to an [i]-type vowel as in 'see'. It is usually without friction, except when voiceless as mentioned above, but it may also have friction when it is voiced, if the vowel /iː/ as in *see* follows; this is particularly so when a very close variety of /iː/ is used, since the prime requirement for /j/ is that the tongue shall move from a higher and/or fronter position than that needed for the vowel which follows. This does not happen, except idiosyncratically, in RP but it commonly does so in Scottish accents and others such as Welsh where /iː/ has this very close, front characteristic.

The phoneme sequence /hj/ as at the beginning of *hue*, is commonly realized by a single voiceless palatal fricative sound [ç], so /hjuː/ = [çuː]. It is possible to contemplate this sound as representing a single, new phoneme in contrast with /t, d, h/ etc. in *too*, *do*, *who*, etc., but it is more economical and in tune with our intuition to regard it as the realization of /hj/, parallel with /fj, dj, nj/ etc. in *few*, *due*, *new*, etc.

/w/

Like /j/ this entails a vocalic glide, this time from a close or half-close back-rounded position to the position of whatever vowel follows, and if /w/ is lengthened it gives rise to an [u]-type vowel as in 'too'. The sequence /hw/ is no longer at all widespread in the RP pronunciation of *which*, etc., plain /w/ being usual, so that *which* and *witch* are identical. But in those accents where /hw/ occurs (Scottish, Irish, American) it is usually represented by a single voiceless labiovelar fricative [ʍ]. Again, as with [ç], it is not profitable to consider this sound as representing an extra phoneme but rather a sequence /hw/ parallel to /sw, tw, θw/ etc., as in *sway*, *twenty*, *thwart*, etc.

Marginal consonants

In addition to the phonemes considered above there are several sounds used more or less regularly in English which cannot be considered central to the language for one of two reasons. Either they are basically borrowed sounds, borrowed, that is, from another language and used only in words belonging to that language, although used in speaking English, or on the other hand they are sounds which can of themselves carry meaning in an English context but cannot be incorporated into English words in the way that /p, t, k/ etc. can. An example of a borrowed sound in the above sense is [x], the voiceless velar fricative, which occurs most commonly in the word *loch*, basically a Gaelic word, and also in the name *Bach*, basically German, and perhaps in *bach*, *fach*, basically Welsh. This sound (like [ç] mentioned on p. 145 in *light*) could also be considered an allophone of /h/. In Scottish, where [h] and [ç] also occur this is a sensible solution and *loch* would then be /lɔh/, but in general English where it is of very restricted occurrence (and very frequently replaced by /k/) it is reasonable to consider it a marginal sound.

Examples of sounds which have meanings of their own and which cannot be incorporated into English words are the alveolar click [ʇ] and the lateral click [ʖ]. Earlier [ʇ] was called the 'Tut-tut' click in order to identify it and this indicates well enough the meaning of sympathy or reproof which is directly associated with this click (or a series of them); similarly [ʖ], characterized as the 'Gee-up' click, has a clear meaning of its own, though since the thinning of the horse population it is more often used to express approval than to encourage horses. Neither, however, occurs outside this usage, and they therefore differ from regular phonemes of the language, such as /p, t, k .../ in two respects: one, that they have a meaning of their own, which /p, t, k .../ do not, and two, that they do not have any flexibility in combining with other phonemes in order to form many different words, which /p, t, k .../ do.

Vowels

In dealing with consonant sounds in English we have seen that the number of phonemes does not vary greatly from one accent to another. Many do not have /h/, Cockney does not have /θ/ and /ð/, but apart from this all the phonemes are represented in all accents, though their realizations may be quite varied. The same is by no means true of vowels – there is a good deal of variation in the number of phonemes and even more in the ways in which the phonemes are realized. Nonetheless it is useful to have a central accent from which to describe the variation and we will again use RP, which has twenty or twenty-one phonemes, as follows:

/iː/	peat	/uː/	fool	/ɪə/	pier
/ɪ/	pit	/ɜː/	furl	/ɛə/	pear
/e/	pet	/eɪ/	fail	/ɔə/	pour
/æ/	pat	/əʊ/	foal	/ʊə/	poor
/ʌ/	putt	/aɪ/	file	/ə/	banana
/ɑː/	part	/aʊ/	foul		
/ɒ/	pot	/ɔɪ/	foil		
/ɔː/	port				
/ʊ/	put				

Of these, /ɔː/ and /ɔə/ are not often separated: relatively few RP speakers make a contrast, for instance, between 'paw' with /ɔː/ and 'pour' with /ɔə/; most pronounce such words identically and therefore have twenty rather than twenty-one phonemes, but some still make the contrast and it must be reckoned with.

The /ə/ phoneme, commonly called 'schwa' from the Hebrew, exemplified in the first and last syllables of *banana*, is special in two ways: first, it is the most frequent RP vowel phoneme, and second it occurs only in unstressed syllables, so that in the words *beckon* /ˈbekən/, *adorn* /əˈdɔːn/, *sofa* /ˈsəʊfə/ it is always the other syllable which is stressed (ˈ is placed before the stressed syllable). It is almost possible in RP to consider [ə] as an allophone of /ʌ/; most occurrences of /ʌ/ are exclusively in stressed syllables, e.g. *comfort* /ˈkʌmfət/, *abundant* /əˈbʌndənt/, *loveable* /ˈlʌvəbl/, and if that were always so we could say that [ʌ] was the stressed allophone and [ə] the unstressed one. However in a few cases /ʌ/ occurs in unstressed syllables, e.g. *hiccough* /ˈhɪkʌp/, *uphold* /ʌpˈhəʊld/, *unfortunate* /ʌnˈfɔːtʃənət/, where [ə] will not do – notice *hiccough* with [ʌ] and *gallop* with [ə], *uphold* with [ʌ] and *oppose* with [ə]. So /ə/ must be considered to be a separate phoneme in RP, though in many other accents, e.g. Yorkshire, Lancashire, American, this is not so.

/aɪ, aʊ, ɔɪ/ are with few exceptions always realized as *diphthongs*, that is, a change from one vowel quality to another, and the limits of the change are roughly indicated by the two vowel symbols. This should not be taken to mean that they are sequences of phonemes; each functions in exactly the same way as the other vowels which are not diphthongal and is to be considered a unit phoneme. The phonemes /eɪ, əʊ, ɪə, ɛə, ʊə/ are usually realized as diphthongs in RP but not necessarily in other accents. /iː, ɑː, ɔː, uː, ɜː/ incorporate the mark [ː] which indicates that in RP they are longer than the remaining vowels /ɪ, e, æ, ʌ, ɒ, ʊ/; compare *deed* /diːd/ and *did* /dɪd/.

The following pages give descriptions of typical realizations of RP vowels together with an indication of the range of variation in other accents both in numbers of phonemes and in the actual sounds used. Where mention is made of a particular accent for illustrative purposes, it is to be understood that the broadest form of the accent is intended.

/iː/

This phoneme, found in *see*, *unique*, *receive*, is most often realized as a slight diphthong in RP, though it may also have a monophthongal realization. Both these are shown on Figure 56 in relation to the cardinal vowels (p. 107). An arrow indicates the direction and extent of the change of vowel quality in diphthongs. The change of quality in the diphthong is not very great in RP and often escapes casual notice. Diphthongization may be much greater in other accents, for instance, in Cockney and Birmingham; on the other hand in many Scottish and Welsh accents a monophthong approximating cardinal [i], the closest front vowel, and perceptibly closer than the average RP monophthong, can be heard. These variants are also shown on Figure 56.

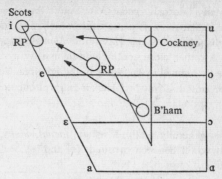

Figure 56: /iː/ variants

/ɪ/

RP realizations of /ɪ/, as in *wit*, *mystic*, *village*, are short and monophthongal. Figure 57 shows the area in which they generally fall. In other accents the vowel may be closer than in RP,

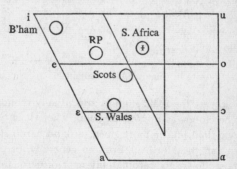

Figure 57: /ɪ/ variants

for example in Birmingham and the Midlands generally, where it is nearer to cardinal [i], the wide diphthongization of /iː/ making room, as it were, for the close realization of /ɪ/. On the other hand a considerably more open vowel, nearer to cardinal [ɛ], is common in South Wales, and a more central vowel in many Scottish accents. In South African and much American English there is a contrast, which does not exist in British English, between, e.g. *finish* and *Finnish*; the first vowel of *finish* is a rather close central vowel, usually symbolized [ɨ] whereas the first vowel in *Finnish* is in the RP area. Such accents must be accounted as having [ɨ] as an extra phoneme.

/e/

In RP /e/ is generally realized, in *set*, *meant*, *many*, etc., as a short, front vowel between cardinals [e] and [ɛ], see Figure 58.

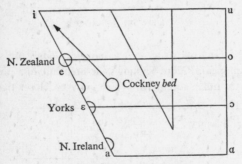

Figure 58: /e/ variants

In other accents the realization is also usually monophthongal but may be closer, as in New Zealand, where it is typically as close as cardinal [e], or more open, around cardinal [ɛ], as in Yorkshire and the North of England generally, or more open still, almost down to cardinal [a] in Northern Ireland and South Wales. In addition diphthongal realizations can also be heard in Cockney in words such as 'bed, men', where the quality changes from about the RP area in the direction of [i].

/æ/

/æ/, as in *pat*, *plait*, *cash*, is realized in RP as a short vowel between cardinal [ɛ] and cardinal [a], as shown in Figure 59. Generally it is monophthongal but there may be a diphthongal

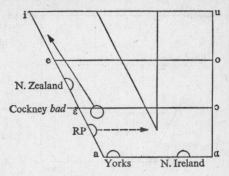

Figure 59: /æ/ variants

glide from that position to a more central one. Some accents, like Cockney and Birmingham, have a closer vowel, about cardinal [ɛ], and in New Zealand it is usual to hear a closer vowel still. On the other hand many accents of the West and North of England have a vowel, sometimes referred to as the 'flat a', about cardinal [a], and in some Scottish and particularly N. Irish accents the corresponding vowel is often well back towards cardinal [ɑ]. Cockney again often has a diphthong in words such as *bad*, *man*, in which the movement is from about cardinal [ɛ] up towards [i].

/ʌ/

In RP, /ʌ/ as in *bus*, *come*, *rough* is generally realized as a short almost open central vowel, as shown in Figure 60. Older speakers tend to favour the back part of the area shown there and younger speakers the front part. Cockney has a vowel which is open and front, about cardinal [a], whereas in many Irish accents /ʌ/ is represented by a true back, open vowel. Jamaican English also typically has a back vowel and slightly closer than the Irish quality. South Wales often has a vowel somewhat closer than RP and more towards cardinal [ɛ]. In educated Yorkshire and

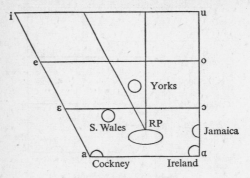

Figure 60: /ʌ/ variants

much other Northern speech and also in most American pronunciation the vowel is central and above half-open. In broader Northern accents /ʌ/ is not distinguished from /ʊ/ as in *put* so that *cud* and *could* are identical.

/ɑː/

The vowel /ɑː/ of *half*, *part*, *pass* in RP is an open, rather back vowel (see Figure 61) and it is relatively long. A very much fronter vowel, close to cardinal [a] is usually heard in Yorkshire, differing from the /æ/ variant (Figure 59) only in being long, so that *ham* and *harm* are differentiated mainly by vowel length. In accents as far apart as Cockney and Tyneside a truly cardinal [ɑ] is heard, and a very typically South African trait is an /ɑː/ variant which is almost as close as cardinal [ɔ]. Many Scottish and N. Irish accents do not distinguish /æ/ and /ɑː/, so that *father* and *gather* are exact rhymes, and these accents have one phoneme missing in this area. This is not the case with N.

English when the /æ/ variant is used in words such as *pass*, *after*, *laugh*, etc.; there *is* an /ɑː/ variant, as we have seen, which enables a distinction to be made between *ham/harm* and *gather/father*, but a different selection is made: RP selects /ɑː/ in *pass*, *laugh*, etc., whereas N. English (and others, e.g. most American accents) select /æ/.

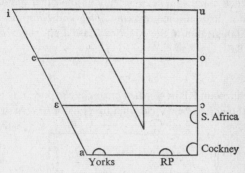

Figure 61: /ɑː/ variants

/ɒ/

In RP this is realized in, e.g. *pot*, *what*, *cost* as a short, back, open or almost-open vowel (Figure 62). Cockney typically has a

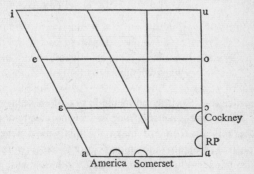

Figure 62: /ɒ/ variants

slightly closer vowel than this whereas in Somerset and the West Country generally, as well as in Ireland, a fronter vowel is heard, and in America the vowel may be quite close to cardinal [a]. In Jamaican English there is no contrast between /æ/ and /ɒ/, and therefore no distinction can be made between *hat* and *hot*, both having a vowel similar to the Somerset variant shown in Figure 62. In some American accents on the other hand /ɒ/ and /ɑ:/ are not distinguished, making *bomb* and *balm* identical. In both the Jamaican and the American case a phoneme is missing vis-à-vis RP.

/ɔ:/

This is realized in RP in words such as *caught*, *port*, *talk* as a long monophthong just below cardinal [o] (Figure 63). As was men-

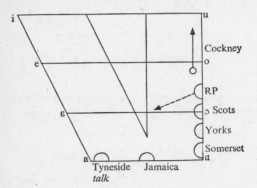

Figure 63: /ɔ:/ variants

tioned earlier (p. 153), this phoneme is not often separate from /ɔə/, in which case *saw* and *sore* are pronounced identically. Many speakers who do not make the distinction nevertheless use a diphthong [ɔə] (also shown on Figure 63) as a realization of /ɔ:/ before pause. When this is the case both *saw* and *sore* are pronounced [sɔə] and both *caught* and *court* are pronounced [kɔ:t]. Other RP speakers use the monophthongal pronunciation

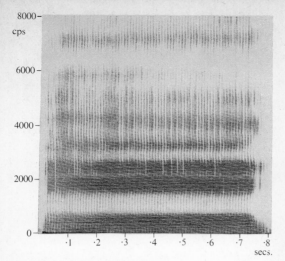

Plate 1. Spectrogram of [ɪ]

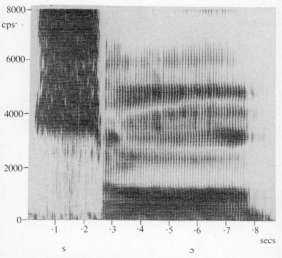

Plate 2. Spectrogram of 'saw' [sɔ]

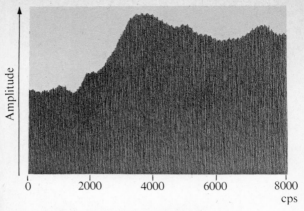

Plate 3. Amplitude section of [s]

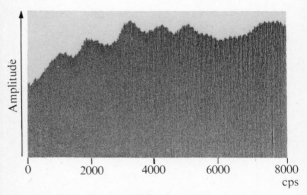

Plate 4. Amplitude section of [f]

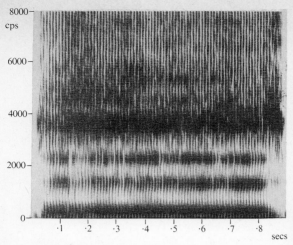

Plate 5. Spectrogram of [z]

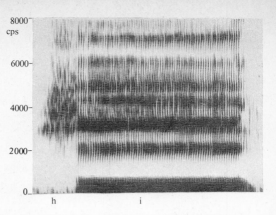

Plate 6. Spectrograms of [h] before [i, ɑ, ɔ]

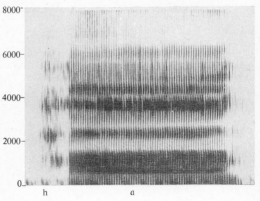

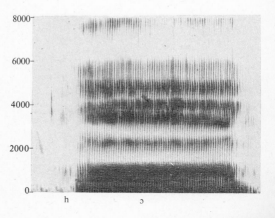

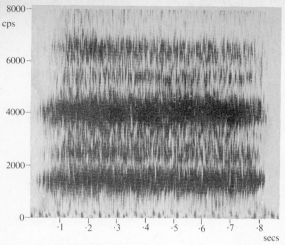

Plate 7. Spectrogram of [x]

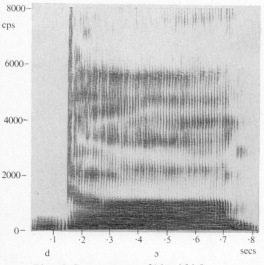

Plate 8. Spectrogram of 'daw' [dɔ]

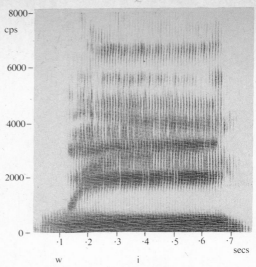

Plate 9. Spectrogram of 'we' [wi]

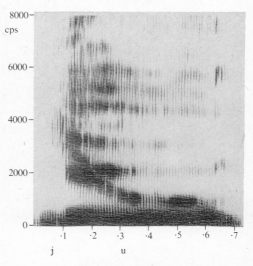

Plate 10. Spectrogram of 'you' [ju]

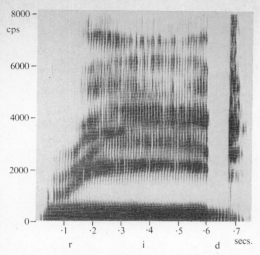

Plate 11. Spectrogram of 'reed' [rid]

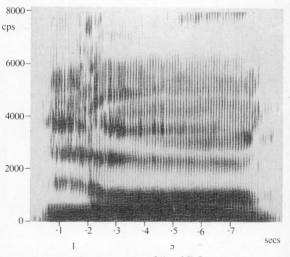

Plate 12. Spectrogram of 'law' [lɔ]

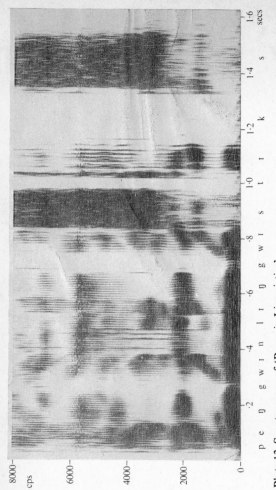

Plate 13. Spectrogram of 'Penguin Linguistics'
[peŋgwɪn lɪŋgwɪstɪks]

at all times. Cockney commonly has two diphthongal allophones of this phoneme; in final position it is similar to the RP diphthong of Figure 63, though usually ending in a more open position; in non-final position as in *caught*, etc. the diphthongal movement is towards the closer position of [u]. The Yorkshire pronunciation is between cardinals [ɔ] and [ɑ] and the Somerset pronunciation typically opener still. Many Scottish accents have no contrast between /ɔː/ and /ɒ/, in which case *cot* and *caught* are identical, with a vowel about cardinal [ɔ]. Jamaican English has no contrast between /ɔː/ and /ɑː/, *port* and *part* being identical, and this accounts for the position shown for Jamaican on Figure 63. In both these cases one phoneme is missing vis-à-vis RP. The opposite is the case for Tyneside pronunciation, because this has an extra phoneme. In RP, *fork* and *talk* rhyme, in Tyneside they do not; Tyneside *fork* has a vowel very similar to RP [ɔː], but in *talk*, *walk*, *call*, etc. the vowel used is an open one very close to cardinal [a], and it is to be noted that this is not a variant of /ɑː/, since Tyneside *calm*, *farm*, etc. have an open back vowel of cardinal [ɑ] quality. So Tyneside must be accounted as having an extra phoneme /aː/ in addition to /ɑː/ and /ɔː/.

/ʊ/

RP /ʊ/ is realized in, e.g. *wood*, *could*, *put* as somewhat more central and closer than cardinal [o], as in Figure 64. There is no

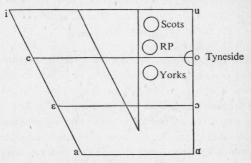

Figure 64: /ʊ/ variants

great variation in other accents, but Tyneside has a true back
cardinal [o] quality, and many Yorkshire and American accents
have a vowel somewhat opener than RP, which may or may not
have lip-rounding. From Birmingham northwards to the Scottish border /ʊ/ and /ʌ/ are not distinguished in the broadest
accents. In Scotland, on the other hand, /ʊ/ and /uː/ are not
distinguished in many accents, both being typically realized with
a vowel more central than cardinal [u]; and in a few Scottish
accents /ʊ/, /uː/ and /ɪ/ are all realized with the /ɪ/ variant.

/uː/

In RP, /uː/ most often has a diphthongal realization as shown in
Figure 65, but it may be given a monophthongal pronunciation
slightly lower and more central than cardinal [u]. In the sequence

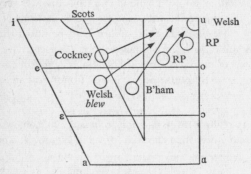

Figure 65: /uː/ variants

/juː/, as in *you, music* the monophthong or the beginning of the
diphthong is usually more central than in Figure 65. In Scotland
the vowel is still more central or even front. Various accents
have wider diphthongs than RP; for example Cockney may have
a much more fronted beginning point and Birmingham a more
open and central one. In RP and most other accents *blue* and
blew are identical, but in most of Wales they are distinguished.

In *blue* the vowel is a monophthong identical with cardinal [u], but in *blew* a wide diphthong is used as shown on Figure 65, and this diphthong, which may be symbolized /ɪu/, must be accounted an extra phoneme in this type of pronunciation.

/ɜː/

In RP the /ɜː/ of, e.g. *bird*, *hearse*, *word* is typically a long, mid, central vowel as shown on Figure 66. In Cockney and

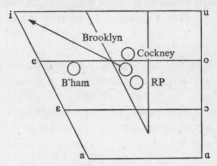

Figure 66: /ɜː/ variants

Australian English a vowel noticeably closer than this is frequent and in both Birmingham and New Zealand speech a half-close vowel fairly close to cardinal [e] but with lip-rounding (i.e. secondary cardinal [ø]) can be heard. In Tyneside speech /ɜː/ is not distinguished from /ɔː/, *shirt* and *short* being identically pronounced with a vowel like RP /ɔː/ (Figure 63). In *rhotic* accents (i.e. those in which /r/ occurs before consonants and before pause) such as Western and South-Western English, Irish, and Mid-Western and Western American English a retroflex [ɹ] is used in words such as *bird* and this represents the sequence /ər/. The exact quality of this retroflex sound varies from area to area. In Somerset and much American pronunciation it is similar to RP [ɜː] with added retroflexion; in north-western English (e.g. Blackburn) the underlying quality is a good deal closer than

[ɜː] (also with retroflexion), and in much of Ireland an underlying vowel close to cardinal [ɔ] accompanies the retroflexion. In
Brooklyn and parts of the Southern States of America retroflexion does not occur but rather a diphthong which starts in a
central position and changes toward [i].

Where other accents have /ɜː/ Scottish accents have the
sequences /ɪr/, /er/ or /ʌr/, so that the words *bird, heard, word* do
not rhyme. Scottish, therefore, does not have /ɜː/ as a phoneme
and yet makes more distinctions than RP can because it has
retained /ɪ, e, ʌ/ in such words and because it is rhotic.

/ə/

This, as we have said, is the commonest English vowel phoneme
for the reason that it has replaced many other vowels over the
centuries, e.g. /ɒ/ in *contain* /kənˈteɪn/, /æ/ in *postman* /ˈpəʊst-
mən/ etc., etc. and the process is still alive in the sense that words
such as *and, can, of, at* typically have /ə/ when they are unstressed,
which is most of the time.

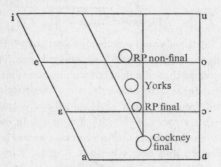

Figure 67: /ə/ variants

There are two major allophones in RP, one central and about
half-close which occurs in non-final positions, e.g. in *about* and
callous, and one central and about half-open which occurs before
pause, e.g. in *sailor, sofa* (Figure 67). Other non-rhotic accents

differ from this mainly in the quality of final /ə/; in, for example, Yorkshire the final /ə/ has a quality closer than RP, and in Australian English a closer vowel still can be heard in final position, differing little from non-final variety. On the other hand Cockney typically has an almost fully open central vowel in final position.

Rhotic accents distinguish words such as *beta* and *beater* by the use of /ə/ in the first case and /ər/ in the second, which non-rhotic accents in general do not. However, there is one non-rhotic accent, Tyneside, which has a contrast between, for example, *dresses* and *dressers* on the basis that the first has the half-close, non-final type [ə] in the second syllable of *dresses* and a much more open, Cockney-like vowel in the second syllable of *dressers*.

/eɪ/

In RP this is generally realized in, e.g. *day*, *late*, *vein* as a diphthong moving from a position between cardinals [e] and [ɛ] to a typical RP [ɪ] position (Figure 68). The change of quality is not

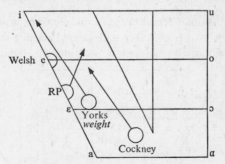

Figure 68: /eɪ/ variants

very great but usually perceptible. In other accents the pronunciation is monophthongal; in much of Wales and Northumberland, for instance, a long vowel of cardinal [e] quality is found and in most of Yorkshire a somewhat more open vowel occurs. On the other hand the diphthongal movement may be much more extensive, as for example in Cockney and Birmingham where the beginning point is an almost open vowel.

In various scattered areas of Britain, parts of Yorkshire, of Lancashire and of South Wales, for example, words such as *wait/weight* and *rain/reign* are distinguished by the use of a monophthong of approximately cardinal [e] quality in *rain, wait* and of a diphthong of the type [ɛi] in *weight, reign*, originating somewhere near cardinal [ɛ] and moving in the direction of cardinal [i]. Such accents have two phonemes, /eː/ and /ɛi/, and can therefore make distinctions not open to RP with the single /eɪ/ phoneme. In at least one area of Scotland words such as *meet/meat/mate* are all distinguished, *meet* having [i], *meat* háving a monophthong in the cardinal [e] area, and *mate* also a monophthong in the cardinal [ɛ] area. In this case too there is an extra phoneme which enables a distinction to be made amongst words which in RP all have /iː/, like *meet, meat*.

/əʊ/

The most common RP realization of this phoneme in words such as *go*, *dough*, *coat* is probably a diphthong starting at a typical RP [ɜː] position, i.e. mid-central, and moving slightly up and

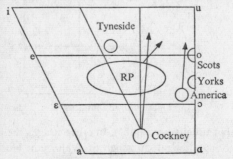

Figure 69: /əʊ/ variants

back to RP [ʊ], but the starting point may vary a good deal as shown in Figure 69. Those diphthongs which have the more retracted beginning point are more typical of older speakers and those with the fronter beginning point of younger. Other accents have a monophthongal pronunciation: Scottish and Welsh often have a vowel of cardinal [o] quality, parts of Yorkshire one rather more open, and Tyneside a half-close central vowel with lip-rounding (symbol [ɵ]). Many other accents have diphthongs of various kinds, some with back beginning points like [ou], which can often be heard in American English, some with central or even front beginning points, e.g. Cockney, which at the same time usually has a more central end point.

In those accents, e.g. many American and Scottish ones, which distinguish *horse* from *hoarse* (as RP does not), it is not a question of an extra phoneme but simply of the use of /ɔː/ in *horse* and /əʊ/ in *hoarse*.

/aɪ/

This diphthong in words like *buy*, *fine*, *sight*, etc. has a realization in RP with an open or almost open beginning point which varies from central to front and moves towards RP [ɪ] (Figure 70). In *fire*, *fiery*, etc., the realization is often monophthongal,

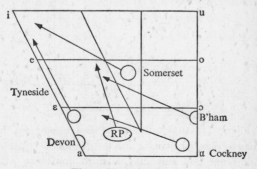

Figure 70: /aɪ/ variants

with the quality of the diphthong's starting point. In Devon a long monophthong somewhat opener than cardinal [ɛ] is common. Other accents have diphthongs with a wide variety of starting points ranging from just below cardinal [ɔ] in Birmingham, through about cardinal [ɑ] in Cockney and [ɜ] in Somerset, to just below cardinal [ɛ] in Tyneside. Welsh and Tyneside both have end points at cardinal [i], whereas Cockney often has a much more open one. In most Canadian accents there are two very noticeably different allophones of this phoneme, one which is used when fortis consonants follow, e.g. in *tight*, *rice*, which is very similar to the Somerset diphthong shown in Figure 70, and the other when lenis consonants follow (*tide*, *rise*) or in open syllables (*tie*, *rye*), which has a much more open and front beginning point, near cardinal [a].

/aʊ/

In RP, words such as *now*, *drought*, *fowl* have a diphthong which begins somewhat further back than for /aɪ/ and changes towards

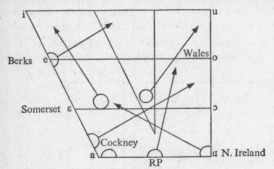

Figure 71: /aʊ/ variants

RP [ʊ] (Figure 71). In words such as *shower*, *showery*, the realization may be monophthongal with the quality of the diphthong's beginning point and this may lead to confusion with /ɑː/; *showery* and *starry* are exact rhymes in such pronunciations, which are not uncommon but *fiery*, even with its monophthongal pronunciation, will be distinguished from them by its fronter quality. The broadest form of Cockney also has a long monophthong of about cardinal [a] quality, but less broad forms have a diphthong starting rather above cardinal [a] and changing towards cardinal [ɔ] or closer. In S. Wales a diphthong can be heard with a central and not very open beginning point but ending at cardinal [u]. In N. Ireland on the other hand the beginning point is often cardinal [ɑ] and the end point a rounded front vowel close to cardinal [œ]. In Somerset and generally in the West of England a diphthong can be heard which begins about cardinal [ɛ] and ends near cardinal [y], i.e. close, front and with lip-rounding. In Berkshire the beginning point is often closer than this, at cardinal [e], and the end point a close, central vowel with lip-rounding. Canadian accents again have two distinct allophones; before fortis consonants, as with /aɪ/, the beginning point of the diphthong is central and slightly closer than that of the Welsh variety in Figure 71, whereas elsewhere it is similar to that of RP, c.f. *lout/loud*.

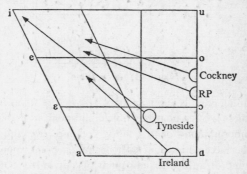

Figure 72: /ɔɪ/ variants

/ɔɪ/

In words like *boy*, *join*, *voice* RP has a diphthong which starts around cardinal [ɔ] and moves towards [ɪ] (Figure 72). The

starting point in Cockney is typically a little closer than this and
the end point more open. Conversely, in Tyneside the starting point
is more open and more central whilst the end point is about cardinal [i], and a fully open and back starting point may be heard in
much of Ireland. On the whole the range of variation for /ɔɪ/ is
much less than for the other diphthongs discussed above.

/ɪə/

There are two main allophones of /ɪə/ in RP, corresponding to
those of /ə/ (Figure 67). Before pause, as in *fear*, *idea* the end point
of the glide is a half-open central vowel and elsewhere, e.g. *fierce*,
really, it is somewhat closer than this (Figure 73). In both cases

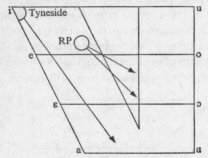

Figure 73: /ɪə/ variants

the beginning point is about as for RP [ɪ]. Before /r/, as in *weary*,
fearing, there is often no perceptible diphthongization, but rather
a long monophthong of [ɪ] quality, compare *fear* and *fearing*.
Some other accents have a closer beginning point, more like [i]
than [ɪ], and/or an opener end point; Tyneside has both. In S.
Wales all these words may be heard with the sequence /jɜː/ rather
than /ɪə/, the main difference being in the relative lengths of the
two vocalic elements: in /jɜː/ the first is much shorter than the
second, in /ɪə/ they are more nearly equal in length. In rhotic
accents 'r'-words are pronounced as /iː/ or /ɪ/ + /r/; in America

it is generally /ɪr/ in *dear*, etc., in Scotland generally /iːr/. In words with no 'r', such as *idea*, /iː/ or /ɪ/ + /ə/ is used.

/ɛə/

In *scare, scarce*, etc. RP has a diphthong which starts at cardinal [ɛ] or below and moves to a more central but equally open position (Figure 74). Before /r/, e.g. in *vary, wearing*, a monophthongal

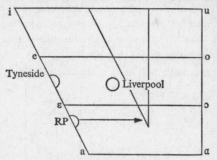

Figure 74: /ɛə/ variants

allophone is frequent, of the quality of the diphthong's starting point. The same monophthong is common in all positions in Yorkshire, and a closer quality, nearer cardinal [e] is normal on Tyneside. Liverpool and environs have a vowel which is similar but considerably centralized, and this is used for both /ɛə/ and /ɜː/; it follows that in this pronunciation no distinction is made between, e.g. *fare* and *fur*, and one phoneme is therefore missing. Rhotic accents have a sequence of either /eɪ/ or /e/ + /r/ in all these /ɛə/ words; in Scottish /eɪr/ is usual, in America /er/. In Western England /er/ is also usual but in this case the sequence is most often realized as a single retroflex sound with an underlying [ɛ] vowel quality, a so-called 'r-coloured [ɛ]'.

/ɔə/

As mentioned earlier /ɔə/ as an independent phoneme, differentiating *pour* from *paw* /pɔː/, is quite rare in RP. It occurs in 'r'-

words like *pour*, *score* whereas /ɔː/ occurs in non-'r'-words such
as *paw*, *saw*, but /ɔə/ does not necessarily occur in all 'r'-words;
the only place where /ɔə/ is regularly distinguished from /ɔː/, even
by those few who make the distinction is before pause, so it is
quite unusual, though not unheard of, for *caught* and *court* to be
distinguished on this basis in RP. Rhotic accents, of course, make
this sort of distinction regularly but it is not common elsewhere.
The West Riding of Yorkshire provides an example: all non-'r'-
words have the rather open back vowel shown in Figure 63, whereas 'r'-words have a diphthong beginning near cardinal [o] and
changing towards central [ɜ] (Figure 75).

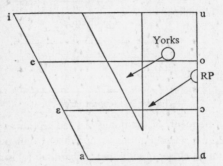

Figure 75: /ɔə/ variants

/ʊə/

This occurs in RP in words like *lure*, *endure* and is realized as a
diphthong changing from the normal [ʊ] quality to a central and
more open position (Figure 76). A monophthongal pronunciation
is again found regularly before /r/ in, e.g. *alluring*, *furious*, having
the quality of the diphthong's beginning point. Rhotic accents use
/r/ in 'r'-words, with either /uː/ or /ʊ/. /ʊ/ is found in America and
/uːr/ in N. Lancashire, for example. In non-'r'-words like *skua*,
fluent it is usually /uː/ + /ə/. Non-rhotic accents may have monophthongal realizations, e.g. a long vowel more open than RP [ʊ]
can often be heard in Yorkshire, but more usually diphthongs

occur with a beginning point corresponding to the /uː/ variant of the accent and changing to /ə/. So Tyneside changes from very close back to open central.

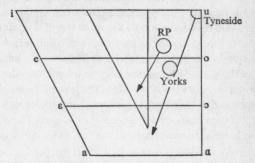

Figure 76: /ʊə/ variants

The brilliance of the brain

This account of the individual phonemes of English gives some idea of the complexity of the sound aspect of language, but it is far from complete; we have not yet considered the part which stress plays, the factor differentiating *incite* from *insight* /ɪnˈsaɪt, ˈɪnsaɪt/, nor the part which length plays in differentiating, for example, *Wonnnderful!* /ˈwʌnːːdəfļ/ from *wonderful* /ˈwʌndəfļ/, nor the part which pitch plays in separating *I don't know* from *I don't, no*. We shall look at these and other factors in the following chapters, but we have already seen enough to realize the magnitude of the task that the human brain performs every hour of every day without apparent thought or strain.

One of the great dreams of the communications engineers is to build a machine which will recognize speech, so that if you speak into a microphone connected to the machine it will produce, say, a readable text of what was said; given an acoustic input the machine would produce an accurate linguistic record. It was first imagined that it would be possible to analyse the acoustic record mechanically, and abstract features typical of particular phonemes as you went along, resulting in a more or less continuous phonetic transcription, but imagine the difficulties in the light of what we have seen in English. First of all, the same man, even if he is aiming at the same pronunciation of the same word, does not necessarily exactly repeat himself; then he uses different allophones in different situations, for example [t] and [ʔ] for /t/, or [əi] and [ai] for /aɪ/ in the Canadian case mentioned on p. 168. Already the machine must have some knowledge of the variability of one man's pronunciation due to inherent inaccuracy and to the influence of context. But then suppose that a second man speaks into the microphone, having the same accent as the first. He nevertheless has a different voice quality, he sounds a different person, and this difference would find its place in the acoustic record; the machine would have to know what differences to ignore in making its interpretation. And if a third man, with a different accent, does the speaking, the difficulties are of quite another order. Figure 77

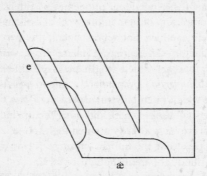

Figure 77: Overlap of /e/ and /æ/ realizations

shows the areas of different realizations of /e/ and /æ/, taken from Figures 58 and 59. The overlap between these areas is considerable and therefore, ignoring individual differences, the same sound, having the same acoustic features, might represent /e/ in one speaker and /æ/ in the other. To cope with this the machine would need to know two quite separate things: first, how that particular sound related to other sounds in the vowel system of the particular speaker, and second, whether /e/ or /æ/ was more likely in a particular context: if we hear [ɛ] in *bad* in *It wasn't bad*, we know that it is unlikely on grounds of meaning that the speaker meant *It wasn't bed* and this immediately sets up expectations of what vowel he is likely to use when he really wants to say *bed*. These kinds of information would have to be built into the machine before it would have any chance of solving its problem: then change from a man's to a woman's to a child's voice and the whole cycle starts up again. In practice machines have been constructed to do simple tasks such as recognizing the ten spoken digits, but a change of voice is always likely to disorientate the machine completely, and there is no likelihood at all in the near future that a machine will be built to recognize natural speech in a wide range of voices.

Yet we can orient ourselves to thousands of different speakers of different sex and different ages and different accents, with all the acoustic differences that these imply, in a fantastically short space of time. The first few words are hardly out of the speaker's mouth before we have adjusted all our controls to cope with his particular acoustic output and make sense out of it. How we do this is imperfectly understood, but part of the explanation lies in the way in which spoken language is structured, the way in which sounds are organized to serve their purpose of communication; and we shall now turn to this in the following chapter.

6. A Language and Its Sounds

The white flag of truce may indeed be a shining white flag, but it may just as well be a piece of torn sheet or a dirty white scarf or even a piece of newspaper; whatever their nature – within limits: it is no good waving a rifle – these different things fulfil the same function, they represent the same intention. A phoneme is represented by different concrete sounds at different times. On p. 144 we mentioned that the various [h] sounds in *heart, hat, hunt, heat*, etc. are all different, being simply strong voiceless varieties of the following vowels; to show this we can represent them as [ɑɑːt, æ̣æt] etc. This means that there are as many different [h] sounds as there are vowels which can follow. Try some of those words and notice that the [h] sounds are really different. Now all these *different* sounds represent the *same* /h/ phoneme; there is only one /h/ phoneme in the same way that there is only one flag of truce, but both are represented by different concrete objects at different times. We have already seen (p. 122) that the actual sounds which represent /h/ are technically known as the *allophones* of /h/, so [ɑ, æ] etc. are all allophones of /h/.

The allophones of a phoneme are never in contrast with each other, that is, they can never make a difference of meaning between one word and another: if I use [ɑ] instead of the normal [æ] in the word *hat* it may sound a bit peculiar, but the word will still be recognizable as *hat* and not *bat* or *sat*. This lack of contrast, or lack of distinctive power, of the allophones of one phoneme comes about in two main ways: if [ɑ] only occurs before the vowel [ɑː], and [æ] only occurs before [æ], and so on, they can never possibly distinguish meanings; for this to happen the two sounds *must* be capable of occurring in exactly the same environment, as do [s] and [t] in *sack* and *tack*, or [l] and [d] in *lay* and *day*. Allophones which *never* occur in the same environment (like [ɡ], [æ] etc.) are said to be in *complementary distribution*. Other examples of allophones in complementary distribution are the different [l] sounds in *clearly* (p. 121), or [t] and [ʔ] as allophones of /t/ in *tight corner* (p. 122). However, there are also cases where two different sounds *do* occur in the same environment and yet are never distinctive; for example, when I say *Good night*, the [t] sound at the end may be exploded or not, sometimes I release it and sometimes I hold on to it. Now these are obviously two different sounds, one having an explosion and one lacking it, and both occur in the same environment – at the end of *Good night* – but even so they do not make a difference of meaning: *Good night* is *Good night* whether you have an exploded or unexploded [t] sound at the end of it. In a case like this, when allophones of a phoneme *do* occur in the same environment, but without distinctive force, we say that the allophones are in *free variation*.

Our decisions are not made purely on distributional grounds; we take phonetic features into account as well. If we did not it would be difficult to decide how the aspirated [pʰ, tʰ, kʰ] of *pin*, *tin*, *kin* should be related to the unaspirated [p, t, k] of *spy*, *sty*, *sky* (p. 132). The unaspirated [p] is in complementary distribution not only with the aspirated [pʰ] but also with aspirated [tʰ] and [kʰ], since none of them occurs after /s/. So we decide to group the two [p]'s together as representing the same phoneme because they are both bilabial stops and thus more similar to each other than either is to the [t] and [k] sounds. More thorny is the question: why do we take unaspirated [p] in *spy* to represent the /p/ phoneme? Why not the /b/ phoneme? After all [b] does not occur after /s/ either, so it too is in complementary distribution with unaspirated [p], and one of the important things about /b/ is that it is never realized with aspiration in any position. The answer in such cases is that you choose arbitrarily: in English we have opted for the /p/ phoneme; Danish phoneticians faced with the same situation in Danish have opted for /b/. In practice it makes little difference because whatever you do you are left with one phoneme which does not occur after /s/, /p/ in Danish and /b/ in English; it would be necessary to bear this in mind, however, in making any comparison of the distribution of /p/ and /b/ in English and Danish.

In dealing with an unknown language one has to approach the drawing up of a phoneme inventory in this way, considering the sounds, looking at their distribution and finding out whether they can make differences of meaning or not, and then grouping them together as representing the same phoneme. At best it is a hazardous and difficult operation. In one's own language it is much easier to proceed from larger to smaller units – to start with whole utterances and break them down by comparisons into smaller and smaller elements until finally you arrive at something which cannot be broken any further, and this is the phoneme. In fact, this is the basis for our intuitive perception of the phoneme; we *know* that /str/ at the beginning of *stray* is divisible into /s/ + /t/ + /r/ because the /s/ is dispensable, cf. *tray*, so is the /t/, *ray*, so is the /r/, *stay*, but when we try to divide further there is no comparison that allows us to divide /s/ or /t/ or /r/ in two, and we have therefore arrived at the minimal units or phonemes.

Even this process is not fool-proof, there are problems which remain and have no single solution. For example, the problem of /tʃ/ in *chair* /tʃɛə/; it would seem that /t/ is dispensable, leaving *share* /ʃɛə/, and /ʃ/ is dispensable, leaving *tear* /tɛə/, and therefore this is a sequence of /t/ + /ʃ/ just as /tr/ in *tray* is a sequence of /t/ + /r/. Yet we do not feel about /tʃ/ as we feel about /tr/, we would be quite happy to accept it as a unit. Why? The reason is partly to do with /dʒ/, partly to do with the sort of sequence /tʃ/ would be. /dʒ/ in *jay* /dʒeɪ/ cannot be treated so easily as /tʃ/ because the /d/ is not dispensable; if we omit it we get /ʒeɪ/, but /ʒ/ is not a permitted initial phoneme in English (it occurs only in a few borrowed words like *gigolo, genre*) so this is not satisfactory; but it would be odd to treat one of this correlated pair as a sequence and the other as a unit. Then, if we treat /tʃ/ as a sequence we will find that it is an odd sort of sequence; parallel to the /tr/ sequence we have /kr, pr, fr, dr/ etc. What have we that is parallel to /tʃ/? Nothing; no /kʃ, pʃ, fʃ, dʃ/ or any other sequence of consonant + /ʃ/. And similarly with /dʒ/. So for both these reasons /tʃ/ and /dʒ/ are generally taken to be unitary, despite the separability of /tʃ/ by the comparison method.

System and structure

By operating this method of comparison, plus the other considerations referred to above, we can arrive at a system of phonemes for a particular accent, such as the Received Pronunciation system set out on pp. 129 and 153. What we mean by *system* here is a set of items which can replace each other in a given framework and from which we must select when we want to fill that framework. In fact what we find is not one system but several. In the first place we can talk of a consonant system and a separate vowel system, because consonants typically replace each other but do not replace vowels; in the framework /set/ *set* we can replace /s/ by /p, b, d, g, l, m, n, j, w, dʒ/ to get *pet, bet, debt, get, let, met, net, yet, wet, jet*, but we cannot replace /s/ by, for instance, /ɑː/ or /ɜː/. Similarly we can replace /e/ in *set* by /iː, ɪ, æ, ɒ, ɔː, ʊ, uː/ etc. to get *seat, sit, sat, sot, sort, soot, suit*, but we cannot replace it by /k/ or /f/. Within these two separate systems we can see *subsystems*; for example, the subsystem of initial consonants, which excludes /ʒ/ of *rouge* and /ŋ/ of *ring*, since they do not occur at the beginning of a word, and the subsystem of final consonants, which excludes /h/. Within the vowel system there is the subsystem of final vowels, which excludes /e, æ, ɒ, ʌ/ because they do not occur before a pause; or the subsystem of vowels occurring before /ŋ/ which includes only /ɪ, æ, ʌ, ɒ/ as in *sing*, *sang*, *sung*, *song*. And so on.

Besides this interest in systems and subsystems, we are interested in the way in which the units from the systems are put together to make up the forms of the language – the *sequences* in which they operate. This is no longer a matter of one item being replaced by another, but of linear sequence; and we want to know what sequences of phonemes are permitted in the language and what are not. If an utterance starts with /t/ any one of a large number of phonemes may follow: /r, w, j/ amongst the consonants, and any of the vowels; if the utterance starts with /ð/, as in *though*, then a vowel must follow (and not all of the vowels); if it starts with /tj/, the only thing that can follow is /uː/ as in *tune* /tjuːn/. This study of the arrangement of items and the constraints which operate in these arrangements is a study of *structure*. The two aspects of system and structure are inseparable; we derive a vowel system, for instance, from a set such as *seat*, *sit*, *set*, *sat*, etc., but the items in this set are structures of the language, i.e. sequences of phonemes found in the language, so we derive a system from a particular place in a structure. Conversely, we define a structure as a particular sequence of phonemes, say /s + iː + t/ in *seat*, so system and structure are entirely dependent one upon the other.

Systemic/non-systemic

As we have seen, differences of sound may or may not correspond to differences of system: the Cockney diphthong in *late*, [aɪ], is different in sound from the RP diphthong [eɪ] in the same word, but this is not a difference of system because there is a regular correspondence between Cockney [aɪ] and RP [eɪ]; that is to say, *any* word containing [eɪ] in RP (such as *day*, *ache*, *pain*, etc., etc.) will automatically contain [aɪ] in Cockney. On the other hand, when we consider Scottish /kɔt/ for both *cot* and *caught*, which are differentiated in RP as /kɒt/ and /kɔːt/, we cannot say that the single Scottish vowel will *always* correspond to RP /ɔː/, or *always* correspond to RP /ɒ/. In the word *cause* the Scottish /ɔ/ corresponds to RP /ɔː/, whereas in *moss* it corresponds to RP /ɒ/. In other words, the Scottish vowel system has one phoneme fewer than the RP system in this case, whereas RP and Cockney have the same number, even though the /eɪ/ phoneme in *day*, etc. is realized differently in the two accents.

Differences which affect systems (such as the RP /ɒ, ɔː/ *v.* Scottish /ɔ/) are *systemic*; those which do not affect systems (like the RP [eɪ] *v.* Cockney [aɪ]) are *non-systemic*. Other systemic differences amongst English accents would be Cockney /f/ for RP /f/ and /θ/ in *fin, thin*; lack of /h/ in many accents compared with its occurrence in others; RP and /ʌ/ /ʊ/ compared with Yorkshire /ʊ/ in *cud, could*; S. Wales /eː/ and /ɛi/ distinguishing *wait*, *weight* compared with RP /eɪ/ in both. Other examples of non-systemic differences are the New Zealand [ɛ] in *bad* compared with Yorkshire [a]: Cockney [aʊ] in *go* compared with RP [əʊ] or Scottish [oː]; the use of dark [ɫ] in Scottish against clear [l] in Irish; and the use of a rolled or flapped [r] in Scottish against the frictionless continuant [ɹ] of RP, etc.

We can also see *subsystemic* differences, that is, differences which apply only at certain points in structure and not at others; for example, in *seat v. sit* or *heap v. hip* both Cockney and RP have /iː/ *v.* /ɪ/ and any difference in the realizations of those phonemes is non-systemic. But before [ɫ], in *heel v. hill* or *field v. filled*, Cockney no longer has a contrast between /iː/ and /ɪ/; one vowel only, [ɪ], is used in both words of the pair, so that *heel* and *hill* both sound like *hill*; but RP still preserves the contrast between /iː/ and /ɪ/ in this position, and therefore the difference as between Cockney and RP in this particular position is systemic. So far as the overall system is concerned both RP and Cockney have an opposition between /iː/ and /ɪ/ in most positions, i.e. the replacement of /iː/ by /ɪ/ would cause a change in meaning (*seat/ sit, deed/did*, etc.), but in Cockney the opposition is *neutralized* before [ɫ] since only one of the two vowels occurs and there is therefore no possibility of a distinction in meaning between *field/ filled*, *heel/hill*, etc. In American accents /e/, /æ/ and /eɪ/ are distinguished in *bet, bat, bait*, as they are in RP. But before /r/ as in *merry, marry, Mary* the opposition is neutralized and only one vowel /e/ is used in all three words. In German, /t/ and /d/ are in opposition at the beginning of words but not at the end, so *Deich* ('dyke') and *Teich* ('pond') are distinguished, but not *Rad* ('wheel') and *Rat* ('advice') which, despite their spelling, are both /raːt/, and the opposition is neutralized. In the same way the opposition between /p/ and /b/ in English is neutralized after /s/ where only what we agree to call /p/ occurs.

Selectional differences

Besides systemic and non-systemic differences amongst different accents of the same language there is another type of difference exemplified by the Northern and Southern pronunciation of words like *glass, laugh* which have /æ/ in the North and /ɑː/ in the South. This is not a systemic difference because both North and South have /æ/ and /ɑː/, /æ/ in *man* and /ɑː/ in *half* (with non-systemic differences of realization, of course). It is a matter of selection: of the two available phonemes /æ/ and /ɑː/ the North selects one and the South the other. This is not a conscious selection; the reasons for it lie in the history of the language. In a particular word or set of words a change takes place in one accent but not in another. In the areas where *glass, laugh*, now have a long /ɑː/ the original pronunciation was with /æ/, just as in *cat*, but over the years the *glass, laugh* set split away from the *cat, man* set and came to be pronounced /glɑːs, lɑːf/. No such change took place in the North, but it is important to notice that words such as *half, farm* developed to /ɑː/ in both North and South so that the /æ/ v. /ɑː/ opposition was maintained for both. Similarly broad Tyneside has retained the original /uː/ in many words like *out, now*, *town* (contrary to RP /aʊ/) but nevertheless has /aʊ/ in other words like *bough*, *row*.

Selectional differences may affect large sets of words, as they do in the /æ/ *v.* /ɑː/ and /uː/ *v.* /aʊ/ examples above, or they may affect only a single item; the pronunciation of *night* on Tyneside as /niːt/ rather than /naɪt/ (whereas *bright*, *light*, etc. all have /aɪ/) is perhaps an example of this. In any case the set of words affected may be quite small, as in the set of *one*, *among* and a few others which in much of the North have /ɒ/ and rhyme with *gone*, *song* whereas in the South they have /ʌ/ and rhyme with *fun*, *sung*. In Northern (and other) accents *either*, *neither* have /iː/ and rhyme with *breather*, whereas in RP they have /aɪ/, and this is a set of just these two items. A slightly larger set is the /ɒ/ *v.* /ɔː/ set in words like *salt*, *fault*, *Austria* and perhaps *off*, *often*, where Northern speakers have /ɒ/ and Southern speakers may have /ɔː/, but the set is more extensive if we take into account the type of American pronunciation which also has /ɔː/ in, for example, *dog*, *coffee*, *loss* and a good many others.

This sort of difference may also occur within one accent and it then generally affects single words or small sets. For example, *economic* may have /iː/ or /e/ at the beginning, *graph* may have /ɑː/ or /æ/ in RP (and this may extend to *photograph*, *autograph*, etc.), *Persia, Asia* may have /ʃ/ or /ʒ/ medially, and so on. Quite a lot of cases are no doubt due to spelling pronunciation and/or relative unfamiliarity of the word. The pronunciation of the word *England* by a few speakers with /e/ rather than /ɪ/ at the beginning is probably a spelling pronunciation, like *hoopoe* as /huːpəʊ/ rather than the ornithologist's /huːpuː/.

Cases of selectional differences must be carefully differentiated from cases of neutralization of oppositions. It is easy to fall into the trap of thinking, for instance, that when *straw* is /strɔː/ in most accents but /ʃtrɔː/ in parts of W. Ireland, the difference between /s/ and /ʃ/ is one of selection, but it is not, because the Irish speaker has no other option in this position; whenever /t/

follows, /ʃ/ is the only possible precursor, just as /s/ is the only possible precursor in the other accents. If it were a selectional difference both options would be open to both accents; in RP *pass*, *glass*, /ɑː/ is selected, it is not conditioned by the following /s/, since *gas*, *mass* have /æ/; similarly the Northern /æ/ in *laugh*, *after*, *staff* is not conditioned by the following /f/, since *half*, *scarf* have /ɑː/. The /s/ v. /ʃ/ case is a neutralization for both accents of the opposition /s/ v. /ʃ/ before /t/; the /æ/ v. /ɑː/ case is a true selectional difference.

Comparing accents

These differences of selection are bound to make us wonder what it is we are doing when we compare, say, the vowel system of one accent with that of another. It is all very well to say that RP has /uː/ and /aʊ/ and Tyneside has /uː/ and /aʊ/ and that therefore they are in this respect systemically equivalent, but how do we decide to group together for systemic purposes a phoneme of one accent and a phoneme of another which may be realized in very different ways? The answer is that we take into account for this kind of comparison the stock of words which they hold in common, and when we say that both RP and Yorkshire have /æ/ and /ɑː/ what we are saying is that in most of the words where the sound [æ] occurs in RP the sound [a] occurs in Yorkshire, and that in most of the words where the contrasting RP sound [ɑː] occurs, the equally contrasting Yorkshire [aː] also occurs. We are working less with sound qualities than with equivalence of occurrence in a common set of words. In view of differences of selection we cannot expect that the set of words containing /æ/ in one accent will be exactly the same as the set containing it in the other, but that is not necessary. So long as the set of equivalent words is larger than any sub-set (like the 150 or so in the *glass*, *laugh* sub-set) then it is fair to identify the phoneme of one accent with that of another.

Indeed it is much more revealing to proceed in that way, on the basis of word-sets, than purely on the basis of similarity of sound. Figure 78 represents the vowel systems of two different accents of

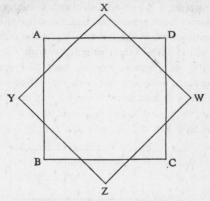

Figure 78: Two accents with different realizations of the same system

the same hypothetical language and their different realizations. Each has four phonemes in contrast with each other and we may suppose that they are systemically equivalent. The realization of

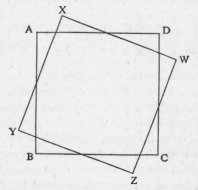

Figure 79: As in Figure 78, with X and A, etc. closer in realization

phoneme X is just as similar to that of phoneme A as to that of
phoneme D and so on. How are we to decide whether to equate
X with A or with D? We can do so only on the basis of the words
in which they occur: if X and A both occur in a large number of
words common to both accents we link them together as representing the same point in the pattern; if, on the other hand, X
shares more words with D than with A, we link X and D. And
this applies, too, in the more extreme case of Figure 79. This
represents the same situation but with realizations of X much
closer to A than to D, and so on. Even so, if X and D occur in a
very similar word-set and X and A do not, then it is much more
revealing to equate X and D than X and A.

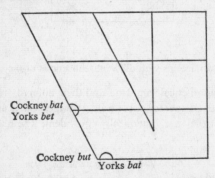

Figure 80: Identical realization of different phonemes

Take the case of Yorkshire /e/ and /æ/ in *bet*, *bat*, and Cockney
/æ/ and /ʌ/ in *bat*, *but* shown in Figure 80 (abstracted from Figures
58, 59, 60). Exactly the same vowel sounds may occur in Yorkshire *bet* and Cockney *bat*, and in Yorkshire *bat* and Cockney *but*.
If it were a matter of similarity of sound we should be obliged to
say that cardinal vowel [ɛ] represented the same point in the vowel
systems of Yorkshire and Cockney, but in fact in Yorkshire [ɛ]
appears in *bed*, *head*, *said*, *mess*, etc., whereas in Cockney it appears in *bad*, *had*, *sad*, *mass*, etc. and to ignore this would be to

falsify the total picture and to give a wrong idea of the way in which the various vowels contribute to the language. If we want to compare the vowel system of one *language* to that of another, we are bound to proceed largely on the basis of sound similarity because there is no common word stock to consider, but within one language it would be foolish to take account merely of systems of sound without any thought for the job that these sounds are doing.

In comparing accents which are systemically different one method would be simply to say: 'Accent X has ten vowel phonemes and accent Y nine'; this tells us something but not very much. Another method would be to say: 'Accent X has phonemes A, B, C, D, and Accent Y has A, B and D'. This tells us a little more but it still does not tell all we would like to know. Take the case of comparing RP and any Northern accent which does not have the /ʌ/ *v.* /ʊ/ opposition in *cud, could*. We could put it this way:

$$\text{Yorks } /e \sim \text{æ} \sim \text{ʊ} \sim \text{ɒ}/$$
$$\text{RP} \quad /e \sim \text{æ} \sim \text{ʌ} \sim \text{ʊ} \sim \text{ɒ}/$$

(The sign $\sim$ means 'is in opposition to'.)

But we are left wondering how the two fit together. What words does this extra /ʌ/ of RP occur in? We can make the presentation much more explicit by arranging it in this way:

$$\frac{\text{Yorks}}{\text{RP}} \quad /e \approx \text{æ} \approx \frac{\text{ʊ}}{\text{ʌ} \sim \text{ʊ}} \approx \text{ɒ}/$$

This is to be interpreted to mean: both Yorkshire and RP have /e, æ, ɒ/ in opposition in largely the same sets of words, *pet, pat, pot*, etc., and in addition there is a set of words, all of which have /ʊ/ in Yorkshire, but some of which have /ʌ/ and some /ʊ/ in RP. We now know the area in which the systemic difference lies with regard to the word stock of the language. Similarly:

$$\frac{\text{S. Wales}}{\text{RP}} \quad /\text{iː} \approx \frac{\text{eː} \sim \text{ɛi}}{\text{ei}} \approx \text{ɑː}/$$

means that in RP there is a set of words containing /eɪ/ which in S. Wales (and other accents, p. 166) is split between two contrasting phonemes /eː/ and /ɛɪ/, e.g. *wait, weight*.

Those American accents which do not have an /ɒ ~ ɑː/ distinction (i.e. they do not distinguish *bomb* from *balm*, etc.), but do use /ɔː/ in words such as *dog, loss, coffee*, etc. as well as in *law, thought*, etc. may be compared with RP as follows:

$$\text{American} \atop \text{RP} \quad /iː \approx \frac{\text{ɑː} \sim \text{ɔː}}{\text{ɑː} \sim \text{ɒ} \sim \text{ɔː}} \approx \text{uː}/$$

Because /ɑː/ and /ɔː/ appear both above and below the line this must be taken to mean that some American /ɑː/ words (like *balm*) have /ɑː/ in RP but some have /ɒ/ (e.g. *bomb*), and also that some American /ɔː/ words have /ɔː/ in RP (e.g. *law*) and some have /ɒ/ (e.g. *dog*).

The situation may be more complicated. Tyneside has no contrast between /ɜː/ and /ɔː/; all /ɜː/ words and most /ɔː/ words have the same pronunciation, so *shirt = short*. But some words which in RP have /ɔː/, have /ɑː/ in Tyneside (e.g. *walk, talk, call*) and this /ɑː/ is in contrast with both /ɔː/ and /ɑː/. This situation can be represented as follows:

$$\text{Tyneside} \atop \text{RP} \quad /iː \approx \frac{\text{ɔː} \sim \text{ɑː}}{\text{ɜː} \sim \text{ɔː}} \approx \text{ɑː}/$$

This means that there is a set of words which in Tyneside is divided on the basis of a contrast /ɔː ~ ɑː/, but which in RP is divided differently, on the basis of a contrast /ɜː ~ ɔː/. The use of /ɔː/ both above and below the line, but in reverse order, guarantees that there are at least some words that have /ɔː/ in both accents (e.g. *short*), that there are some which have /ɔː/ in Tyneside and /ɜː/ in RP (e.g. *shirt*), and that there are some which have /ɔː/ in RP and /ɑː/ in Tyneside (e.g. *walk*).

Phonemes and sounds

The phoneme principle is useful in bringing relative simplicity out of great complexity of sound, and the study of different phoneme systems, whether among the accents of one language or in different languages, can be revealing as to the ways in which languages work. What we must avoid is thinking that the phoneme is the be-all and end-all of phonetic study; it is not and it is dangerous to think that it is. If we transcribe *beat* and *bead* phonemically as /biːt/ and /biːd/ that is one thing, and quite useful too. But if we then come to imagine that the difference between those two words as we hear them is entirely a matter of the difference between /t/ and /d/, as the transcription might suggest, then we have gone off the rails, because the perceptual difference between the two words lies as much in the relative lengths of the preceding /iː/ as in the consonantal ending. In /biːt/ the vowel is much shorter than in /biːd/ and this contributes a great deal to our recognition of one word or the other. We do not symbolize the length difference in a phonemic transcription because it is a *conditioned* difference: whenever a fortis consonant follows in such words the preceding vowel is shorter than when a lenis follows. We could, if it were only a question of words such as these, transcribe them /bit/ and /biːt/, showing the difference in vowel length but not the concomitant consonantal difference. But in fact we need, the /t ∼ d/ distinction in other places, e.g. *too*, *do*, so we prefer to symbolize the /t ∼ d/ difference in *beat*, *bead* too, and leave the vowel length difference to be deduced from a general rule. An inventory of phonemes implies a set of rules which will enable us to deduce an actual pronunciation from the phonemic transcription, and the phoneme is an organizational convenience rather than a basic unit in perception.

A second danger is to imagine that when we have dealt with everything that we can deal with in phonemic terms we have then accounted for the language, so far as its sound aspect is concerned.

This is far from the truth. Many of the meaningful differences of sound in a language simply cannot be accounted for on a phoneme basis, and to carry the phoneme principle too far, to try to make it carry more than it is able, is to reduce its utility in those areas where it has a real part to play. It is time now to move on to those aspects of sound where the phoneme principle has less importance.

Pitch

Different rates of vibration of the vocal cords are, as we have seen, closely related to differences of fundamental frequency and to differences of perceived pitch. These different perceived pitches are used in all languages that we know of in order to make differences of meaning, but there are two fundamentally different ways in which they are used in various languages. Firstly, in languages like English, French, German, Spanish and many others, pitch operates on whole utterances; in the sentence *You told him* if the pitch falls from *told* to *him* the effect is of a statement; if it rises, the effect is of a question *You told him?* The component words are the same; the fact that they are uttered with a different pattern of pitch does not prevent our recognizing them as the same in the two cases. Yet the total meanings of the two utterances are different. We may do the same thing on a single word, e.g. *No* as a statement, with the pitch falling, and *No?* as a question, with it rising, but again it is the same word that we are using, and we are using it as a whole utterance. This use of pitch to distinguish whole utterances without interfering with the shape of the component words is known as *intonation*.

In a second large group of languages, the *tone* languages, pitch operates on words, to change their shape and alter their meaning. If in the National Language of China (Mandarin) the syllable /mɑ/ is said with the pitch falling (as for English *No* as a statement) it means 'scold' but if it is said with rising pitch (as English

No?) then it means 'hemp'. These are quite different words of unrelated meaning, unlike English *No* which retains its basic meaning whatever pitch changes take place on it. Very many American Indian languages, and many in S. and W. Africa and S. E. Asia, are tone languages. Nearer home, we have Swedish and Norwegian: Swedish, for example, has two words *Anden* distinguished by tone: the first falls in pitch on both syllables, and means 'soul'; the second has a fall in pitch only on the first syllable, with the second low, and means 'the duck'.

In both intonation and tone languages the contrasts of high *v.* low or fall *v.* rise or whatever they may be are purely relative. This is necessarily so since the same contrasts must be available to all speakers of the language, men, women and children, and obviously a child has a much higher range of pitch than a man. The exact musical notes, therefore, are not important but only the

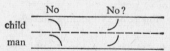

Figure 81: Relativity of pitch change

relation between them. Figure 81 shows rise in pitch and fall in pitch, as for English *No?* and *No* or Chinese /ma/ ('mother') and /ma/ ('scold') in the respective pitch ranges of man and child. Furthermore, the contrasts within the speech of a single person

I	don't	know	I	don't	know	I	don't	know

Figure 82: Relative pitch in one voice

are also relative; for example, we may say the sentence *I don't know* with various intonation patterns, but three possibilities are illustrated in Figure 82. The pattern is recognizably the same in each case, starting low, jumping higher, then falling; but the

ranges are different. The similarity of pattern throughout ensures
that the sentence is understood as a plain statement in all three
cases; the difference in range in the three different utterances corresponds to a difference of feeling on the part of the speaker. The
first may sound grim, the second casual or apathetic, the third
categorical, and these differences, however we label them, stem
from the difference of range.

Tone languages have the added complication that as well as the
tonal use of pitch to differentiate word meanings as described
above, they also use pitch in a way similar to the intonation
languages. Mandarin has four basic tones, high level, rising from
low to mid, rising from mid to high, and falling from high to low.
They can be represented as in Figure 83. But range may be used as

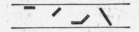

Figure 83: Tones in Mandarin

in English – the utterance may, for example, be confined to the
top part of the pitch range to express impatience, or to the bottom
part to express repetition of someone else's statement. In these
cases the contrast between the tones will be preserved, but within
the restricted pitch range, see Figure 84. In some tonal systems a

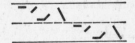

Figure 84: Tone and range in Mandarin

particular pitch may be interpreted as a high tone in one part of
an utterance and a low tone in another; this is the case in Luganda
in which each syllable has a 'high' or a 'low' tone but in which
the general trend in an utterance is downwards. Figure 85 shows
an utterance consisting of successive 'high' and 'low' tones.
Syllable number 2 is 'low' compared with syllables 1 and 3, but

the same pitch on syllable 5 must be reckoned 'high' in relation to the preceding and following syllables.

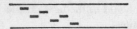

Figure 85: High and low tones in Luganda

Something like the phoneme principle can be seen at work in both intonation and tone languages; features which are perceptibly different can be grouped together because of similarity of function. For example, one characteristic pitch movement in English is a fall-rise, e.g. *soon* ∨ . If this is followed by a pause the whole pattern is heard, e.g.

We must visit her soon.

But if there is no following pause the pattern is reduced to a fall from high to mid, though with no change in meaning:

We must visit her soon, in any case.

We group the two perceptually different pitch patterns of *soon* together, as we group allophones of a phoneme together, on the grounds that they have the same function, the same meaning; they are doing the same job.

Similarly the low-rising tone of Mandarin occurs in its full form only before pause, elsewhere it is represented by a low-level pitch, so /lao/ 'old' has this tone in its full form in /taː lao/ 'he's old' , but not in /lao peŋjɔu/ 'old friend' In Cantonese a high-falling tone which occurs before pause is represented elsewhere by a high-level tone. Again these different tones can be brought together into one *toneme*, as different sounds are brought together in one phoneme.

Pitch phenomena are rather complex both in tone and intonation languages, but by recognizing the separability of range and pattern, the relativity of pitch contrasts, the toneme idea and the fundamentally systemic nature of intonation patterns, they can be reduced to order in much the same way as the welter of sounds. More will be said in the next chapter about both inton-ation and tone systems.

Stress, loudness

Stress is the name given to the stronger muscular effort, both respiratory and articulatory, which we can feel in connection with some syllables as opposed to others in English and other languages. For instance, *August* has more effort on the first than the second syllable, we hit it harder; but *august* has the greater effort on the second syllable. In English, therefore, stress is a significant factor since it is an essential part of word-shape; words easily become unrecognizable if the stress is wrongly placed. In other languages, although there may be differences in the amount of effort on one syllable and another, these dif-ferences are not necessarily significant in the same way as in English, as we shall see in Chapter 7.

The auditory correlate of stress is loudness, the stressed syllables tend to sound louder than the unstressed, but the relation is an uncertain one. When we say the word *incite* in isolation we usually do so with falling intonation on the stressed syllable, thus ⎯·⎯❯ and the syllable with the fall stands out more from the effect of the pitch change than from that of greater loudness. Similarly in *insight* we quote it with a fall from the first to the second syllable: ⎯❯·⎯ and the first syllable stands out. If we remove the pitch difference by saying the words on a monotone the difference of loudness is hardly enough of itself to distinguish the words, and if we say *insight* with the rising pitch of surprise: ⎯·⎯·⎯ the second syllable may well sound louder than the first even though we can clearly feel that the muscular effort is greater on the first syllable. It is clear from this that stress alone and the part it plays in loudness is not enough to make the sort of sound difference which can be regularly perceived and used in language. Apart from the great help that pitch gives – and this is an aspect of pitch which should be separated from its purely intonational use described in the last section – you may have noticed in dealing with the examples above that there is also a relation between stress and syllable length. The /ɪn-/ of *incite*, i.e. the unstressed syllable, is perceptibly shorter than that of *insight*, where it is stressed, even though there is little or no difference in the length of the second syllable /-saɪt/ in the two words. So length may help, along with pitch and stress/loudness, to make clear distinctions which are useable in language.

We can see another difference which may operate in conjunction with stress in the contrast between *content* ('happy') and *content* ('that which is contained'). In RP and various other accents the first, unstressed syllable of the adjective has /ə/ as its vowel /kənˈtent/, whereas in the noun, where the first syllable is stressed, the vowel is /ɒ/, /ˈkɒntent/. The stress effort on the first syllable has preserved an original /ɒ/, which, when the stress is on the second syllable, has been obscured to /ə/. This does not happen in all accents; typically in Northern speech /ɒ/ is retained whether the syllable is stressed or not, and in such cases the additional pointer to the place of stress provided by a difference of vowel is not available. But in all accents, the use of /ə/ rather than other less obscure vowels in unstressed syllables is a feature of English in some cases, either as a result of historical change, e.g. *postman* /ˈpəustmən/, *breakfast* /ˈbrekfəst/, or of present-day alternation of /ə/ with other vowels in running speech, e.g. *can* as /kən/ or /ˈkæn/, *I can try* /aɪ kən ˈtraɪ/, as against *Yes I can* /jes aɪ ˈkæn/.

The point about this combination of stress, pitch, length and vowel quality is that it can be used in language to make some syllables stand out more than others. How this relatively greater prominence of some syllables over others is used in language we shall see further in Chapter 7.

Apart from this narrowly linguistic use of respiratory and articulatory energy in connection with stress, there is the question of general loudness. First, each of us has his own preferred level of loudness: some people speak very quietly as a rule, others much more loudly – everyone can think of examples along these lines. But we are also all capable of varying the general loudness of our speech for purposes of communication. Sometimes it is inappropriate to use our normal conversational loudness, in church, for instance, and we then use less energy and produce speech which is quieter all round. On the other hand, it is sometimes necessary to speak more loudly than usual, for example, if we are in a noisy place, or delivering a public lecture. Then we push harder from the lungs and produce larger articulatory movements. Inappropriate loudness levels may cause trouble, as when a public speaker talks so quietly he cannot be heard, or when a sudden lull in party chatter catches someone still speaking at the higher level adopted to deal with the surrounding noise.

Also, we can vary our loudness from utterance to utterance, or within utterances, for effect. In saying *It was scandalous* the syllable /ˈskæn-/ will always be stressed, but the amount of energy used on it may be only as much as is needed to distinguish it from the unstressed syllables around, or it may be very much greater than that, if we wish to express outrage. Or, in saying something like: *John told me – John Smith, that is – that he* ... the parenthetical expression will often be said more quietly than what surrounds it, simply to underline that it *is* a parenthesis.

Length

The length of sounds, the length of syllables, the length of words and the length of utterances (in the sense of the time spent over them) are all variable, and the variations are used for linguistic purposes. Vowel length, as we have already seen (p. 154), plays a part in distinguishing /iː/ from /ɪ/, /ʌ/ from /ɑː/ etc. in RP and other (but not all) English accents. In English, however, the qualities of the long and the short vowels are often different, /iː/ and /ɪ/ for instance, so length is not the only distinctive feature, perhaps not even the main one. In other languages vowel length or consonant length alone may be distinctive. In Finnish, for example, there are eight basic vowel qualities, all of which are distinctively long or short, and the quality when long is just the same as when short. Finnish consonant length is also distinctive. Both types are demonstrated in the series /tuleː/ 'comes', /tuːleː/ 'blows', /tulleː/ 'ought to come', /tuːlleː/ 'ought to blow'.

Length differences which are not distinctive but conditioned, e.g. the *bead*, *beat* difference mentioned on p. 189, may, as we have seen, play quite a big part in our recognition of the following consonant. This is true also of consonant length; notice the difference in length of /n/ in *send* against *sent* or /l/ in *felled* against *felt*. In *send* and *felled*, where lenis /d/ follows, the /n/ and /l/ are much longer than in *sent* and *felt* where fortis /t/ follows, and the length of /n/ and /l/ are powerful cues to distinguishing /t/ from /d/. Bear in mind too what was said earlier (p. 129) regarding the relative shortness of the lenis consonants as compared with the fortis; so /z/ in *rise* is noticeably shorter than /s/ in *rice*.

In the previous section we noticed that syllable length may help in the perception of stress, like the length of /ɪn-/ in *incite* and *insight*. Syllable length in English is also closely related to rhythm. Rhythm in English and in various other stress languages – though not all – is based on the stressed syllable. Utterances are broken up into groups of syllables each of which contains one and only one stressed syllable. For example, compare *The man laughed* and *The manager laughed*; the syllables /mæn/ and /lɑːft/ are stressed in both, but the length of /mæn/ is very much shorter in 'manager' than in 'man', because there is a rather

strong tendency for the syllables between stresses to be compressed into the same time; so we say the word *manager* in not
much more time than *man* and therefore the syllable /mæn/ is
very different in length in the two cases. Further, unstressed
syllables which precede the stress are said particularly quickly,
which is the case with *the* here, and the /ɪn-/ of *incite*. The point
about all this is that as we listen, the relative lengths of syllables
are a further help to the identification of stress; and the way in
which syllables are grouped together by this rhythmic principle
is used, as we shall see in Chapter 8, to underline certain syntactic
groupings.

Then, too, there are differences of syllable length which are
more connected with the direct expression of attitude, for
example, the lengthening of /n/ in *Wonnnderful!* /ˈwʌnːːdəfl̩/, mentioned above, p. 173. From the phonemic point of view this is
simply /n/, the length is not distinctive in the sense that the long
/ll/ of Finnish is distinctive, i.e. distinguishing one word from
another, but the added length does contribute to meaning, even
if its contribution is different in kind from that of the phoneme
per se. The lengthening of /e/ in *Terrible!* has just the same effect.

Tempo, the relative speed or slowness of utterances, is obviously related to length. Again, as with loudness, people vary
in their average tempo; some of us speak more quickly, some
more slowly, though there is probably less difference than with
loudness if we leave aside pauses and hesitations. But we can
again use differences of tempo for both expressive and other
purposes. If in saying *He was a big, strong bear of man*, we slow
the whole thing down and lengthen out all the syllables we get a
stronger impression of this bear-like character than if we say it
at normal tempo. If in *He's very precise, very finicky*, we speed
the whole thing up we again underline the meaning of our
utterance by the faster tempo. The quieter utterance mentioned
in the last section in relation to parentheses may be accompanied or replaced by fast tempo for the same purpose, e.g.

When I went there – on Saturday it was – I ... the parenthesis will probably be marked by both reduced loudness and increased speed as compared with what surrounds it (and very likely by low pitch range).

Affected as they are by systemic, non-systemic, rhythmical, affective and tempo considerations, the absolute lengths of sounds and syllables are extremely variable but if these various categories are clearly separated, the complexity of the concrete data can be simply and sufficiently accounted for.

Vowel, consonant and syllable

We can think of vowels as sounds, characterizing them by their articulatory features – voice, open articulation, non-laterality, etc. – or their acoustic features – well-defined formant structure, periodic vibration, etc.; but we can also think of them as purely linguistic units, counters which do a certain job, irrespective of how they sound. So the [æ] in *sat* may be viewed as a sound and we can describe it articulatorily or acoustically or in terms of the cardinal vowels; but we can also think of it simply as a member of a system, an item whose sole interest is the fact that it can occur in a particular framework in contrast to other items. The first is a purely phonetic view, a descriptive process couched in the terms of disciplines which are not primarily linguistic – physiology, acoustics, audition – whilst the second is a strictly *phonological* view, looking at sounds for the *functions* they perform in the language rather than their nature as sounds.

From this latter point of view vowels are a class of phonemes which occupy similar positions in words and other structures, and consonants a class which occupy other positions. It has often been said that vowels are typically central in the syllable and consonants typically marginal, and there is clearly some truth in that; if we split a word like *consignment* /kən'saɪnmənt/ into syllables (without enquiring too closely into what 'syllable' means) we no doubt arrive at /kən-ˈsaɪn-mənt/ where indeed the vowels are central and the consonants surround them. But if we want to establish vowel and consonant as phonological categories we should derive them from a phonological unit. How are we to define the syllable phonologically? We could define it as an articulatory unit, for instance by counting peaks of activity of the breathing muscles which correspond fairly well to our ideas of syllable; we could define it auditorily by counting peaks of audibility; we could perhaps define it acoustically through the highly interrelated acoustic activity within short stretches of about syllable length; but these would be phonetic categories, defined in extra-linguistic terms, and not phonological.

Our first acquaintance with the notion of 'syllable' probably involved the teaching that a syllable was something that contained a vowel, with or without surrounding consonants. This gives a clue to a phonological treatment of the syllable. Why derive vowel and consonant from syllable? Why not derive vowel and consonant independently and then build the syllable up from them? This can be done quite satisfactorily by simply considering the sequence of phonemes in a language without reference to syllables. When we do so we find that the phonological classes of vowel and consonant can be established by the fact that there are two sets of phonemes which occur in different places, and these correspond to our ideas of what vowels are and what consonants are. Once this is done we can define the syllable by saying that it is a unit containing one and only one vowel either alone or surrounded by consonants in certain numbers and certain arrangements. In English we can say that the vowel of the syllable may be preceded by up to three consonants and followed by up to four, abbreviated in the formula (CCC)V(CCCC); the vowel may occur alone, as in *I* (aɪ); it may have one, two or three consonants before it, as in *pie*, *spy*, *spry* /p-, sp-, spr-/ and one, two, three or four after it, as in *tech.*, *techs.*, *text*, *texts* /-k, -ks. -kst, -ksts/.

Why do we need a unit 'syllable' at all? What is its usefulness?

In the first place the syllable is there in the language whether we like it or not; verse is regularly based on numbers of syllables, scripts have been devised on a syllabic basis, e.g. Cretan Linear B; it is there and, unlike the word, it is clearly a phonological unit – we can and do derive it from utterance – so we ought, for the sake of self-respect, to be able to define it rather than simply accept it as given. Secondly, it is useful as the largest unit we need to consider in explaining how phonemes are permitted to combine together in a language. Once we have investigated the structure of the monosyllable we can account for all larger units as sequences of syllables; in other words, with few exceptions nothing occurs in these larger units which cannot be accounted for as the result of stringing together single syllables. If in English the sequence /kststr/ occurs, as in *fixed string*, we account for it, not by laboriously trying to discover a structure within it, but by making a syllabic division and saying that it consists of /kst + str/, both of which are accounted for in our English syllable formula above. The third reason for wanting the syllable is that it is convenient in phonology to have a hierarchy of units, each built up from the next smallest one; our minimum unit is the phoneme; then comes the syllable, made up of phonemes in certain arrangements; then perhaps, as in English, comes the rhythm group mentioned on p. 197 in connection with stress and consisting of a sequence of syllables; then the intonation group, consisting of a sequence of rhythm groups and unified by the pattern of intonation it carries; and perhaps beyond that a larger group still, consisting of a sequence of intonation groups.

The greatest beauty of this view of the syllable is that it enables us to account for the different ideas that speakers of different languages have about syllables. The phonological view of the syllable requires a separate definition for each separate language; there is no universal phonological syllable. If one took an articulatory view, a universal syllable would be possible, but it would bear a poor relation to the rather clear idea that speakers of a given language have of what constitutes a syllable within it. The speaker of one language may know quite certainly that a particular sequence of phonemes constitutes one syllable, but the speaker of a different language may be equally certain that the same sequence constitutes two or even three syllables. For example, the English sequence /klʌb/ *club* is undoubtedly monosyllabic to an Englishman, but the Japanese, in borrowing it into their language, have given it three syllables /kurabu/, and the reason is precisely that the Japanese syllable does not permit /kl/ as a sequence, nor /b/ before anything but a vowel. In just the same way, when most English speakers first attempt the initial /kn/ of German *Knabe* 'boy' they insert a vowel and make it /kənaːbə/, i.e. three syllables rather than two (as it is for Germans), because /kn/ is no longer a permitted initial sequence in English.

If, as suggested here, the basic importance of the syllable is that it is the minimum unit of phonological structure, it is small wonder that we are conscious of its reality, since our constant use of our native language has familiarized us with what is permitted and what is not in the phoneme sequences of that language, and this knowledge is summed up in our awareness and acceptance of the syllable. In just the same way we can account for our recognition and acceptance of the phoneme as the minimum unit of phonological system.

Systems and patterns

Faced with a list of the phonemes of a language or an accent of a language is there anything we can do to classify them by showing similarities and differences between them? Is there any pattern among them which we can bring out and which would help us to understand the ways in which they do their job of giving concrete form to the meanings of the language? Certainly there is; we have just seen how an investigation of the way in which phonemes follow each other in sequences allows us to separate out two large classes, vowel and consonant, which are important and interesting just because of the different parts they play. We can go further than this and investigate differences of behaviour within these classes. For example, looking at the vowels of English (RP) we find that the vowels /ɪ, e, æ, ʌ, ɒ, ʊ, ə/ are different from the remainder in not occurring in stressed, final syllables unless followed by a consonant; so /ˈsɪtɪ/ *city* is possible because the first /ɪ/, whilst stressed, is followed by a consonant, and the second /ɪ/ is not stressed. But */sɪˈtɪ/ is not possible, nor */sɪˈte/, */sɪˈtæ/ and so on (* shows a form which does not occur). All the other vowels do occur in these conditions: *guitar* /gɪˈtɑː/, *ado* /əˈduː/, *dismay* /dɪsˈmeɪ/ etc., etc. Then /e, æ, ʌ, ɒ/ do not occur finally at all, whereas /ɪ, ə, ʊ/ do, in unstressed syllables, though /ʊ/ is rare, e.g. *happy* /ˈhæpɪ/, *sofa* /ˈsəʊfə/, *thank you* /ˈθæŋk jʊ/. Next, /ə/ does not occur in stressed syllables, whilst /ɪ/ and /ʊ/ do, and /ɪ/ occurs initially in English words, e.g. *ill*, whilst /ʊ/ does not.

All these differences of occurrence seem meaningful, they tell us something about the working of the language. But what about /e, æ, ɒ, ʌ/? It is not easy to separate them on similar grounds; if we say that /e/ is separable because it does not occur before final /ŋ/, as the others do in *sang, song, sung*, this does not seem so interesting. It would not surprise me if a word /seŋ/ turned up tomorrow, perhaps a technical word in some activity I know nothing about, and I would accept it happily, in a way quite different from my attitude to anything like */sɪˈtæ/. Similarly, in relation to consonants it seems sensible to take account of the fact that /ŋ/ and /ʒ/, as in *song, measure*, do not occur initially in native words, even though there is clearly a difference between them: we can contemplate borrowed words with initial /ʒ/ such as *gigolo, Jeanne* with equanimity, but not words with initial /ŋ/. It is probably not accidental that /p/ is never followed by /w/ initially, or that /t/ and /d/ are not followed by /l/ in the same position, that /s/ is the only phoneme which can precede two other consonants initially, as in *spray*, *stew*, *squad* /sprei, stjuː, skwɒd/, and that /ð/ as in *though* never occurs in initial consonant sequences at all. But are we to give the same significance to the fact that /w/ does not occur initially before /ɔɪ/, or /z/ before /j/ except in learned words like *zeugma* /ˈzjuːgmə/, or that initial /gj/ is represented only by the heraldic term *gules*? Surely not, but it is difficult to see why some of these constraints strike us as revealing, whilst others seem to be entirely accidental. No clear answer has been given to this but our intuition tells us that some of these facts are pertinent to the economy of the language, and others are mere accidents. Until such time as a formal method for recognizing what is pertinent and what accidental can be formulated, we must rest content with our intuitive ideas.

A quite different way of looking at the similarities and differences in our phoneme inventory is the method of *distinctive features*. This method is not purely phonological, not based purely on the function of phonemes, but rather one which takes into account the types of difference, articulatory or acoustic, between the phonemes in the inventory. So, in English the differences between /p, b, m/, /t, d, n/ and /k, g, ŋ/ can be accounted for in terms of three general articulatory features: stop *v.* nasal, fortis *v.* lenis, and place of articulation (labial, apical, dorsal). This can be shown in the form of the matrix below, where [+] indicates possession of the feature, [−] lack of it and [o] inapplicability of it.

	p	b	m	t	d	n	k	g	ŋ
stop	+	+	−	+	+	−	+	+	−
nasal	−	−	+	−	−	+	−	−	+
fortis	+	−	o	+	−	o	+	−	o
lenis	−	+	o	−	+	o	−	+	o
labial	+	+	+	−	−	−	−	−	−
apical	−	−	−	+	+	+	−	−	−
dorsal	−	−	−	−	−	−	+	+	+

Obviously there is a good deal of redundancy here; any [+] on

the stop line implies a [—] on the nasal line, and any [+] on the
fortis line, a [—] on the lenis. We can get rid of this in the following way:

	p	b	m	t	d	n	k	g	ŋ
nasal/non-nasal	—	—	+	—	—	+	—	—	+
fortis/non-fortis	+	—	o	+	—	o	+	—	o
labial	+	+	+	—	—	—	—	—	—
apical	—	—	—	+	+	+	—	—	—
dorsal	—	—	—	—	—	—	+	+	+

The differences in place of articulation are not at first sight
binary oppositions like the nasal/non-nasal or fortis/non-fortis
differences, but they can easily be reduced to binary oppositions
as follows:

	p	b	m	t	d	n	k	g	ŋ
nasal/non-nasal	—	—	+	—	—	+	—	—	+
fortis/non-fortis	+	—	o	+	—	o	+	—	o
labial/non-labial	+	+	+	—	—	—	—	—	—
dorsal/non-dorsal	—	—	—	—	—	—	+	+	+

The independent apical category has now disappeared and
/t, d, n/ are characterized as non-labial and non-dorsal. But
there is no compelling reason why we should have chosen to get
rid of apical/non-apical rather than one of the other categories.
Is there any way in which the same effect can be produced less
arbitrarily? To some extent, yes, by substituting more general
articulatory categories for the more specific labels of labial and
dorsal. So we postulate a neutral position of the tongue and refer
to variations from it. Coronal/non-coronal would mean a raising
of the tip and/or blade of the tongue above this neutral position
and anterior/non-anterior an obstruction in front of the hard
palate. Applying this we get:

	p	b	m	t	d	n	k	g	ŋ
nasal/non-nasal	—	—	+	—	—	+	—	—	+
fortis/non-fortis	+	—	o	+	—	o	+	—	o
coronal/non-coronal	—	—	—	+	+	+	—	—	—
anterior/non-anterior	+	+	+	+	+	+	—	—	—

Now let us introduce the set /f v, θ ð, s z, ʃ ʒ, h/. Immediately we need one extra feature-category to distinguish these fricatives from the stops /p, b, t, d, k, g/. Let us call it continuant/non-continuant. But we also need a feature to separate /θ/ from /s/ and /ð/ from /z/, all of which are coronal and anterior. Call this strident/non-strident (/θ/ and /ð/ making much less friction noise than /s/ and /z/). Now we have:

	p	b	m	t	d	n	k	g	ŋ	f	v	θ	ð	s	z	ʃ	ʒ	h
nasal/non-nasal	—	—	+	—	—	+	—	—	+	—	—	—	—	—	—	—	—	—
fortis/non-fortis	+	—	o	+	—	o	+	—	o	+	—	+	—	+	—	+	—	o
coronal/non-coronal	—	—	—	+	+	+	—	—	—	—	—	+	+	+	+	+	+	—
anterior/non-anterior	+	+	+	+	+	+	—	—	—	+	+	+	+	+	+	—	—	—
continuant/non-continuant	—	—	+	—	—	+	—	—	+	+	+	+	+	+	+	+	+	+
strident/non-strident	o	o	o	o	o	o	o	o	o	—	—	—	—	+	+	+	+	—

If we now add /tʃ/ and /dʒ/ to the list we do not need an additional feature-category since they can be characterized as both non-continuant and strident. For the remaining four consonants /l, r, j, w/ one extra feature is needed, call it glide/non-glide; all these are glides, /l/ is coronal and coronal, /r/ is coronal and non-anterior, /j/ is non-anterior and non-coronal and /w/ is anterior and also non-anterior (i.e. it has lip-rounding, which makes it anterior, whilst its back-tongue raising can be disregarded). So all the English consonants can be separated one from another and characterized in terms of presence or absence or irrelevance of seven distinctive features as follows:

	p	b	m	t	d	n	k	g
nasal/non-nasal	—	—	+	—	—	+	—	—
fortis/non-fortis	+	—	o	+	—	o	+	—
coronal/non-coronal	—	—	—	+	+	+	—	—
anterior/non-anterior	+	+	+	+	+	+	—	—
continuant/non-continuant	—	—	+	—	—	+	—	—
strident/non-strident	o	o	o	o	o	o	o	o
glide/non-glide	—	—	—	—	—	—	—	—

If the feature-categories are valid this is a useful way of summing up essential differences between any consonant and any other consonant; if we consider /p, t, j/ in the last matrix above we find:

```
p  —  +  —  +  —  o  —
t  —  +  +  +  —  o  —
j  —  o  —  —  +  o  +
```

/t/ and /p/ are clearly very similar in that they have six out of seven features in common (/t/ is coronal, /p/ non-coronal); whereas /t/ and /j/ are very dissimilar, with only one feature, non-nasal, in common. But if we select our distinctive features with a view to keeping down their number and making them widely applicable, as we have done here, we have to accept the results, and one is inclined to wonder whether the fact that /p/ turns out more similar to /j/ than /t/ does, by the single feature of non-coronal, is of any real importance, or whether it is simply an irrelevance produced by the selection of features.

The set of distinctive features used above still produces redundancies; for example the nasal/non-nasal feature, which separates /m, n, ŋ/ from the rest, and the continuant/non-continuant feature, which separates /p, b/ etc. from /f, v/ etc., are redundant as applied to /m, n, ŋ/. The fact of nasality implies continuity, and so far as the English nasals are concerned they do not need to be characterized as both. On the other hand, if we wish to extend our list of distinctive features to cover all possible oppositions

	v	θ	ð	s	z	ʃ	ʒ	h	tʃ	dʒ	l	r	j	w
—	—	—	—	—	—	—	—	—	—	—	—	—	—	—
—	—	+	—	+	—	+	—	o	+	—	o	o	o	o
—	—	+	+	+	+	+	+	—	+	+	+	+	—	—
—	+	+	+	+	+	—	—	—	—	—	+	—	—	+
—	+	+	+	+	+	+	+	+	—	—	+	+	+	+
—	—	—	—	+	+	+	+	—	+	+	o	o	o	o
—	—	—	—	—	—	—	—	—	—	—	+	+	+	+

in all languages, as some scholars do, then nasal need not imply continuant; in many African languages the sequences [mb] and [nd], as in names like *Mboya, Ndola*, are to be considered as realizing single phonemes, because in these languages no other consonant sequences are permitted in initial position. If /mb/ and /nd/ are in opposition to /m/ or /n/ and /b/ or /d/ in these languages, then they must be characterized as both nasal and non-continuant, since /m, n/ are nasal and continuant, and /b, d/ are non-nasal and non-continuant.

Distinctive features have been presented here in mainly articulatory terms, but they can also be presented as oppositions between acoustic features, e.g. grave and acute, referring to the predominance of the higher or lower part of the spectrum, and compact and diffuse, referring to energy concentrated in the central part of the spectrum as opposed to concentration in a non-central part.

There can be no theoretical preference for either presentation; in both cases oppositions are characterized in terms taken from outside the purely phonological sphere, and if properly handled both may be more revealing than a more narrowly descriptive approach. French has /p, b, t, d, k, g/ voiced and voiceless stops at labial, dental and velar places of articulation. It also has /m, n/ labial and dental, and /ɲ/ the palatal nasal, as in *agneau*, ('lamb'). And it has /f, v, s, z, ʃ, ʒ/, labio-dental, alveolar and palato-alveolar fricatives. In terms of conventional places of articulation we need *bilabial*, for /p, b, m/, *labio-dental* for /f, v/, *dental* for /t, d, n/, *alveolar* for /s, z/, *palato-alveolar* for /ʃ, ʒ/ and *palatal* for /ɲ/. But by broadening our articulatory frame we can show a parallelism among the different series which no doubt increases our insight into the French consonant system:

	p	t	k	b	d	g	m	n	ɲ	f	s	ʃ	v	z	ʒ
nasal/non-nasal	—	—	—	—	—	—	+	+	+	—	—	—	—	—	—
voiced/non-voiced	—	—	—	+	+	+	○	○	○	—	—	—	+	+	+
continuant/non-continuant	—	—	—	—	—	—	+	+	+	+	+	+	+	+	+
anterior/non-anterior	+	+	—	+	+	—	+	+	—	+	+	—	+	+	—
apical/non-apical	—	+	—	—	+	—	—	+	—	—	+	—	—	+	—

This shows that /p, t, k/ differ from each other in exactly the same way that /b, d, g/ differ from each other and /m, n, ɲ/, and /f, s, ʃ/ and /v, z, ʒ/. So /ʃ/ and /ɲ/ are to /k/ and /g/ as /f/ and /m/ are to /p/ and /b/, or as /s/ and /n/ are to /t/ and /d/, despite the palato-alveolar articulation of /ʃ/ and the palatal articulation of /ɲ/ compared with the velar articulation of /k/ and /g/. We may truly represent this parallelism in French like this:

p	b	m	f	v
t	d	n	s	z
k	g	ɲ	ʃ	ʒ

rather than:

p	b	m				(bilabial)
			f	v		(labio-dental)
t	d	n				(dental)
			s	z		(alveolar)
			ʃ	3		(palato-alveolar)
					ɲ	(palatal)
k	g					(velar)

This is another instance of the possibility of bringing simplicity from complexity and, provided that we do not oversimplify in using distinctive features, we can benefit from them. However, it is easy to oversimplify. For example, in the final English matrix on p. 206 the feature coronal is essential to /t/ as opposed to /p/ and /k/, but what is the position if /t/ is realized as [ʔ], glottal stop, as it so often is in English, say, in *setback*, or even in Cockney *wa'er*? That is certainly not coronal, and it is difficult to see a way of including the glottal and the alveolar realization of /t/ in one feature-category, except perhaps negatively by saying that what characterizes /t/ is the absence of /p/ and /k/ features.

If a satisfactory scheme of distinctive features can be established which will account for all the oppositions which are used in the languages of the world – and the number of such features need not be very large – it would have great importance for the typology of languages from the phonetic point of view. It would give us a much better chance of making fair comparisons between the systems of one language and those of another, and we would be a good deal nearer than we are at the moment to being able to order languages in terms of their similarities and differences by reference to a coherent and universal framework.

Different interpretations

We have mostly spoken so far as if there was agreement amongst different analysts as to the systems and structures of a particular language, but this is not so, and the differences of interpretation which exist may sometimes make it seem as if the uncertainties in phonetic and phonological analysis are greater than in fact they are. Regarding the consonants of English, for instance, there is virtual unanimity on the system, the only place of disagreement being as to whether /tʃ/ and /dʒ/ are sequences or single-unit phonemes and by far the majority of analysts agree that they are unitary.

There is by no means the same agreement about the vowel system. If we apply one widely accepted American analysis we would have only /ɪ, e, æ, ɒ, ʊ, ə/ as vowels in RP; /iː, ɑː, ɔː, uː, ɜː, eɪ, əʊ, aɪ, aʊ, ɔɪ, ɪə, ɛə, ʊə/, which have been included in the vowel system in this book, would be interpreted as sequences of vowel + consonant. So /ɑː, ɔː, ɜː, ɪə, ɛə, ʊə/ are to be /æ, ɒ, ə, ɪ, e, ʊ/ + /h/; Sam is /sæm/ and psalm is /sæhm/ and so on. /iː, eɪ, aɪ, ɔɪ/ are to be taken as /ɪ, e, æ, ɒ/ + /j/, so that sit is /sɪt/ and seat is /sɪjt/ etc.; and /uː, əʊ, aʊ/ are /ʊ, ə, æ/ + /w/, so pull is /pʊl/ and pool is /pʊwl/ and so on. This has two advantages: it shortens the vowel inventory very considerably, by thirteen items in fact, from nineteen to six (/ʌ/ is taken to be the stressed allophone of /ə/, so cut = /kət/), and it fills certain gaps in the patterns of occurrence of /h, j, w/: all three, as we have so far understood them, occur only before vowels, as in who, you, we

/huː, juː, wiː/, but by this interpretation all three can occur finally and before consonants, as in *awe*, *ought*, *I*, *ice*, *owe*, *oak* /ɒh, ɒht, æj, æjs, əw, əwk/, bringing them into line with most of the other consonants, which also occur in these positions.

This interpretation raises two difficulties, however. Though simplifying the phoneme inventory it complicates the task of explaining the structure of consonant clusters in English syllables, which, as we have seen, is a necessary part of the phonological statement of a language, so that for words like *aunts*, *waists*, *coaxed* we are faced with the clusters /-hnts, -jsts, -wkst/ rather than the simpler /-nts, -sts, -kst/. Secondly, it raises the question of whether the interpretation is in harmony with the native speaker's intuitive feeling for his language, and if not, whether this feeling has any relevance to the analyst's job of presenting the sound picture of the language. Is he entitled to produce an analysis which takes no account of the native speaker's intuitions or even goes contrary to them, relying on principles of economy, simplicity, elegance in his work, or should he be seeking for explanations which satisfy a native as well as making sense in phonological terms? Does he construct the system, or does he look for a system actually present in his material? This is a very, very old argument and has been irreverently referred to by linguists as the 'hocus-pocus' *v.* 'God's truth' argument.

It is unlikely that complete agreement can be reached. Some workers see themselves as creators of systems and structures, putting their materials together this way and that until they find an arrangement which satisfies them; others see themselves as discoverers, searching out something which is hidden, yet is there to be found. Even the most convinced 'God's truth' man is bound to find himself from time to time in the position where *he* has to make the decision, the language obstinately refuses to do it for him; for example, in allotting the unaspirated [p] of *spy* to the /p/ or /b/ phonemes (p. 177). And the true 'hocus-pocus' man will no doubt flinch from allotting the same unaspirated [p] to the /t/ phoneme merely because it is in complementary distribution with [tʰ] (as well as with [pʰ] and [kʰ]). It would be dangerous totally to ignore the native speaker's own ideas about his language, particularly when those ideas are shared by many others, because competence in a language implies a working knowledge of the systems and structures and rules of that language; the speaker will not be able to express that knowledge in precise, analytical terms any more than he can easily give a verbal explanation of the meaning of a word like *charity*, but he can use the word, he knows in practice where it fits in and where it does not, and similarly he knows a good deal about the working of sounds. One should look pretty hard, therefore, at any solution which does not satisfy a speaker of a language as to its rightness, because there may be something important behind his feeling.

Up to now we have assumed that the phoneme is essential to phonetics, because of its power to bring relative simplicity to the otherwise confusing variety of actual sounds which every language contains, and also because it seems to be something whose existence is easily recognized by the native speakers of a language. We may sometimes disagree about whether a certain sequence of sounds represents one phoneme or two, or which phoneme a particular sound represents, but such difficulties as these have not persuaded us to abandon the idea of the phoneme as a powerful aid in investigating the systems and structures of phonology.

However, one very influential modern view of language, the transformational-generative view, has grave doubts about the value of the phoneme. According to this view, the syntax of a language provides us with strings of words and other grammatical elements, such as prefixes, suffixes, singulars, plurals and tenses. These strings would be represented in a way corresponding much more to a spelling than to a phonemic transcription. For example, the word *criticize* might be represented as KRITIK + īz (as opposed to the phonemic /ˈkrɪtɪsaɪz/). The phonological part of the grammar then provides rules for turning this into an actual pronunciation in any accent of the language. One rule would have to be where to place the stress – on the first syllable in most accents, but on the last in some Scottish accents; another would cause the second κ to be pronounced [s] before ī; another would turn ī into [aɪ] in RP and [ɑɪ] in Cockney; and so on. So there is a jump from the rather abstract, spelling-type representation of the syntactic strings to an actual (allophonic in our terms) pronunciation, and the phoneme is by-passed.

The advantages of this approach are that every word or other grammatical element is always represented in the same way, and that the rules for turning this representation into an actual pronunciation can be formulated in such a way that they show up interesting regularities. So KRITIK is always KRITIK in its syntactic representation (just as *critic* is always *critic* in our own spelling) and this is very necessary in an orthography of any kind. Likewise īz is always īz, even in *criticism* = KRITIK + īz + M, and the rules for turning κ into [s] and ī into [aɪ] (for *criticize*) or [ɪ] (for *criticism*) are applied later. There would be little point to the rule 'κ = [s] before ī' if it applied only to *critic*, *criticize*, *criticism*, but in fact it applies to many more, for example *mystic* + *ism*, *medic* + *ine*, *romantic* + *ize*, etc., and therefore has general value.

The pair *opaque* and *opacity* exemplify the same rule, and they also exhibit a vowel alternation which can again be accounted for by a general rule applicable also in cases like *vain/vanity*, *sane/sanity*, *tenacious/tenacity*, etc. The point of the syntactic representations and the phonological rules is to reveal various interesting and important features about the pronunciation of the language – the relation between kindred forms, the relation between stress and sound sequences, as in *photograph/photography*, etc. – and a good deal that is new and satisfying has already come from this approach.

Yet there is something lost if the phoneme is abandoned. It is important to know that different accents of a language have different numbers of phonemes, because it means that some people have fewer possibilities for making distinctions between words and some have more, and this is a fact of the language which should not be glossed over. The real solution in the long term is to combine the two approaches to the benefit of both, and there are already hopeful signs of this happening.

7. Languages and *Their* Sounds

The previous two chapters showed what a varied thing one language is from the point of view of the sounds it employs. The present chapter will give some idea of the great variety of phonetic means that different languages use for their common purpose. This common purpose is communication. Each language has its own special grammar and its own special vocabulary, both tailored to its communication needs, and the purpose of the sound systems and structures which the language has at its command is to give an audible form to grammatical and lexical distinctions. How this is tackled will be treated at greater length in the following chapter. Here our aim is to try to show how very variously different languages draw upon the total stock of sounds and sound features which the human vocal tract is capable of producing, and how differently they have organized themselves for the job of giving a shape to the distinctions of meaning that the grammar and vocabulary provide.

Nothing in this chapter is intended to dim the picture presented in Chapter 6 of the great variety both of system and of sound within one language, but we will have to present simple systemic arrangements of phonemes as representative of a language in order not to overcomplicate the comparisons we shall be making between different languages; readers should remember that when, for instance, we say that Italian is a seven-vowel language we are a) talking about vowel phonemes, not allophonic realizations, and b) not implying that the sort of differences of system which occur in English do not occur in Italian, but simply that a seven-vowel system commonly occurs amongst Italian accents.

Vowel systems*

The minimum vowel system always takes the form

i   u

a

and systems of this form are attested in Classical Arabic and Greenland Eskimo. Perhaps the commonest vowel system of all adds two other vowels to this minimum triangle to give a five-vowel system of the type

i   u

e   o

a

which is found in Spanish, Modern Greek, some dialects of Arabic, including Egyptian, Czech, Latin (this is where the five vowel letters of the Roman alphabet come from), etc. It is very common for there to be only one vowel of the openest position in a particular language; so whilst close front /i/ is parallelled by close back /u/ and mid front /e/ by mid back /o/, there is no partner for /a/ in either of the two systems mentioned above, and its realization is commonly between front and back, i.e. between cardinals [a] and [ɑ]. But there may be opposition at this lowest level, so in Persian the system is

i   u

e   o

a   ɑ

* In these vowel patterns the cardinal vowel symbols are used but without implying any fixed quality. /i/ is simply the closest front vowel *in the system*, /u/ the closest back vowel and so on.

and /a/ is realized somewhat like RP /æ/ and /ɑ/ like RP /ɒ/. The seven-vowel system of Italian has three degrees of opening at the front and back plus /a/ alone at the openest level, so:

```
        i           u
        e           o
        ɛ           ɔ
              a
```

and Igbo has four degrees at both front and back:

```
        i           u
        e           o
        ɛ           ɔ
        a           ɑ
```

whilst in Tswana it seems that there are four degrees of opening at front and back plus /a/ at the openest level, making a nine-vowel system in all:

```
        i           u
        ɪ           ʊ
        e           o
        ɛ           ɔ
              a
```

In all these systems we find firstly, a vertical contrast between different degrees of openness and, secondly, a horizontal contrast between front *v.* back or rounded *v.* unrounded. It is quite common to find not simply a front/back distinction but one which is front/central/back, or front-unrounded/front-rounded/back, or front/back-unrounded/back-rounded at one or more of the different degrees of opening. Portuguese, for example, has

```
        i           u
        e           o
        ɛ     ə     ɔ
              a
```

whilst N. Welsh has

i	ɨ	u
e		o
ɛ	ə	ɔ
	a	

and many Scottish accents have

i		u
e	ɪ	o
ɛ	ə	ɔ
	a	

In all of these the contrast is front/central/back. Some French accents have:

i	y	u
e	ø	o
ɛ	œ	ɔ
a		ɑ

and Finnish **has**

i	y	u
e	ø	o
a		ɑ

whilst Danish has

i	y	u
e	ø	o
ɛ	œ	ɔ
	a	

and in all three the contrast is front-unrounded/front-rounded/back.

The front/back-unrounded/back-rounded is the least common of these possibilities but it occurs in Vietnamese:

i	ɯ	u
e	ɤ	o
ɛ	ʌ	ɔ
	a	

and in Turkish both front-rounded and back-unrounded are in contrast with front-unrounded and back-rounded, so:

$$i \quad y \quad ɯ \quad u$$
$$e \quad ø \qquad o$$
$$a$$

Notice here that the symmetry present in all the other systems is broken: it could be restored by situating /a/ between /ø/ and /o/, but there seems to be little justification for this. Symmetry is very frequent in vowel systems but it is not invariable, nor is it an absolute requirement, and one should beware of forcing a factitious symmetry in order to keep the picture tidy.

Additional vowel features

In the vowel systems mentioned so far, the differences between the vowels are differences of quality linked to differences of tongue and lip position, but other features may be used to increase the number of distinctions which can be made at the vowel place in the syllable. These are nasalization, length and diphthongization. It may be well to mention that nasalization in this context refers to a quite independent feature of vowel quality: we may get nasalization of vowels in English and other languages either all the time, as a personal characteristic, or when nasal consonants adjoin them, but there are no differences of meaning in English which can be attributed to the presence or absence of nasalization, and it is therefore non-systemic. Systemic nasalization may characterize the same number of vowels as there are in the non-nasal system, but usually there are fewer nasalized than purely oral vowels; in Burmese the seven oral vowels

$$i \qquad u$$
$$e \qquad o$$
$$ɛ \qquad ɔ$$
$$a$$

are in contrast with only five nasalized vowels:

$$i \qquad\qquad u$$
$$e \qquad\qquad o$$
$$a$$

/ɛ/ and /ɔ/ being missing from the nasalized system; and in Portuguese the eight-vowel oral system, mentioned above, goes with a five-vowel nasalized system:

$$i \qquad\qquad u$$
$$e \qquad\quad o$$
$$ə$$

In French the nine-vowel oral system mentioned earlier is complemented by only three (or in some accents four) nasalized vowels:

$$e \quad (\text{œ}) \quad o$$
$$a$$

Diphthongization and length are similar to each other in effect: the short steady-quality vowel is contrasted on the one hand with a change of quality and on the other with prolongation, and one can see in English how sometimes diphthongization and sometimes length are used to carry the same contrast. So Cockney [aː] in *out* is parallel to RP [ɑʊ], and Scottish [oː] in *go* to RP [əʊ]. A diphthong, as we have seen (p. 154), is phonetically a vowel glide or a sequence of two vowel segments which functions as a single phoneme. Not all such sequences or glides are to be considered as diphthongs. In French, for example, the sequences [ai] and [aːi] occur in *haïr* ('to hate') and *paille* ('straw') but neither constitutes a diphthong because neither occurs in the variety of contexts which other vowel phonemes of the language can occupy; so [ai] is taken to be a sequence of vowels /a/ + /i/, just as /ʊɪ/ is in English *suet*, and [aːi] is interpreted as vowel + consonant,

/a/ + /j/, parallel with the sequences /ɛ/ + /j/ in *vieille*, /i/ + /j/ in *fille*, /u/ + /j/ in *nouille*, etc. which also occur.

In general when a particular vowel quality regularly precedes or follows all or most of the other vowel qualities of the language, it is to be interpreted as consonantal in function; that is the case with /j/ in the French examples above, and it is also the case with English /j/ and /w/ which can be followed by /iː, e, æ, ɑː, ɒ/ etc. in *yield*, *yet*, *yak*, *yard*, *yacht*, etc. Quite apart from the fact that /j/ and /w/ occupy the same sorts of position that the other consonants occupy – *yet*, *wet*, *met*, *let*, *set*, *bet*, etc. – it would be extravagant to add this large number of phonemes (/jiː, je, jɑː, jɒ/ etc.) to the already long vowel inventory, and would produce absolutely no profit. But in the case of /eɪ, aɪ, ɔɪ/ and /əʊ, aʊ/ and /ɪə, ɛə, ɔə, ʊə/, again apart from their occupying the same positions that the other vowel phonemes occupy, the second elements of the diphthongs, /ɪ, ʊ, ə/, follow only a few of the other vowels in the inventory and are therefore not at all parallel with the case of /j/ or /w/ + vowel in English or the case of vowel + /j/ in French. In a language such as Finnish, where with few exceptions any one of the eight vowels may follow any other, in sequences such as /ia, ɑi, uo, ou, eu, ue/ etc., there is obviously no advantage in regarding these sequences as diphthongs, and similarly the long vowels of Finnish must be taken to be a special case of one vowel following another, i.e. /aa, uu, yy/ etc. In Portuguese and Burmese both nasalization and diphthongization occur: in addition to the oral and nasalized vowels mentioned above, diphthongs of the /ai, au/ type occur both oral and nasalized, with a distinctive function.

In the Germanic languages, including English, both genuine diphthongs and long vowels exist side by side with short vowels; in Danish the nine vowels of the system shown above are all found long and short with slight differences in quality and there are in addition the diphthongs /ai, au, ɔy/. Other vowel glides such as /eu, øu, iu, ɔu/ which also occur, must be interpreted as vowel + /v/ since they do not occur freely in the same sorts of context as the remaining vowels and diphthongs. In English the correspondence between short and long is less tidy: /ɪ, æ, ɒ, ʊ, ə/ have traditionally been linked to /iː, ɑː, ɔː, uː, ɜː/ and this leaves /e/ and /ʌ/ with no long partner; a neater arrangement would be to exclude /ə/ as being typically unstressed, whereas the others all bear stress, and equate /ʌ/ with /ɜː/ and /e/ with the diphthong /ɛə/, which in any case is often monophthongal in realization. But English has come very far from the clear long/short relationship which obtained in the Old English system:

$$
\begin{array}{ccc}
i & y & u \\
e & & o \\
\varepsilon & & \\
& a &
\end{array}
$$

All of these occurred both long and short and the correlation was a simple one. In modern English the correlation is by no means so clear-cut and it is doubtful whether there is any profit in trying to pair off the longs and shorts. Much more revealing of the functional, rather than purely phonetic, relationships amongst vowels in English is the approach mentioned on p. 213 where a link is made between vowels on the basis of alternations in related words. So /aɪ/ is linked to /ɪ/ because of *precise – precision, imply – implicit, bile – bilious*, etc., and /iː/ is linked to /e/ because of *extreme – extremity, deep – depth, please – pleasant*, etc. But this is very much a matter of the total economy of a particular language and as such runs beyond the scope of a purely phonetic approach.

Triphthongs are sequences of three vocalic segments functioning as a single vowel phoneme: they are rare in language and most sequences of this kind are analysed as phoneme sequences also. In English the /aɪə, aʊə/ sequences of *fire, power* have sometimes been referred to as triphthongs, but they do not behave like other vowel phonemes, being much more restricted in the contexts in which they appear, and therefore they are considered as sequences of /aɪ/ and /aʊ/ with /ə/. On the other hand it is possible to argue that the sequence /juː/ in English *tune* is a single phoneme – and therefore a diphthong – and that /jʊə/ in *pure* should also be treated as a single phoneme, which would make it a triphthong, but the case is by no means certain, and the more usual view is that these both constitute sequences of phonemes /j + uː/ and /j + ʊə/. In Mandarin [iao] and [uai] as in [ˌɕiao] ('small') and [ˈkuai] ('fast') are certainly monosyllabic and might be taken for triphthongs were it not for the fact that neither can be followed by /n/ or /ŋ/ or /r/, as the other vowels and diphthongs of Mandarin can. This implies that the final vocalic segment is functioning consonantally as the end of the syllable, just as /n, ŋ, r/ are, and that the correct analysis is as sequences of phonemes /ia + w/ and /ua + j/. In Tyneside English it is not uncommon to hear the sequence [ieə] in words like *late* and this is undoubtedly a triphthong since it occurs in just the same contexts as the other vowels and diphthongs of the accent.

Consonant systems

We may look at consonants either from the point of view of their functioning in the language, or of their phonetic features. The two views do not necessarily coincide, but both generally force us to consider a number of subsystems rather than a single overall system. So in English /w, j, r, l/ form a functional subsystem in that they are the only consonants to occur as the third term in an initial consonant cluster, e.g. /skw, stj, spr, spl/; /s/ is the only consonant which can occur initially in such clusters; and /p, t, k/ (plus /f/ if we include *sphragid*) are the only intermediate possibilities. Phonetically we have a subsystem of stops, of fricatives, of liquids, of nasals. It is these phonetically determined subsystems that we shall look at first.

Stops

All languages have pure plosive consonants at two places of articulation at least, either /p/ or /t/ and /k/. It is much more common to find three different places /p, t, k/ as in English, French, German, Danish, Portuguese, etc. Four places are less common; Greenland Eskimo has /p, t, k, q/, Hungarian /p, t, c, k/ and Hindustani /p, ṭ, ṭ, k/. It is rare to find five separate places but Tamil has /p, ṭ, t, ṭ, k/ and Arabic /b, t, k, q, ʔ/. Where there are more stops than this in a particular language, it is the result of other factors than differences of place. One obvious factor is a voiced/voiceless or lenis/fortis difference as in /p, t, k, b, d, g/, variously realized in French, German and Danish, but it should be noted that such distinctions do not necessarily affect all stop places in a language; for example Arabic has /t/ linked with /d/ and /k/ with /g/, but /b/ has no corresponding /p/. Another factor is affrication as in English /p, t, k, tʃ/ or Hungarian /p, t, c, k, ts, tʃ/ or Polish /p, t, k, ts, tɕ, tʃ/; in Polish the voiced/voiceless distinction applies to all of these consonants and the total of stops is elevated to twelve.

Differences of air-stream mechanism can also be a multiplying factor: in Georgian /p, t, k, ts, tʃ/ are doubled by the egressive pharynx-air mechanism, giving the ejectives /p', t', k', ts', tʃ'/, and the voiced/voiceless distinction raises the total to fifteen. In Zulu, fortis/lenis, affrication and three different air-stream mechanisms are used to multiply the number of stops: /p, t, k/ *v.* /b, d, g/ is a fortis/lenis distinction; then /p', t', k'/ are ejective, as in Georgian; then the mouth-air mechanism adds the three clicks /ʇ, ʗ, ʖ/, alveolar, retroflex and lateral (i.e. *not* at the same three places of articulation as the other stops above). These basic clicks are further differentiated by combining the mouth-air mechanism with the lung-air mechanism in three different ways: first, the click is 'nasalized' by allowing voiced lung-air to pass out through the nose during its performance, giving /ĩ, c̃, ʖ̃/;

secondly, the soft palate is raised preventing the same voiced lung air from escaping nasally: this gives the voiced clicks /ᶢǀ, ᶢǁ, ᶢǃ/; and thirdly, the click is followed by a puff of voiceless lung air, giving the aspirated clicks, /ǀh, ǁh, ǃh/. A combination of the lung-air and the pharynx-air mechanisms is responsible for /ɓ/, the voiced bilabial implosive (the alveolar and velar implosives do not occur). Affrication contributes /tʃ', dʒ, kx'/ and also the *lateral affricates* /tɬ'/ and /dɮ/. In addition, the homorganic nasal consonant can be prefixed to /p', t', k', b, d, g, tʃ', dʒ, tɬ', dɮ, kx'/ giving /mp', nt', ŋk'/ etc.: these sequences are monophonemic in Zulu, just as the affricates or the aspirated clicks are, so the grand total of stop phonemes in Zulu, due to these intersecting features, is no fewer than thirty-eight.

Another general way in which stop phonemes may be multiplied is by secondary articulations, so that the primary articulations of the contrasting sounds are the same, but their secondary articulations are different. Such differences may spill beyond the stop category and may characterize larger or smaller sets of sounds; in Arabic /s, z, t, d/ are matched by a so-called 'emphatic' set /ṣ, ẓ, ṭ, ḍ/ which differ in that they are velarized, that is, they have the same primary place of articulation as the corresponding non-emphatic set but with added raising of the back of tongue; this causes a difference of transition from vowel to consonant or consonant to vowel and it is this which largely accounts auditorily for the distinction between them. In Russian there are two much larger sets which are distinguished by secondary articulation; these are the so-called soft and hard consonants. The soft consonants are all characterized by a raising of the front of the tongue high towards the hard palate in addition to their primary articulation, whilst the hard consonants have velarization like the Arabic emphatics mentioned above; the contrast is between palatalization and velarization, and it affects fourteen basic consonant articulations: /p, t, k, b, d, f, v, s, z, ʃ, m, n, l, r/, giving twenty-eight separate phonemes. The addition of the consonants /g, ʒ, x, ts, tʃ/, which do not participate in this hard/soft correlation, makes a total of thirty-three consonant phonemes in Russian.

Fricatives

It is quite common for fricative systems to have more places of articulation than the stops: we saw that with the latter it is rare to have as many as five places, but English has five fricative places /f, θ, s, ʃ, h/, so has German /f, s, ʃ, x, h/, and so has Polish /f, s, ɕ, ʃ, x/, whereas all three have only three places for pure stops. Arabic has six: /f, s, ʃ, x, ħ, h/ against five for stops; Spanish and Russian four /f, θ, s, x/ and /f, s, ʃ, x/ respectively against three for stops. Italian and French have the same number of places for stops and fricatives, i.e. /p, t, k/ and /f, s, ʃ/; so does Eskimo: /p, t, k, q/ and /f, s, x, χ/. Other languages have fewer fricative than stop places; Hungarian has /f, s, ʃ/ against /p, t, c, k/.

Languages sometimes have the same general features operating to multiply the fricatives and the stops: in French, for example, the voiced/voiceless feature operates for both sets: /p, t, k/ v. /b, d, g/ and /f, s, ʃ/ v. /v, z, ʒ/. Similarly in Hungarian this distinction runs right through both systems: /p, t, c, k, ts, tʃ/ v. /b, d, ɟ, g, dz, dʒ/ and /f, s, ʃ/ v. /v, z, ʒ/. In English the four fortis fricatives /f, θ, s, ʃ/ have their lenis counterparts /v, ð, z, ʒ/, but /h/ does not, and this is usual in all languages where /h/ occurs. Spanish has /p, t, k/ contrasting with /b, d, g/, but the fricatives /f, θ, s, x/ have no voiced correlates, and in Finnish /s, h/ have no voicing contrast, whilst /v/ has no corresponding /f/. In Arabic /s, x, ħ/ have voiced counterparts /z, ɣ, ʕ/ but the remainder /f, ʃ, h/ do not. We have already seen that the soft/hard distinction operates on /f, v, s, z, ʃ/ in Russian, and the emphatic/non-emphatic contrast affects /s, z/ in Arabic as well as /t, d/. On the whole, however, fricatives tend to be less differentiated in this kind of way than stops are; Spanish has the voiced/voiceless correlation for the stops but not for the fricatives; Georgian has a three-way distinction amongst the stops – voiced/voiceless-aspirated/voiceless-ejective – but only the voiced/voiceless difference in its fricatives. Zulu, with its highly differentiated stop system, has only the voiced/voiceless distinction for /f, v/ and /s, z/, whilst /ɬ/ and /ʃ/ have no voiced counterparts.

Nasals

These are still less differentiated than fricatives; the maximum number of places of articulation for nasals is four, for instance in Eskimo with /m, n, ŋ, ɴ/ corresponding to the stop places /p, t, k, q/. More commonly there are three places, as in English and German /m, n, ŋ/ or French, Italian and Spanish /m, n, ɲ/ or Punjabi /m, n, ɳ/. Often enough only two nasal places occur: /m, n/, as in Greek, Persian, Turkish; and in several American Indian languages only one occurs, either /m/ or /n/. Russian distinguishes hard and soft /m, n/ on the same basis as the stops and fricatives, and Burmese has voiceless /m̥/, alongside voiced /m/, but such manner distinctions are very rare amongst nasals.

Laterals

Most languages have one and only one lateral, /l/, as in English, French, German. Japanese is one of the few languages which have no lateral at all. There are rather more cases of languages with two laterals; for example Spanish and Italian have /l/ and the palatal lateral /ʎ/, in *calle* ('street') and *miglia* ('mile') respectively, and Punjabi has /l/ and the retroflex lateral /ɭ/. Russian, of course, has soft and hard /l/, and various languages have both /l/ and its voiceless fricative equivalent /ɬ/: Welsh, for example, as in *Llanelli*, and also Sesuto. A few have /l/ and its voiced fricative counterpart /ɮ/, e.g. Xhosa, but no language is recorded as having more than two laterals.

Rolls, flaps

In many languages /r/ is represented by a rolled or flapped consonant at either the alveolar or, less commonly, the uvular place of articulation. Some kinds of Dutch, for example, have an alveolar roll, and some a uvular roll. It is very unusual to have the two rolls /r/ and /ʀ/ in contrast but this does happen in Provençal. In Urdu and other Indian languages the alveolar flap /ɾ/ and the retroflex flap /ʈ/ are distinctive; in Welsh the voiced flap [ɾ] contrasts with the voiceless one [r̥], as in *Rhossilly*, but this latter is generally taken to be /hr/ phonemically; and in Spanish the flap /ɾ/ is in contrast with the roll /r/ in *pero* ('but') and *perro* ('dog'). Russian again has soft and hard /r/ and Czech has both /r/, which is a plain alveolar roll, and /ṛ/, spelt 'ř' as in *Dvořak*, which is a post-alveolar roll accompanied by strong friction. No more than two contrasts are ever found, roll against roll, or flap against flap, or flap against roll, and as with the nasals they are much less differentiated than the stops or fricatives.

Frictionless continuants

In many languages, /w, j, r/ are realized generally as non-fricative gliding sounds, for instance in English when /r/ is a post-alveolar frictionless continuant, or in Danish, where it is a uvular frictionless continuant. /w/ mostly has labio-velar articulation, as in English and French, but it may be a labio-dental frictionless continuant as in Dutch. Russian has no independent /w/ and both hard and soft /r/ are rolled, so it has only /j/ in this category; German equally has no /w/ as distinct from /v/ but it has /j/, and /r/ may be realized as a uvular frictionless continuant or fricative. Urdu has /j/ and a labio-dental frictionless continuant /ʋ/ (but no separate /v/). French /r/ is frequently a uvular frictionless continuant /ʁ/, and in addition to /w, j/ French also has a labio-palatal /ɥ/ as in *huit* ('eight') in contrast with the others, which is very unusual. At the other end of the scale Georgian has no frictionless continuants at all.

Phonotactics

Phonotactics is the term used to refer to the way in which phonemes combine together in a particular language. It is possible to imagine two different languages with the same inventory of phonemes but whose phonemes combine together in quite different ways, and it is therefore not sufficient merely to list the phonemes. If in languages any phoneme could follow any other phoneme with equal probability there would be no place for phonotactics, but in fact there are powerful constraints operating in all languages, and each language has different rules governing the sequences of phonemes which may and may not occur. These rules can be summed up by stating the syllable structure of a language, and all longer stretches can be explained as a succession of syllables, since in principle no sequences occur in these longer stretches which cannot be accounted for in this way.

The (CCC)V(CCCC) structure of the English syllable (p. 200) is the most general statement of the possibilities of sequence. Within that framework we need to know which of the consonants can occur singly or in clusters both before and after the vowel which is the syllable's centre. For example, all consonants occur singly before the vowel except /ŋ/; /ʒ/ is rare but does appear in rather recent borrowings like *gigolo*, *jabot*. Clusters of two consonants before the vowel have one of two forms: /s/ + C in *stay*, *swim*, *sleep*, etc. or C + /w, j, r, l/ as in *twin*, *beauty*, *cream*, *plain*, etc., but not all the possibilities suggested by these still rather general formulae occur in fact; */sr, sb, sʃ/ and others are not found, nor are */tl, hr, fw, ʃj/ and others. /ʒ/ does not occur in initial clusters at all, as one might expect from its rarity as a single initial, /v/ only occurs with /j/, as in *view*, /h/ only with /j, w/ as in *huge*, *which* (in those accents where *which*, *witch* are distinguished) and /w, j, r/ are not found as the first of two consonants – /l/ would be the same were it not for /lj/ in *lute* if it is distinguished from *loot*. Three-term initial clusters have a more restricted form which is a combination of the general two-term possibilities: the first consonant must be /s/ and the last must be one of /w, j, r, l/; the middle consonant is one of /p, t, k, f/ as in *splash, stew, square, sphragid*, but again not all possible combinations of these occur, e.g. */spw, stl, sfj/ and others.

Clusters after the vowel are much more complex than those before, partly because of the way in which English makes grammatical use of consonantal terminations to express plural, past tense and ordinal numbers, as in *texts*, which gives /-ksts/, *jinxed* /-ŋkst/ and *sixth* /-ksθ/. Without these inflectional endings there would be no more than three consonants in final as in initial sequences but since *texts*, etc. are undoubtedly monosyllabic, the grammatical complexity of the words does not relieve us of the necessity of explaining the structure of this and other final clusters. Let us take the case of the rhotic accents, such as West Country or Irish, in which /r/ occurs before other consonants, e.g. *serve, hurt*; all single consonants except /w, j, h/ may occur finally in the syllable; two-term final clusters are of five main types as follows:

C + /t, d, s, z/	*apt, begged, since, cleanse*, etc.
/l/ + C	*bulk, elf, bulge, help*, etc.
/r/ + C	*earn, work, warm, birch*, etc.
/m, n, ŋ/ + C	*nymph, plunge, ink*, etc.
C + /θ/	*width, fifth*, etc.

Altogether there are 75 of these two-term clusters (58 in non-rhotic accents) as compared with 44 initial two-term clusters.

Three-term final clusters number 69 (or 49 in non-rhotic accents); they consist of one of the two-term clusters exemplified above, preceded or followed by another consonant. Examples are /-pts/ *crypts*, /-nzd/ *cleansed*, /-nθs/ *tenths*, /-ndʒd/ *plunged*, /-rmθ/ *warmth*, etc.

Only 9 four-term final clusters occur (7 in non-rhotic accents) and they all consist of one of the three-term clusters with the addition of /s/ (in 7 cases) or /z/ or /t/ (in one case each). Examples are /-lfθs/ *twelfths*, /-mpts/ *exempts*, /-ksθs/ *sixths*, /-mpst/ *glimpsed*, /-rldz/ *worlds*. All of these are the product of grammatical complexity. If from the total of 153 consonant clusters we were to subtract all of those which were found only in complex words we would be left with only 58 (51 two-term and 7 three-term). This is a measure of the complication that the grammatical use of consonantal affixes brings to the task of phonological explanation, or perhaps one should say a measure of the ready contribution of phonology to the making of grammatical distinctions.

In Russian the syllable can be generalized as (CCCC)V(CCCC), but here, because the same sort of grammatical complexity operates more in initial position, the initial clusters are more numerous and more complex than the final ones. In particular /vz/ and /fs/ both represent a grammatical prefix, which gives four-term clusters of the type /vzdr-/ and /fskl-/, to the number of 18, all quite unfamiliar in English terms. Amongst the three-term clusters, familiar-looking items such as /skr-/ and /spl-/ occur alongside others like /tkn-/ and /fsk-/; there are 83 of these compared with only 6 in English. Similarly, two term clusters are more numerous and less easily generalized than in English; they number 188, compared with only 44 in English, and contain items such as /sk-, bl-, kt-, fp-, lg-/. Altogether, then, there are 289 initial consonant clusters in Russian as compared with 50 in English.

On the other hand Russian has only a few more final clusters than English, 5 four-term, e.g. /-mstf/, against 7 in English; 25 three-term, including /-kst, -ktr, -str/, as against 48 in English; and 112 two-term, e.g. /-ks, -pt, -fk, -kr/, against 75 in English; the totals being 142 for Russian and 130 for English. Of the Russian total, 39 are accounted for by the grammatical process of dropping a vowel in an inflected form of a word; for example, the noun-ending /-stvo/ loses the vowel in the genitive plural resulting in the final cluster /-stf/ which would not otherwise occur; all the final four-term clusters are of this kind.

A language with quite a different syllabic structure is Persian. In general terms the syllable is CV(CC), that is, there must be a consonant before the vowel, and there may be 0 to 2 consonants following it. One three-term cluster /-mbr/ may occur, but only in a few borrowed French words like /septembr/ and there is always the possibility of splitting the cluster by adding a vowel, /september/, so we may discount this. Despite this general simplicity of the Persian syllable, the structure of the final two-term cluster is very much freer than it is in either English or Russian. Persian has 23 consonants, so the total possibility for two-term clusters, if we exclude the double occurrence of a phoneme, e.g. /-bb/, is $23 \times 22 = 506$. In fact, no fewer than 182 of these actually occur, well over one-third of the total. By contrast English has 24 consonants, giving a total possibility of $24 \times 23 = 552$, but of these only 75 occur finally, about one-seventh of the possible combinations. The constraints which govern consonant sequence in two-term clusters are much more stringent in English than they are in Persian, where one finds, for instance, a great many reversible clusters of the type /-br, -rb and /-ql, -lq/, in grammatically simple words; in English this occurs too, e.g. /-st, -ts/ in *rest*, *quartz* but not to any great extent, there being a total of only three such cases, /-sp, -ps/ in *rasp*, *lapse*, /-sk, -ks/ in *ask*, *axe* added to /-st, -ts/ above, and another one if we take into account consonantal in flection, namely /-zd, -dz/ in *used*, *adds*.

Syllable structure in other languages may be simpler still; Cantonese for example has the structure (C)V(C), where no consonant sequences occur within the syllable at all. However, the initial and final consonant places are very differently filled; whereas in English all but the consonants /h, ŋ, j, w/ may occur both initially and finally in CVC syllables, i.e. 20 out of the total of 24, in Cantonese only 6 out of a total of 20 occur in both positions, since only /p, t, k, m, n, ŋ/ occur in final position, the remainder being confined to initial position. This kind of restriction is found in its most extreme form in languages whose syllable structure is (C)V, such as Tswana, where the syllable may consist either of a vowel alone or a vowel preceded by a single consonant; but no syllable is closed by a consonant and therefore all of the consonants occur initially in the syllable and none at all finally. Incidentally, sequences such as /nt-/ and /ŋk-/ are found in Tswana, but this does not imply that consonant sequences are permitted, since the nasal is always syllabic in such cases, and bears a tone in exactly the same way that each vowel of the language bears a tone; the word /nta/ ('louse') has the tone pattern ‾‿— just as /noka/ ('river') does, but in /nta/ the falling tone is on the /n/ and in /noka/ it is on the /o/. Whenever the nasals bear tones they must be accounted as being a part of the vowel system, so that /nta/ has the structure VCV rather than CCV; when they do not bear a tone they belong to the consonant system, so /noka/ has the structure CVCV.

(C)V is the simplest syllable structure that occurs. Obviously no language has simply V, with no consonants at all, but less obviously V(C) does not occur: that is, there is no language, so far as we are aware, in which consonants are permitted after the vowel unless they are also permitted before it.

Stress

Stress may be fixed in relation to the words of a language, or it may be free; in Polish it is fixed, being tied to the penultimate syllable, and in Czech it is fixed on the first syllable. In French, isolated words have stress on the last syllable, but unlike Czech and Polish a word does not retain its stress in longer utterances unless it happens to come at the end of a phrase, so that stress in French is a mark of the final syllable of a phrase rather than a word. In none of these cases is it possible for stress to distinguish between one word and another, as it may be in languages with free stress. English stress is free in the sense that one cannot predict simply from knowing the number of syllables in a word which syllable the stress will fall on: it may be on the first, as in *trouble-someness*, *parachute*, *pillow*; or the second, as in *polite*, *ideally*, *potentially*; or the third as in *congregation*, *international*, *possibility*, and so on. Because of this freedom it is possible for stress to be contrastive in cases like *billow*, *below* and *insight*, *incite* (though such cases are very rare and apparently accidental). More common are the regular noun/verb differences – *convert*, *convert*; *import*, *import*; *subject*, *subject*, etc.; and the effects of certain word-endings on the place of stress, e.g. *-ation* always has the word-stress on its first syllable, so *imagine* (second syllable) and *imagination* (fourth syllable), and *-ity* attracts the stress to the preceding syllable, so *sensitive* (first syllable) and *sensitivity* (third syllable).

This type of regularity is rather common in free-stress languages, but the rules for its application generally involve listing the forms which show the regularities and those which do not, as for English *invoice* where noun and verb forms are identical. In Persian, stress is almost always on the last syllable of the word but there are exceptions to this which fall into two categories: first, a few grammatical words like /ˈhætta/ ('even') and /ˈzirɑ/ ('because') and exclamations such as /ˈzenhɑr/ ('behold'), and secondly, various complex words in which prefixes and suffixes disturb the final stress; for example, the verbal prefix /mi-/ takes the stress in /ˈmiræftæm/ ('I was going'), and the vocative suffix /-ɑ/ attracts the stress to the syllable before it, e.g. /pɑdeˈʃɑhɑ/ ('oh king!'). It is necessary therefore in Persian to list the words and affixes which prevent the general rule of final stress from operating, but this is a task which is very much simpler than it is for English.

English is not restricted to a single stress per word; longer words and compounds often have two or even more stressed syllables. So, *civilization* /ˈsɪvɪlaɪˈzeɪʃən/ has stress on its first and fourth syllables, and *co-worker* /ˈkəʊˈwɜːkə/ on its first and second. Comparison of the two words *education* and *educated* show a difference of stressing which has to be taken into account. In both of them the first and the third syllables are stressed in the sense that they have greater articulatory energy than the other syllables, but in *education* there is more insistence on the third syllable and in *educated* on the first, and we say that this syllable has primary stress and the other has secondary stress. The secondary stress is indicated by lowering the stress mark, e.g. /ˌedjʊˈkeiʃən, ˈedjʊˌkeɪtɪd/.

It has been suggested that a further degree of stress should be recognized to account for compounds of the type *motor-car designer*, where the primary stress would be on the first syllable, secondary stress on the second syllable of *designer* and tertiary on *car*, but this does not seem to be necessary provided the effects of *accentuation* are recognized, and these are a feature of the utterance rather than of the word. Suppose that in answering the question *Who wants to go there?* we say *No one wants to go there*, then the likely pitch/stress pattern would be ＼ . . . . which is very much what we have for *motor-car designer* also. The point about this is that the word *No-one* is accented and not merely stressed: that is, it is made to stand out by means of a fall in pitch added to its stress, whereas *wants* and *go*, even though they are stressed, do not stand out in at all the same way. Similarly in *motor-car designer* the first syllable /məʊ-/ has the fall in pitch which accents *motor*, whereas *car* and *designer* have only stress. Accentuation, as we have said, is a feature of the utterance, giving prominence to those parts which are semantically important; stress is a feature of the word and is just as much a part of its shape as the sequence of constituent phonemes is. The two are certainly related in those languages which have stress as a word feature, even though it is fixed, because the features of pitch which mainly constitute accentuation centre around the naturally stressed syllable of the word to be accented: in the example above *No one* has its first syllable stressed and it is on this syllable that the fall in pitch which accentuates it occurs. So also in French, *personne* has fixed stress on its final syllable and in the utterance *Personne ne veut y aller* ('No one wants to go there'), it would be on this syllable that the pitch-fall corresponding to the one on *No-one* above would occur.

We do not speak in isolated words; we utter sequences of sounds, stresses, pitches which can, by a rather sophisticated process, be analysed into sequences of words, in much the same way that we can abstract grammatical categories such as subject, predicate and the like. To a large extent word-stress is an abstraction of the same kind: we deduce from the facts of accentuation that a word has such and such a syllable stressed because when it is accented in an utterance the features which show us it is accented cluster round a particular syllable. The phrase *Very probably* may be uttered with the following three stress/pitch patterns (amongst others): and in all three cases both words are accented. The three different pitch patterns are used to convey different meanings, but each also has the single function of accenting the two words, and the pitch features which tell us they are accented can best be described from a particular syllable in each word – this is the syllable that we take to be stressed, and indeed when we use a single word as a complete utterance it is on this syllable that the accenting pitch features are centred. So, in *Stupid! Ridiculous! Idiotic!* we have the same fall in pitch, but related to the first, second and third syllables respectively and it is this which leads us to the conclusion that these are the stressed syllables, more than any extra loudness associated with them. The same argument can be used to show that the word in French has fixed stress on the final syllable, since the corresponding French words *Stupide! Ridicule! Idiot!* would each normally have a fall in pitch on the last syllable; but there is also the possibility in French of producing extra emphasis by placing the fall in pitch on the *first* syllable in each case which is certainly not a possibility in English or in any other stress language, and this underlines the irrelevance of stress to word-shape in French.

In Japanese, pitch is identifiable as giving a general shape to the word, much as stress does in English. Some (but not all) words have one syllable or a sequence of syllables on a higher pitch than the following syllable or syllables, e.g. /sajɔnara/ ('good-bye') $\underline{}\,\overline{}\,\overline{}\,\underline{}$. The last high-pitched syllable is critical; from it the pattern of the whole word can be deduced: all syllables before it are on the same high pitch except the first syllable of the word, and all syllables following it are on a lower pitch. The first syllable may itself be high, in which case the rest of the word is low in pitch $\overline{}\,\underline{}\,\underline{}\,\underline{}$. This critical last high pitch is free in its occurrence: it can occur on any syllable of a word except the last (and in utterances it can occur there if the following syllable is not itself high). The big difference between English and Japanese is that in the latter some words do not have any high pitch, whereas in English every word has at least one stress. Differences of stress occur in Japanese too but they are predictable in terms of the pitch pattern of the word, the higher the pitch the louder the syllable. Danish has the same stress system as English with the addition that each stressed syllable may or may not have the 'Stød' or glottal stop added to it (in fact, it is rarely a complete stop but rather a short period of creaky voice). So *Maj* ('May') is /maiʔ/ and *meg* ('me') is /mai/; *Mand* ('man') is /manʔ/ and *man* ('one') is /man/. Originally the Stød was connected only with monosyllables but this is no longer so: *Ænder* ('ducks') is /ɛnʔər/ whilst *Ender* ('ends') is /ɛnər/.

The concept of stress may be related not only to accentual features of pitch but also to features of vowel quality and features of rhythm. In English, for instance, the very frequent vowel /ə/ of a*bout*, *sof*a, /əˈbaʊt, ˈsəʊfə/ appears only in unstressed syllables whereas the others all occur in stressed syllables.

/ɪ/ occurs very frequently in unstressed syllables too, as in *insanity* /ɪnˈsænɪtɪ/ but it occurs under stress as well. The remaining vowels are much less frequent in unstressed than in stressed syllables, but notice, for example, /e, æ, ɑː, aɪ/ in the first syllables of *sententious, cantankerous, partake, psychology*, and /ɒ, ɔː, əʊ, ɔɪ/ in the final syllables of *pathos, tussore, shallow, alloy*. In Russian, another language in which stress is free, the connection between stress and vowel quality is very strict; some qualities only occur in unstressed syllables and others only in stressed. For example in /ˈprɔdənə/ ('sold') the spelling suggests /a/ and /ɔ/ in the last two syllables but these qualities are found only under stress, and in post-stress syllables their place is taken by /ə/. The same is true of the pre-pre-tonic syllable (two before the stress) but not of the pre-tonic where /a/ but not /ɔ/ or /ə/ can occur, as in /səmaˈvar/ ('samovar') where again the spelling suggests /a/ and /ɔ/ in the first two syllables. Certainly in Russian and to some extent in English this close association of certain vowel qualities with stressed and unstressed syllables has an effect on the perception of stress; if the English word *better* is said with this pitch pattern ⎯•⎯\⎯ , as it may be, the second syllable is louder and longer than the first, yet we do not take it to be stressed since we hear /betə/ and know from experience that /ə/ is associated with unstressed syllables and /e/ mainly with stressed.

Both English and Russian are also examples of languages in which the stressed syllables tend to occur at regular intervals of time. In *Nine famous men* the three stressed syllables /naɪn, feɪ-, men/ occur on a regular rhythmical beat despite the fact that there is an unstressed syllable between the second and third stresses but none between the first and second. The same regularity is present in *Nine ignorant men* when an additional unstressed syllable intervenes between the second and third stresses. This has the effect of compressing the syllables of *famous* and *ignorant* so that they are much shorter than the syllables *nine* and *men*. This compression can be seen in *Ninety famous men* where the addition of an unstressed syllable between the first and second stresses greatly shortens the syllable /naɪn-/ as compared with the original monosyllable *nine*. This regularity of occurrence of the stress is by no means absolute; in *Nine terrifying men* it is clear that the interval between the second and third stress is longer than that between the first and second: the number of syllables and sounds which can be articulated in a given space of time is limited. But the strong tendency to have the stresses occurring on a regular beat is certainly there; it has a considerable effect on the duration of sounds and syllables and it gives a very typical rhythmical character to the languages in which it operates. Furthermore, like the association of stress and vowel quality, it affects our perception of the stressed syllables in speech; contrast *To write in verse*, where *write* and *verse* are stressed, with *To write 'inverse'*, where *write* and *in-* are stressed; *write* is shorter in the first than in the second example because of the following unstressed syllable, and our judgement as to whether /ɪn/ is stressed or not relies at least to some extent on the relative length of *write*.

Just because a language has stress as part of its make-up it does not necessarily have a stress-based rhythm, as in English or Russian. Spanish is a language in which the stress is free to the extent that it can occur on any one of the last three syllables of a word, though not earlier; *termino* ('end') is stressed on the first syllable, *cerveza* ('beer') on the second and *celebrar* ('celebrate') on the last. But there is no tendency whatever in Spanish for the stressed syllables to fall at equal time intervals; on the contrary the rhythm of Spanish is dominated by the syllable, and it is the syllables which follow each other at regular intervals, giving a staccato effect to ears accustomed to the variations in syllabic length of a stress-based rhythm. The same syllable-based rhythm is found in French and in Hindi, amongst many others, but it should be noticed that there is no compulsion to have one or other of these rhythmical bases; indeed there is no reason why there should be any rhythmical basis at all in the sense of some feature recurring at regular time intervals, and in a language such as Finnish where both vowel and consonant length are significant any large variations in syllable length such as occur in stress-based rhythms like English, or any approximate equalization of syllable lengths as in syllable-based rhythms like Spanish, would run counter to these very important distinctions of length.

Tone systems

Tone languages differ in the number and the nature of the pitch distinctions which they use to distinguish meanings. In Mende (Sierra Leone) only two tones occur, low and high, and each syllable must have one or other of these; gliding tones do occur, both falling and rising, but these are always on long vowels or a sequence of two different vowels and must be regarded as sequences of low + high or high + low tone. Luganda has three tones, a high, a low and a falling tone which is independent and, since it occurs on short vowels, cannot be regarded as a combination of low + high. Tswana is similar but the falling tone is rare and occurs only on final syllables. Mixteco, a Mexican Indian language, also has three tones, high, mid and low. Mandarin has four, as mentioned earlier, high level, mid-to-high rise, low-to-mid rise (which is low-level unless before pause) and high-to-low fall. Somali too has four tones, but three of these are level, high, mid and low, and only one gliding, a high-to-low fall; Kikuyu and Efik have the same three level tones and fall, but also add a rising glide, giving five tones in all; Cantonese has six tones which can be arranged in two sets of three: a fall, a rise and a level tone in a high and a low register; and Hagu, a dialect of Amoy, has eight tones, four level, three falling and one rising.

In many tone languages every syllable must bear one of the available tones; in Luganda for example each syllable has high or low or falling tone. But in others only a proportion of the syllables carry tones: in Norwegian and Swedish the operation of the tonal contrast between simple and compound tone (p. 191) is confined to words of two syllables or more and therefore monosyllabic words cannot have tone under any circumstances. In Mandarin purely grammatical particles, such as /ma/ which is added in order to turn a statement into a question, are always toneless. Other syllables bear tones in the utterance only when they are accented: Mandarin has an accentuation system similar to that of English in effect but it intersects with the tone system in such a way that only the words which are accented for semantic reasons retain the tones which they would all have in isolation. Cantonese is quite different, since every syllable must have one of the six tones in the system.

Also, tone may intersect with other sound features. Of the eight tones of Hagu, six occur on relatively long syllables and the other two on relatively short ones. The third tone of Mandarin, the low level or low-rising tone, is always associated with a longer syllable than the other tones. In Burmese, syllables with high tone are always rather short and closed by a glottal stop, and syllables with the falling and low tones have long vowels said with breathy voice. In Xhosa there are four tones, high, mid and low levels and a high-to-low fall, but their realization depends to a large extent on the consonant which begins the syllable: one set of consonants, the 'depressors', has the general effect of lowering the tone on the following vowel, and another set of raising the tone. Until this interaction is recognized, the task of accounting for what seems to be a multiplicity of tones is impossibly complicated but once it is realized that some of the tonal realizations are conditioned by the initial consonant, the relative simplicity of the tone system emerges.

In addition to the basic system of tones in a tone language there may also be significant pitch effects which cannot be included in the basic system. In many of the Bantu languages, for example, and in Igbo, a slight general lowering of the actual pitches of the tones at intervals in longer utterances is syntactically significant. After one of these change points there is, as it were, a slight downward shift of key, and all subsequent tones are realized somewhat lower than before. This general lowering of stretches of speech cannot be accounted for on the same basis as the syllabic distinctions of tone and is more akin to the use of pitch which occurs in intonation languages.

Intonation

Intonation patterns are invariably complicated but they too can be reduced to systems and structures by observing the meaningful contrasts which are realized at different parts of the utterance. In English there is a basic three-part structure of the *tone groups* (i.e. the unit of intonation) and in each of these parts a different system of contrasts operates. This can be shown in an example such as *You really mustn't be so mean*. It may be ⠐⠂⠄⠄⠄⠔ , with the last word falling from medium to low pitch; or, holding everything else still, the final fall may be from high to low ⠐⠂⠄⠄⠄⠄⠄⠌ . Instead of a straight fall, the pitch may first rise and then fall on *mean* ⠐⠂⠄⠄⠄⠄⠈⠌ or it may simply rise ⠐⠂⠄⠄⠄⠄⠔ or fall and then rise ⠐⠂⠄⠄⠄⠄⠈⠈ . All of these possibilities form a system which operates in this case on the last word; in general it operates on the last accented word of the tone group, so if in *You really mustn't be so upset about it* the last accented word is *upset* the same possibilities of fall and rise, etc. will occur on the second (stressed) syllable of that word, e.g. ⠐⠂⠄⠄⠄⠄⠈⠌⠄⠄ or ⠐⠂⠄⠄⠄⠄⠄⠄⠄ . Notice that in the last pattern the final rise is not completed on the accented syllable *-set* but is carried by the following unaccented syllables; there are detailed differences in the manner in which the falls and rises, etc. are carried out but the general possibilities remain the same at this place in the tone group. It should also be noticed that the same possibilities are available in monosyllabic tone groups such as *No* $\overline{\quad\searrow\quad}$ $\overline{\quad\diagup\quad}$ $\overline{\curlyvee\quad}$ etc. The last accented syllable of a tone group is known as the *nucleus* or *tonic* and the *nuclear tones* which mark it form a system of their own.

The second part of the tone group's structure runs from the first accented syllable up to the last syllable before the nucleus, so in the examples above it comprises *really mustn't be so* and the possibilities here are different. We may for instance have $\overline{\cdot\,\bullet\,\cdot\,\cdot\,\searrow}$ with the unaccented syllables rising rather than remaining level as before. Or they may fall $\overline{\cdot\bullet\cdot\cdot\,.\,.\searrow}$ or all be low in pitch $\overline{.\,.\,.\,.\,.\,.\searrow}$ and it is clear that this part of the pitch pattern is acting independently of the nucleus and it is acting as a unit. This stretch from the first accented syllable up to the nucleus is called the *head*; sometimes the term 'head' is restricted to the first accented syllable and the remainder is called the *body*, but there seems no reason to make this division since the stretch is functioning as a whole. Unlike the nucleus, which is a single syllable, the head is variable in length; in *You really mustn't be so mean* it has six syllables, two of which are accented, but it may have only one syllable, which must then be accented, as in *What rubbish!* $\overline{\quad\bullet\quad\searrow\quad.}$ or it may be much longer as in *How on earth did you manage to make such a stupid mistake?* $\overline{\bullet\cdot\bullet\cdot\cdot\bullet\cdot\bullet\cdot\searrow}$ where it has fourteen syllables, five of them accented. Its length depends, of course, on the word structure and accent structure of the tone group.

The remainder of the tone group comprises the *pre-head*, i.e. any syllables before the first accented syllable. In our example *You* is the pre-head. Again the possibilities are different at this place, being restricted to low pitch as above, which is much the most common, or high pitch, as in $\overline{\bullet\cdot\bullet\cdot\cdot\cdot\searrow}$ or more usually in a pattern such as *You can't do that* $\overline{\quad\cdot\quad.\quad.\quad\diagup}$. The pre-head is not usually very long but it may be so when the first accented syllable occurs late in the tone group, e.g. *I taught him just about everything he knows* $\overline{.\,.\,.\,.\,.\,\bullet\bullet\bullet\searrow}$.

The only essential part of a tone group, the one which must always be present, is the nucleus; in *No* ⟋⟍ all we have is a rising-falling nuclear tone: there is no head and no pre-head. Neither head nor pre-head may occur without the nucleus and if, in conversation, they do so, it is a sign of incompleteness, perhaps because of interruption. On the other hand, both head and pre-head may occur independently of each other; for example in *What rubbish!* above there is no pre-head and in *It was impossible* ...⟍.. there is no head. For a head to occur there must be at least two accented syllables in the tone group, and for a pre-head to occur there must be at least one syllable before the first accent. This again depends on the accent structure of the tone group; in *Now isn't that kind!* .···⟍ we have pre-head, head and nucleus, but if we take the accent away from *kind* and concentrate it on *isn't* .⟍... there is no head, only pre-head followed by nucleus.

The range possibilities of the whole tone group must also be accounted for since the same general pattern may be found distributed over the whole available range of the voice, or it may be restricted to the top part of the range, or the middle part, or the bottom part. *How nice*, for example, may be ˙⟍ or ˙˙⟍ or •⟍ or •⟍ and it is much more sensible to deal with this by an additional range system than by attempting to do so in the same terms as we account for pre-head, head and nucleus. If we assume that the middle range is normal we can treat the higher restricted range as 'high', the lower one as 'low' and the full range as 'high + low'. This is relatively simple, but there is greater difficulty in accounting for the ranges of the various rises and falls and their combinations which constitute the nuclear tones. From the point of view of pure pitch it seems that a fall may vary continuously in its range, e.g. ⟍⟍⟍⟍⟍ and the problem is to decide whether this corresponds to a continuously varying semantic effect or to a limited number of clear differences of meaning.

British linguists have usually selected a number of falls, which certainly are different in meaning, ranging usually from two to four; and similarly with rising and other nuclear tones. American scholars, however, have widely adopted quite a different practice. They operate with four contrastive pitch levels, 1 usually being low and 4 high and they then account for falls, rises, etc. as movements between these levels, so there may possibly be six falls, as follows ⁚‐⸗⸗⸗ , and similarly with rises. This schema would permit $6 \times 6 = 36$ falling-rising or rising-falling tones. The difficult question remains, though, whether six falling tones are necessary, and if so whether they are sufficient, to express the contrasts of meaning carried by falling tones. Or are the differences of meaning continuous, as the pitch differences are continuous, and do we therefore need a quite different means of expressing continuously varying pitch movements? There is no clear answer to this, but if it turns out that a continuous method is necessary it will pose problems, because we are very much more accustomed to dealing with separate quantities than continuous ones, and much better at it.

The same problem arises in connection with features such as loudness and tempo; can we cut out from the physical continuum a fixed number of degrees of loudness or speeds of utterance corresponding to that number of clearly separate meaning differences, or must we allow for continuous variation here too? On the face of it, features like pitch, loudness and tempo are quite different from features of vowel quality, precisely in that they do vary continuously. In tone languages we can see a use of pitch similar to a significant difference of vowel quality, and in both cases we have a simple criterion for separating one tone or one vowel from another, the difference of meaning between *bad* and *bed* or Mandarin /ma/ ‾‾‾‾ and /ma/ ⟍ . But the differences of meaning between different falls in an intonation language are a horse of a very different colour. There is an obvious affinity of meaning between any fall and any other fall and it would certainly not be surprising if we had to account for continuously varying meaning, but this is a matter in which we must await a better semantic theory before we are able to solve the phonological problem.

Far more work has been done on English intonation than on that of any other language, but it is clear that the tripartite structure of the tone group is neither exclusive to English nor universal in its application. German, Russian and Danish can all be accounted for in terms of pre-head, head and nucleus, but it should not be imagined that the same systems will operate at these three places as operate in English; the number and form of the nuclear tones or of the head and pre-head possibilities vary from one language to another. The fall-rise nuclear tone of English, as in *Please* ‾\/‾ does not occur, for instance, in any of these three languages, and the frequency of occurrence of tones which are similar also varies widely: in Danish the rise-fall nuclear tone is much more common than it is in English, where a plain fall is more frequent, and in Russian a low, level nuclear tone occurs very often, whilst in English such a tone is rare.

In French, however, there is certainly no place corresponding to the pre-head. There is a nuclear place in the sense that meaningful final rises and falls take place at a particular point which is not entirely predictable, so that *C'était très amusant* ('It was very amusing') may be ＿＿--‾‾\ or it may be ＿-‾\＿＿＿ but this is a matter of accentuation rather than of intonation proper and it seems possible that the tone group in French can best be specified as a whole rather than as a combination of independent parts, as in English. This would be relatively easy in unemphatic speech; one common pattern is ＿＿--‾‾\ as in *Ne vous dérangez pas* ('Don't disturb yourself') and this can be specified simply as a rising-falling tune, with the convention that the highest pitch is on the penultimate syllable unless otherwise stated. In *Dîtes-moi tout ce que vous avez fait* ('Tell me everything you did') with the pattern ＿＿-------＿ *tout* would need to be marked as highest in pitch. Also, if the word *monsieur*

were added, the final fall would remain on *fait* and *monsieur*
would be low and level: *fait* would therefore need to be marked.
It might be done as follows: ^*Dîtes-moi* '*tout ce que vous avez*
'*fait, monsieur*, where ^ gives the general shape, the first ' shows
the high point and the second ' the final fall. Similarly a pattern
such as ‾‾‾‾‾‾‾‾‾↘ on *Dîtes-moi tout ce que vous avez fait*,
where *fait* is particularly emphasized, would be: ^*Dîtes-moi tout*
ce que vous avez "*fait*, and ‾↘‾‾‾‾‾‾ would be ^*Dîtes-moi*
"*tout ce que vous avez fait*.

A purely rising pattern, as in *Il y est allé?* ('He went there?')
‾‾‾‾‾‾ could be indicated as ,*Il y est allé* and then a broken
pattern such as ‾‾‾‾‾‾‾↘ in *Il est allé en Amérique* ('He
went to America') would be analysed as a sequence of the rising
plus the rising-falling tone groups: ,*Il est allé* ^*en Amérique*. The
alternative would be to recognize *Il est allé* as the head of a tone
group whose nucleus is *-rique*, but this is only profitable if the
possibilities are different at the two different places, as they are
with the English head and nucleus, and this does not appear to
be so in French.

Sequences of tone groups may show a structure of their own:
in the English sequence *I got up at six, had a cup of tea, and*
settled down to work the pattern may be: [intonation diagram]
and the gradual lowering of the starting pitch of the heads has
the effect of binding the three separate tone groups together
into a larger unit. A subsequent raising of the head pitch will
then announce the start of a new sequence, e.g. . . . *and settled*
down to work. After an hour . . . [intonation diagram] . Exactly the same
sort of thing happens in Russian, whereas in French a sequence
such as *Le matin, après le petit déjeuner, que j'ai pris dans la*
cuisine, je me suis mis à travailler ('In the morning, after breakfast, which I ate in the kitchen, I got down to work') may be
[intonation diagram]   and the whole
thing is held together by a gradual rise in the final pitch of the
tone groups followed by a gradual fall.

It seems possible that deeper investigation of intonation in many languages may reveal widespread or even universal similarities; intonation has often been spoken of as 'gesture-like', more directly linked to meaning than other more arbitrary features of speech. It is certainly very common in European languages at least for a rising tone to be used as a mark of interrogation, as it is in English *No?* ___✔___ but there are cases in which intonation is very much more conventional in its application, as the following chapter will show, and in any case gesture itself is far from being a universal sign language, even though gestures with similar meaning are found over areas larger than single language communities. In the matters of tone-group structure, and the number and frequency of the tonal contrasts used, the present state of our knowledge suggests that there is no universality, and in any case it is wise to postpone the attempt to discover universals until we have thorough analyses of far more languages than are available at present.

8. Sounds Working

What sounds are, how they can be delimited and described, how they fit together in larger structures, how they can be classified and systematized, all these and other aspects dealt with in earlier chapters are fascinating topics, and the phonetician can potter happily along concerning himself only with them. But the true importance of sound is in its relation to the other levels of language study. What does sound do in a language? How does it relate to the grammar of the language and to the word stock? What use do we make of it? It is only when such questions have been answered that the sound aspect of language can be seen in perspective. This chapter will attempt to show how sound contributes to language and to the complex process of communication between human beings that a language serves.

Words and phonemes

In the first place the words that we use in speech are given a recognizable shape by sound; the word *cat* must be /kæt/, or something like enough to it so that by applying our knowledge of our own accent and other accents we can identify the word with ease. If we get into a situation where that is not possible, through gross differences of accent, perhaps, or bad interference by noise or distortion, communication is made difficult or impossible. We must recognize the phonemes and we must recognize their order: /kæt/ is not /kʌt/ *cut*, nor is it /tæk/ *tack* nor /ækt/ *act*. Simple words have a phoneme shape of their own, with the exceptions mentioned below. So too do formatives like the adverb-forming *-ly* /lɪ/ as in *quickly*, *slowly*, or the negative *un-* /ʌn/ in *undo*, *unfinished*, or the comparative and superlative *-er* /ə/ and *-est* /ɪst/ in *brighter*, *lighter*, *brightest*, *lightest*. Sometimes a single grammatical function is represented by more than one phoneme shape; so regular plurals in English have /s/ or /z/ or /ɪz/, as in *cats*, *dogs*, *horses*. Sometimes too, different grammatical functions of related forms are signalled by different phonemic shapes, as for example the noun function of *estimate* /ˈestɪmət/ against the verb function /ˈestɪmeɪt/.

There is a certain amount of tolerance in the matter of phonemic word-shape; there are instances in all languages for example of differing shapes of a word in different circumstances. In most situations in English the word *tin* has the shape /tɪn/ but before the bilabials /p, b, m/ it often changes shape to /tɪm/ as in *Tin Pan Alley*. Similarly /t, d/ may be replaced by /p, b/ in *right place* /raɪp pleɪs/ and *bright boy* /braɪp bɔɪ/ or by /k, g/ in *nutcracker* /nʌkkrækə/ or *broadcast* /brɔːgkɑːst/. So, too, *street* usually has the form /striːt/ but in *Goodge Street* it is more often pronounced /ʃtriːt/ because of the preceding /dʒ/ and following /r/. These changes are apt to look strange in phonetic transcription, but most of the time they pass unnoticed in speech. They are due to the influence of neighbouring sounds and are referred to as *assimilations*. What happens along these lines to the /n/ of *tin* in *tin can*, to the /n/ of *ten* in *tenpence*, to the /z/ of *as* in *as you were*, and why?

There may be omissions, too, without ruining the shapes of words: *postman* may indeed be /pəʊstmən/ but it is more often /pəʊsmən/ with no /t/; *last* in *last out* is invariably /lɑːst/, but in *last man* it is often /lɑːs/; *police* may be /pəliːs/ but is often reduced to /pliːs/. And so on. Some people tend to feel furious about both assimilations and *elisions*, as these omissions are called, if they notice them. They feel that such speech is slipshod or slovenly, not realizing, or forgetting, that this is the way that language behaves and always has behaved. The perfectly normal and acceptable pronunciation of the word *handkerchief* today /hæŋkətʃɪf/ has developed from an earlier form /hændkɜːtʃiːf/ partly by elision of the /d/ and assimilation of /n/ to /ŋ/ under the influence of the following /k/, and partly by weakening of the vowels; and there is no outcry to pronounce *Christmas* or *castle* with /t/, nor *sugar* with /sj/ rather than /ʃ/. Language does what it has to do for efficiency and gets away with what it can. But it cannot get away with too much, and by and large words have to have a more or less invariant selection and ordering of phonemes as part of their shape.

We must not require (and certainly will not find) a unique shape for every word of the language. There are *homophones* – words of different meaning but the same sound – in most languages: in English we have a large ration, e.g. *pear*, *pair*, *pare*; *taut*, *taught*; *site*, *sight*, *cite*; *so*, *sew*, *sow*. And in RP there are more than in the rhotic accents, which would distinguish, e.g. *caught*, *court*; *father*, *farther*; *Mona*, *moaner*, etc. French has the same in *père*, *pair*, *paire* ('father, peer, pair'); *sûr*, *sur* ('sure, on'); *sot*, *seau* ('foolish, bucket'). And German has, e.g., *sein*, *sein* ('to be, his'); *Wetter*, *Wetter* ('punter, weather'), and so on. We may also note that formatives may be homophonous, for example /s, z, ɪz/ are used not only to form plurals in English, as mentioned above, but also to form the third person present tense of verbs, as in *takes*, *finds*, *loses*, and we find not only comparative forms like *brighter* formed with /ə/, but also actor forms like *player*, *taker*, etc.

A language can tolerate quite a lot of homophones provided they do not get in each other's way, that is, provided that they are not likely to occur in the same contexts. This may be a grammatical matter: if the homophones are different parts of speech they are not likely to turn up in the same place in a sentence; it is not easy even to devise ambiguous examples with, say, *bear* n., *bear* v., *bare* or with *caught*, *court*, and such words very rarely interfere with each other. If they are the same part of speech, e.g. *site, sight; pear, pair* they can be tolerated unless they commonly occur in the same area of meaning and in association with a similar set of other words. *Site* may be ambiguous in *It's a nice site*, though a wider context will most likely make the choice plain, but in general it will not associate with the same words as *sight*; it goes with words like *level, plan, house, architect, on the —* and so on, whereas *sight* goes with words like *near, far, clear, sore eyes, at the —,* etc. They are not likely to come into serious collision. If homophones do interfere with each other the language may react either by getting rid of one and using other terms or by modifying one. When English *quean, queen,* became homophonous they did get in each other's way – both nouns, both referring to a woman, one highly derogatory, the other honorific – so we dropped *quean.* On the other hand in French *pommes* may stand for *pommes de terre* ('potatoes') or it may mean 'apples'. So if apples figure on a French menu they are likely to be designated *pommes fruits,* and the ambiguity created by omission in one term is resolved by addition to the other.

Words and stress

Whilst homophony affects some languages more than others, the bulk of word forms in all languages have to be distinguished. This may be a matter of phonemic selection and ordering, but other factors too can contribute. Stress is an integral part of word-shape in English and other languages mentioned in the previous chapter. It is the sole distinguishing factor in pairs like *incite, insight* or *import* v., *import* n. but more often in English the stress difference is accompanied by differences of phoneme selection, so *object* v. and *object* n. are usually /əbˈdʒekt/ and /ˈɒbdʒɪkt/ in RP, though in Northern accents stress is often the only difference: /ɒbˈdʒekt/, /ˈɒbdʒekt/; in *photograph, photography* /ˈfəʊtəˌgræf, fəˈtɒgrəfɪ/ the vowels in the first three syllables are all different with the difference in stress. Such vocalic differences are even more regular in Russian, where, for instance, the vowel differences in /ˈvɔrət/ ('neckband') and /vaˈrɔt/ ('of the gates') are entirely attributable to the stress difference, and where the second and third vowels in [ˈkɔmnətə] ('room') are unstressed allophones of /a/. Other languages do not have these vowel differences correlated with stress: in Greek /ˈpoli/ ('city') and /poˈli/ ('much') the vowels have much the same quality in both stressed and unstressed syllables, as they do in Spanish /ˈtermino/ ('end') and termiˈno/ ('he finished').

In English, stress is much more a matter of general word-shape than of purely distinctive function; often quoted pairs of the type *incite, insight* and *below, billow,* where stress is indeed distinctive, are rare and as it were accidental, but the more regular differences between, e.g., the noun and verb functions of forms like *object, insult, pervert, transport* are examples of stress working as a marker of grammatical differences.

Words and tone

In tone languages tone is an integral part of word-shape, as stress is in English and Russian, and without the correct tone or tones a word will be distorted or even unrecognizable, at least in isolation. Certainly in the case of Cantonese /ˈfan/ against /ˈfan/ the difference of word-shape is totally dependent on tone, whereas in Tswana a word such as /sɪkɔpɛlɔ/ ('key') which has low tone on all four syllables will be distorted but still recognizable if say, a high tone is introduced on one of the syllables, given that no other word of the same phonemic shape but different tonal pattern occurs.

Tonal assimilation occurs in tone languages in a way resembling the assimilation of phonemes mentioned above. That is to say a word has one tonal shape in one situation and a different one in another. For example, Mandarin /ˌhen/ ('very') has the third

tone, low-rising, in isolation and most contexts, but if it occurs
before another word with the third tone, it acquires the second
tone, high-rising, so */ˌhen ˌhɑo/ ('very good') is in fact rendered
as /ˈhen ˌhɑo/. So also /ˈneŋ/ ('be able') usually has the second
tone, but it is said with the first tone, high level, whenever it
occurs between a word with the first tone and another with the
second tone, so we get /ˉtaː ˉneŋ ˈlai/ ('he can come') rather than
*/ˉtaː ˈneŋ ˈlai/. Such changes are not restricted to individual words
such as /ˌhen/ or /ˈneŋ/; the third tone is *always* replaced by the
second tone before a third tone, and the second tone is *always*
replaced by a first tone between a first and a second tone, i.e.
/ˌ ˌ/ → /ˈ ˌ/ and /ˉ ˈ ˈ/ → /ˉ ˉ ˈ/. Regular tonal changes of this kind
do not spoil the shape of the relevant words any more than the
change from /s/ to /ʃ/ spoils the shape of *street* in *Goodge Street*,
and is no more noticeable to the native speaker.

Words and length

Vowel and consonant length can both contribute independently
to word-shape as in the Finnish examples /tuleː/ ('comes'),
/tulleː/ ('ought to come') and /tuːleː/ ('blows'). In stressed
syllables in Italian the contributions of vowel and consonant
length are connected rather than independent, so that a long
vowel is always followed by a short consonant and vice versa, e.g.
/ˈfaːto/ ('fate'), /ˈfatto/ ('fact') and /ˈbruːto/ ('brute'), /ˈbrutto/
('ugly'). In other positions consonant length contributes to
differences of word-shape but vowel length does not; compare
single and double /t/ in /annoˈtaːre/ ('annotate') and /annotˈtaːre/
('grow dark'). In French vowel length contributes in a few cases
like /mɛtre/ *mettre* ('put') and /mɛːtrə/ *maître* ('master') but is
not a regular feature of different word-shapes.

In English, vowel length is sometimes the only factor in differentiating word shape, e.g. Yorkshire *ham*, *harm* [ham, haːm],
but more often a difference of length goes together with a dif-

ference of quality; /iː/ is longer than /ɪ/ in *reed*, *rid* but the qualities are also different. In most Scottish speech length does not contribute to such differences at all, *reed*, *rid*, etc. being distinguished entirely by quality; but Scottish does have a difference, not found elsewhere, between inflected and non-inflected forms such as *teas*, *tease*, which is carried by length only: /tiːz, tiz/.

Consonant length in English is not a part of word-shape except in the case of compounds and derived words, e.g. long /n/ in *pen-knife*, *unknown*, as against short /n/ in *Pennine*, *unasked*; in these cases we generally ascribe the difference to a single occurrence of the phoneme /n/ in the latter examples and a double occurrence in the former but it is the duration of [n] which is the main cue.

Word boundaries

Quite apart from giving words a regular shape by means of phoneme order, stress, tone or length, we may also signal word boundaries in various ways. In English, for instance, we regularly pronounce vowel and consonant combinations differently when a word boundary changes, so that it is possible to distinguish *grey tape* from *great ape*, or *a gnome* from *an ohm*, or *I scream* from *ice-cream*, even though the phoneme sequence and stress are identical and there is no physical pause made between the words. This is done by the use of different allophones in relation to the word boundary: /eɪ/ is longer in *grey* than in *great*, and the /t/ has much more aspiration in *tape* than it has in *great*; the /n/ is firmer and longer in *a gnome* than in *an ohm*; /aɪ/ is longer in *I* than in *ice* and /r/ has more voice in *scream* than in *cream*. Contrasting pairs of this kind are rare but nevertheless word boundaries are often positively marked in this way even though no confusion could possibly result if the marking were omitted. Indeed many of these features of *juncture* are lost at fast tempo without any significant loss of intelligibility, and in much

Scottish speech some of these distinctions are not made at all, *an ohm* and *an aim* being regularly pronounced in a way which strikes the English ear as *a gnome* and *a name*.

In case of necessity we can make the word boundary in *great ape* clear beyond a doubt by using the glottal stop as a special junctural signal /ˈɡreɪt ˈʔeɪp/, but we do not do this all the time. German on the other hand does; any time that a word begins with a stressed vowel at least (and often with an unstressed vowel too), it must be preceded by [ʔ], so in *Leute aller Arten* ('people of all kinds') both *aller* and *Arten* must have initial glottal stop. This is not unequivocally a word-boundary signal since it also occurs within derived words like *ver-alten* ('grow old').

There are other languages which do little or nothing to signal word boundaries in normal speech, e.g. French, where nothing shows that the /z/ of *les affaires* ('business') /lez afɛːr/ belongs to *les*, whilst in *les zéphyrs* ('zephyrs') /le zefiːr/ it belongs to *zéphyrs*, but again if it is essential to make the boundary explicit it can be done by [ʔ] or by pause.

In any event we must not expect that every word boundary will be signalled even in those languages which do it a good deal, any more than that every word of the language should have a distinct shape of its own; there will be homophony in this respect too. So *a tack* is not distinguished from *attack*, nor *a tone* from *atone*, nor perhaps *I can seal it* from *I conceal it*.

Sequence markers

Words are one constituent of sentences, but there are larger constituents consisting of sequences of words which, taken together, fulfil a specific grammatical function. In *That old man in the corner drinks nothing but Guinness*, *that old man in the corner* represents the Subject of the sentence and the remainder the Predicate. In *He ate and drank his fill*, *his fill* is the direct object of both verbs; in *He ate, and drank his fill*, it is the object of *drank* only. In *The umpire, who was blind, gave him out* the relative clause simply describes the one umpire in question, whereas in *The umpire who was blind gave him out* it defines which one of the two umpires is meant. The particular grammatical function may be fulfilled by a single word: in *That old man in the corner drinks* the Predicate is represented by *drinks*; in *John drinks nothing but Guinness* the Subject is *John*. In these cases a single word is doing a job which may also be done by a sequence of words. Words and sequences of this kind may be explicitly marked in pronunciation.

The term sequence is used here rather than phrase or group or the like, because it is grammatically neutral. Sentence elements such as Subject, Predicate, Clause, Phrase, etc. are determined by grammatical not phonological considerations, and no such element is always phonologically signalled; there is nothing in the pronunciation to tell us that *John* in *John dithers* is the Subject of a sentence and that in *John Mathers* it is not. But quite a lot of the time there are pronunciation features which hold sequences together and therefore hint that they are playing a particular unitary grammatical role.

One of these features is accent: in English it is a major marker of the difference between close-knit compound expressions and looser-knit phrases; in *greenhouse* only the first syllable is accented, whereas in the phrase *green house* both are; in *hot-house plant* only *hot* is accented, whilst in *hot houseplant* both *hot* and *house* are. So with *infant teacher, sanitary inspector, lightning conductor*, etc. More generally it is used to show elements of a sentence which are 'given', that is, which are common knowledge between listener and speaker, or are taken to be so. If we say *What did you say his name was* on a rising intonation with only *What* accented it implies (in conformity with the words) that the information has been previously given and a repetition is being asked for; if *name* is accented as well there is no such implication. And if the answer is *I didn't say what his name was* only *didn't* will be accented because the remainder is 'given' in the concrete sense that it has already been said.

Length has two oddly different properties as a marker in English; in the first place it can act as a boundary marker of sequences, and in the second it can serve to hold sequences together which might otherwise be taken to be divided. If the meaning of *Far from being sorry, I was glad they agreed* is 'I was glad *that* they agreed' the length of *glad* is shorter than in the alternative meaning of 'they agreed that I was glad' (corresponding to the insertion of a comma after *glad*), whose length here may be taken to be alternative to a pause. In other cases pause is unlikely and length is the only marker. So in *Two thousand year old horses* there are two possible meanings which can be distinguished solely by the length of /uː/ in *Two*; the first is 'Two horses each of which is one thousand years old', and the second 'An indefinite number of horses each two thousand years old', (this turned out to be the meaning of *The Times* crossheading where this example was found – the horses being in a peat-bog somewhere). If the meaning is $2 \times 1,000$ the /uː/ of *Two* is a good deal longer than when the meaning is $n \times 2,000$, and the extra length of /uː/ has the effect of dissociating 2 from 1,000. Incidentally, a third meaning can be got from the words if accent is also pressed into service, i.e. 'Two thousand horses each one year old'. To get this, the /uː/ of *Two* has its shorter length to connect it with *thousand*, and then *year*, which is not accented in either of the first two examples, is given an accent; this has two consequences: *thousand* is not rushed to the same extent as in *thousand-year-old*, and both *year* and *old* are also longer. A similar type of example occurs when words like *on, in, by* have a close or less close connection with a verb; for example *He climbed on to the top* may mean 'He continued climbing until he reached the top' or 'He arrived on the top by climbing'. In the first meaning both *climbed* and *on* are accented and *climbed* is shorter to show the connection with *on*, whilst *on* is longer to dissociate it from *to*; in the second meaning *on* is shorter and unaccented. Work out the possible meanings of *Five hundred pound notes* and *He looked after the children* and see what the contributions of length and accent are in differentiating them orally.

The second function of length in English is a hesitation function, a signal that an utterance is not complete, that we are having trouble in finding a word or something of that kind. So if we lengthen the /uː/ of *Two* in *Two thousand-year-old horses* beyond what is necessary to dissociate it from *thousand* it signals this hesitation. If we say *It was nice* in quite a final way, but hold on to the /s/ of *nice*, it signals that there is more to come. This particular function of length is often taken over or supplemented by pause and by hesitation sounds. Instead of, or as well as, lengthening the /uː/ of *Two* we may simply pause and in this example that would be sufficient since the unfinished nature of the utterance is amply signalled by the incompleteness of the intonation pattern. Or we may prefer to fill the thinking time with [ɜː] or [əm], or other positive hesitation noises, or we may use any combination of these means. It is very common to hear, for instance, *You, er, – appreciated it?* /juːː ɜːː [silence] əˈpriːʃieitid it/. In cases where intonation suggests that the utterance may be complete, pause alone will not do to hold the floor. If in *It was nice* the /s/ is not lengthened nor [ɜː] etc. used, the listener may fairly conclude that we have finished.

We tend to think that major grammatical boundaries are always signalled by pause, e.g. in *Just after I arrived, the fire-bell rang* where the comma is often equated with pause; but in general, pause alone is not a sufficient signal for sequence boundaries; it must be accompanied by some other feature if it is to be effective. To show that *arrived* finishes a clause its final syllable will be considerably lengthened (compare *Just after I arrived there*, where it is shorter) and usually the intonation pattern will be complete; if pause occurs in association with these, well and good, it is a reinforcement of the boundary signals; but if it occurs without lengthening of *arrive* and with an incomplete intonation pattern the pause will be taken as a hesitation marker. Conversely, lengthening and intonation are usually perfectly effective boundary markers even without physical silence.

However, there are instances where pause is apparently significant. *I agree with you, in some cases. They're very variable* may be structurally altered to attach *in some cases* to what follows rather than to what precedes by having a pause after *you* and none after *cases*, or a longer pause after *you* and a shorter one after *cases*, so giving *I agree with you. In some cases, they're very variable*. Now both of these can be said with exactly the same final lengthenings at the two internal boundaries and exactly the same intonation patterns, but the different pause treatment will point quite unequivocally to a different affiliation for *in some cases*. With tag questions, such as *It was impressive, wasn't it?* the statement and the tag generally have a complete intonation pattern each, but usually no actual pause between. If only a slight pause is introduced, the statement and the tag appear to have been conceived separately rather than as a whole, perhaps corresponding to *It was impressive. Wasn't it?*

Intonation and grammar

There is one aspect of intonation which is tightly tied to the marking of sequences, and that is the fact that a complete intonation unit has a sequence as its domain: the tone group, with its unified structure, is carried by a group of words and the complete tone group confers unity, or at least connection, upon that group. Differences of grammatical structure are therefore reflected particularly by the number rather than the nature of the tone groups used over a given stretch. The difference between *I don't, no* and *I don't know* lies precisely in this; in the first case *I don't* and *no* have separate tone groups, whereas *I don't know* has one unified group, and this corresponds to two propositions as against one.

Whether the actual tone groups used are rising or falling is of no importance, the crucial condition is that there should be two groups in one case and one in the other. In *He ate and drank his fill* we can show in either of two ways that *his fill* is the object of both verbs. First, by using a single tone group for the whole thing, not separating either of the verbs from each other or from the object; or, secondly, we can separate both verbs from each other and from the object, by using three groups: *He ate | and drank | his fill*, rises on *ate* and on *drank* and a fall on *fill*. With the verbs treated alike there is no reason to link the object with *drank* rather than *ate*. But if we split the utterance in two by using one tone group on *He ate* and another on *and drank his fill* we are connecting *drank* more closely to the object than *ate* is: *He ate | and drank his fill* so that *ate* is taken to have no object and *his fill* is the object of *drank* alone.

To mark the descriptive as against the defining relative, as in *The umpire, who was blind, gave him out* the essential is that there should be one complete tone group on *The umpire* and a second on *who was blind*. The defining *The umpire who was blind* . . . has a single group. A different distinction is marked by the same means in *The umpire, being blind, gave him out*, which with three tone groups is equivalent to the descriptive relative (as suggested by the two commas in both); but in *The umpire being blind, he gave him out* the single tone group on *The umpire being blind* encourages the meaning 'Because the umpire was blind', by connecting the constituent words, as it does also in *The umpire being blind didn't help*. Similarly with appositions; two tone groups indicate description as in *Mr Bun, the baker*, whilst a single one indicates definition as in *John Smith the footballer* ('that particular John Smith who is a footballer') or *Dai Jenkins the fish*.

These and other distinctions are manifested by the unifying effect of the tone group, but generally speaking it serves not so much to show distinctions of this kind, but rather to identify in a positive way the major elements of grammatical structure: these would usually be deducible without the help of intonation, as they are in writing to a large extent, but we prefer to make the identifications positive. (There is some relation between punctuation in writing and the delimiting of sequences by intonation, but not a very close one – we mark far more divisions in speech than in writing). The nature of the grammatical elements is very various: it may be Subject/Predicate as in *Several of the neighbours | signed a formal petition*; or Clause/Clause: *When I realized my mistake | I was horrified*; or Phrase/Clause: *As a rule, | I hate it*; and so on. It is instructive to take any few lines of writing and try to decide how it can be divided into sequences by means of intonation. But it must be remembered that not every Subject/Predicate sequence, or Clause/Clause, or Phrase/Clause, or whatever, is divided by intonation; all the examples above may have only one tone group.

Intonation features in a tone language may have exactly the same demarcative function as the tone groups above. For example, if the typical descending sequence of alternate high and low tones in Luganda (p. 193) is followed by a high tone which is higher in pitch than the previous high tone: $\overline{}-\,-\,-\,-\,\overline{}$ this marks a syntactic division of the same order as those quoted for English above.

A second way in which intonation connects with grammar is in choice of tone group. In *People talked about it, sadly*, if we use a falling tune on *People talked about it* and a rising tune on *sadly*, we find that *sadly* is a sentence adverb and the sense is 'It was sad that people talked about it'. But if instead of the rise on *sadly* we have a fall then the adverb is connected directly to the verb, 'they talked about it, and they did it in a sad way'. (If the whole sentence has a single tone group the adverb will also be qualifying the verb directly.) So the choice of rising or falling pitch marks a difference of grammatical connection. So it does, too, in *If you go there, what will you do?* A rise at the end of *If you go there* connects it closely to the following question; a fall slackens the connection and means something like: 'Let's suppose that you go there: what will you do then?' and it would be perfectly possible to reverse the order of the clauses: *What will you do? If you go there*, which would be quite impossible with the rise on *If you go there*.

More common than this signalling of grammatical connection or disjunction is the use of different tone groups to mark differences of grammatical function. *No* and *No?* with falling and rising tone groups respectively are an example of this; the rise shows that a question is being asked, and it is the only thing that shows it (in speech, at any rate: it may well be accompanied by raised eyebrows and a generally enquiring expression). The interrogative form *Isn't it nice* with the falling tune ‿ is more of an exclamation than a question, whereas with a rise on *nice* it is a genuine enquiry. In a tag question such as *It's on Saturday, isn't it?* the tag may have either a rise or a fall; with the rise it approximates a genuine question, but with a fall it is much more rhetorical and requires only confirmation. *He won't pay for anything* may simply mean 'He'll pay for nothing', in which case it has a fall on *anything*, or it may mean 'He won't pay for rubbish', when it has a fall-rise on *anything*. A similar distinction can be made with *if* clauses: *I won't do it if you order me to* may mean 'even if . . . ', or it may mean 'Your ordering me would prevent my doing it'; in the first case *order* has a fall, in the second case a fall-rise. In *Yes, I do* falls on *Yes* and *do* generally indicate agreement; a fall on *Yes* and rise on *do* indicates disagreement.

Differences of tone, as distinct from differences of intonation, can also be used in tone languages to mark differences of grammatical function. If a word of four syllables has as its normal shape a sequence of high-low-high-low ‾ – ‾ – alteration of one of the high tones to low, giving – – ‾ – can be used to show that the word is the object of a verb, or that it is in a relative construction with neighbouring words, etc. Or a low tone might be somewhat raised in pitch, though not so much as to make it identical with high tone, for the same sort of purpose: ‗ – ‾ – .

Intonation and attitude

These distinctions of grammatical function shade imperceptibly into a use of intonation which it is hard to see as grammatical at all in any widely accepted sense of the word, though it is certainly meaningful. When the dentist says *It won't hurt* ·•⌣ the pitch pattern shows encouragement rather than factual prediction; it is a brave attempt to soothe us, to relax us. If the pattern is ·•⧵ it is much more factual, perhaps an objection to the likely ineffectiveness of some punitive measure. A different pattern again, ··⌣ introduces a critical note: 'So what are you making such a fuss about.' These are certainly significant differences – the total meanings are not the same and we do not use them in exactly the same situations – yet they are difficult to see as grammatical differences unless 'grammatical' is extended to cover all differences of meaning.

It is more satisfactory to regard differences of this kind as being differences of attitude on the part of the speaker rather than as differences of grammar. However, there is no sharp dividing line between what is grammatical and what is attitudinal: *Yes, I do* with a fall or a rise on *do* may be thought of as a predominantly grammatical difference corresponding to agreement or disagreement, or it may be thought of as a difference of attitude exactly parallel to the more factual and more critical tunes for *It won't hurt*. Some such differences seem more grammatical, some more attitudinal. Examples which are clearly at the attitude end of the scale are: *I know* as ·⧵ and ·⋏ ; the rise-fall on *know* has implications of archness or shock which are absent from the fall; *You'll fall* ·⋎ is a warning, where ·⧵ is a statement of fact; *What are you doing?* •••⋅ is a more pointed question than ••••, which sounds more sympathetic towards the listener; *Is it fair?* with a falling tune •• ⧵ is more rhetorical than with a rise at the end •• ⌣ . All these are examples of an attitude contrast carried by different selections of nuclear tones, but different selections amongst the available heads and pre-heads are also used for the same purpose. Examples are: *Did you accept it?* .... as against · · · · where the low head implies criticism and the high head does not; *I simply can't believe it* with · · · · ᴺ. is more emphatic than with · · · · ᴺ. ; there is more liveliness in *I've never heard anything so stupid* with · · · · · · ᴺ. than with · · · · · · · ᴺ. ; with the high pre-head *It wasn't* · · ᴺ is exclamatory, but with low pre-head it is not: · ᴺ · · .

Range, tempo and loudness

The range of pitch within which an intonation pattern is performed can be independently meaningful both grammatically and attitudinally. So in *I'd like – it won't take me long – to tell you a story* the restricted low range of *it won't take me long* is a clear signal of interpolation, to differentiate it from the interrupted tune of *I'd like to tell you a story*, and therefore to show that there is a direct syntactic link between *I'd like* and *to tell you a story*. Such interpolations are often accompanied by faster tempo and reduced loudness (p. 199) and any one of the three features can be used alone for this purpose. BBC newsreaders often use a range difference, generally reinforced by pause, to express direct quotation, as in the following: *Mr Smith expressed the view that it was 'a gross extravagance'* . The pause before *a* acts like the opening quotation mark, and the widening of the range marks the actual words of the speaker. This widening is often reinforced by extra loudness.

A particularly interesting use of range is to bind together several successive sequences, each having its own separate tone group, into a larger unit, as in the following: *He looked at it; he admired it; and he bought it. And after he'd bought it ...* . The gradually descending range of the first three tone groups holds them together as parts of a longer sequence corresponding to one section of the narration; the subsequent widening of the range on *And after he'd bought it* marks this off as the beginning of a new section. Similarly in *After I'd seen him, after I'd spoken to him* . . . the lower range of the second group coordinates the two clauses and is more or less equivalent to *and* between them; but if the range is the same for both this may be a new beginning, the second clause correcting the first, and this would certainly be so with a quickened tempo on the second.

Apart from these grammatical functions of range there are obviously attitudinal functions as well; if *Very good* is said in a restricted high range it sounds less than enthusiastic; the same pattern in a restricted low range sounds sincere but not emotional; with a wide range it sounds both sincere and enthusiastic. A response like *Did you?* with a rising tune of very restricted range, whether high, medium or low, tends to sound apathetic or bored: and some widening of the pitch difference between *Did* and *you* is essential if that is to be avoided. A very wide range indicates astonishment: The range difference may apply to the whole tone group, as above, or it may be restricted to the nuclear tone. Compare *I didn't want to go there anyway* with and and where the pre-nuclear part of the tone group has a wide range in each case but the range of the fall differs.

Tempo can be used to express attitude, too, independently of range. Fast tempo may be associated with anger. *What are you doing?* said with quicker than normal tempo sounds at least impatient; and drawling, or slower than normal tempo, has long been associated with relaxation: compare fast, medium and slow utterances of *I can't be bothered*. But slow tempo may be used to underline important parts of the utterance, to show that the speaker regards them as crucial. So in: *I want you to listen to this very carefully* there may be a quite sudden and quite dramatic slowing of tempo on *very carefully*. Conversely, words can be thrown away by an increase of speed; in saying *I'm very well, how are you?* to a friend who has been ill we may dismiss *I'm very well* with fast tempo and immediately switch to slow tempo to express concern in *how are you?*

Differences in loudness are often indicative of differences in strength of feeling; extra loudness may affect whole sequences or only the stressed syllables, so in *It was very, very pleasant* there may be a generally increased loudness over the whole utterance, or affecting only the first syllables of *very* and *pleasant*. And we quite often find a contrast between particularly loud stressed syllables and particularly soft unstressed syllables as in *She was absolutely marvellous* where *ab-* and *mar-* are made especially loud and the remaining syllables virtually whispered. Abnormally reduced loudness over sequences may be illustrated by *Gently, dear* where the softness exemplifies the sentiment required or *It was terrible* where it signals anguish rather than anger.

Voice quality and attitude

The actual way in which the vocal cords vibrate may also be used to express the speaker's attitude. Breathy voice, for instance, is often associated with awe or shock, as when we use it with *No!* in response to some particularly outrageous piece of information; or the same *No!* may be used to dismiss a proposition out of hand. It may suggest ungovernable passion: *I love you*, or the last straw: *Oh, no*. Creaky voice may be used rather like extra loudness to indicate strength of feeling as with *Terrible!* or *Marvellous!* and it may also be used to suggest a considered sort of attitude: *I'm not sure*. It frequently accompanies very low pitches in intonation, but then it is not significant. Falsetto is not uncommon in reaching higher than normal pitches for expressive purposes, so an extra wide fall on *Wonderful!* may drop from high falsetto to very low creaky voice. Whisper over sequences is generally conspiratorial but it may also be used on unstressed syllables in contrast with normal or creaky voice on the stressed syllables, as in *Fantastic!* where *Fan-* and *-tic* are whispered.

A large number of the attitude markers mentioned above may combine together to produce composite effects. So in *Absolutely terrible* we could have the following:

1. Choice of nuclear tone – rise fall.

2. Pitch range: extra high on *Absolutely*: restricted low range on *terrible*.

3. Loudness: normal on *Absolutely*, extra loud on *terr-*, extra soft on *-ible*.

4. Tempo: extra slow on *Absolutely*, normal on *terrible*. Lengthening of *-bs-* in *Absolutely* and perhaps *-e-* in *terrible*.

5. Voice: falsetto on *Absolutely*, creaky on *terr-*, whisper on *-ible*.

The attitude markers are sometimes thought of as luxuries, the icing on the top, with word markers and grammatical sequence markers as the solid cake. But this is hardly true; it is only necessary to listen attentively to the sounds of lively conversation to hear these markers occurring with some frequency. And in one sense at least they are of greater importance than the actual words we use, because if there is any conflict between words and attitude markers, the latter invariably prevail. For example, *Thank you very much* looks civil enough on the page, and so it is in speech unless the attitude markers negative the civility. This can be done by, for instance, saying it in a restricted high range ‾•‾•‾•‾•‾ when it sounds casual; or by saying it extra slowly, when it may sound sinister; or extra quickly, which sounds perfunctory; or extra loudly, which might be from anger. In particular, the enormous use we make of intonation in marking attitudes is constantly acting upon and modifying the basic meanings of the words we use. Take *I love you* again and assume normal loudness, tempo and voice: then ‾•ˋ•‾ is true love; ‾•ˋ•‾ is protest; ‾•ˋ✓‾ has reservations; ‾•••‾ is critical; ‾•ˌ•‾

i.e. 'not just *like* you.' These characterizations are facile, but the point is that the differences are there and we react to them very strongly and very quickly. 'Tone of voice' plays a very big part in our affairs and a great deal of the total information that we communicate is carried by these non-verbal means.

Tone of voice and universals

Perhaps because of the non-verbal nature of attitude markers it is commonly imagined that they, like gesture, are universal in their application, and that what conveys a particular attitude in one language will convey the same attitude in another. But despite our feelings about it, gestures do not have universal application: in much of Southern Europe a backward toss of the head which looks something like a nod, stands for 'No,' and a sideways shake for 'Yes,' and beckoning someone to come nearer is done with the palm facing them rather than facing the beckoner. These are conventions, though they are often accepted over wider areas than that covered by a single language. In just the same way we cannot expect that the sort of attitudes which we express in English by the markers discussed above will necessarily be marked in the same way in other languages, or indeed that another language will express in any way at all the very same attitudes that English expresses. Different languages are not simply different clothings of the same underlying reality; if they were they would resemble codes much more closely than they do, and all we would need in order to transfer from one language to another would be a simple one-to-one key to the code. A language is a very efficient tool which has been developed to deal with situations in a particular place at a particular time and it will have the means to deal with whatever it needs to deal with in that framework; a society which has only one meal a day is not likely to have ready-made terms for breakfast, lunch, tea, supper, dinner, and even within the British Isles one must be cautious in interpreting lunch, tea, dinner at least. So we must certainly not assume that every language will want to be able to express, say, the attitude marked by the fall-rise tone in English, as in *Two* ⤵ , or by breathy voice, as in *No!* On the one hand the language may distinguish several different attitudes within that particular area and on the other it may not differentiate that attitude at all.

This topic is bedevilled by the lack of agreed categories and terms for dealing with attitudes; they have been characterized here by terms such as 'conspiratorial, awe, concern, perfunctory' etc., etc., more with an eye to identifying them to the reader than to classifying them in an orderly scheme, and until some method of dealing with attitudes is developed along very much more scientific lines than is possible at present, we shall not even be able to tell whether this language and that are similar or different in the number and nature of attitudes they can mark. In the meantime we may presume that there are experiences common to the whole of humanity to which reference can be made in all languages and we may be able to identify at least some of these common features and the different methods which different languages use to express them. Provided that we proceed with caution and with a full realization of the incompleteness of our framework not much harm can be done, but any conclusions must remain tentative.

Where we can identify common attitudes, within the above limits, we are on much firmer ground in saying that the means of marking them will differ from language to language. There may be universals; for example, anger might always be accompanied by extra tension of the musculature which could result in extra breath effort and extra loudness; but it need not, since the extra energy could be absorbed in a strained vibration of the vocal cords and no extra loudness. In that case the universal would be the extra muscular effort, and extra loudness and strained vocal cord vibration would be equally likely to represent anger from the listener's end. But we cannot assume that universals of this kind exist, and there are enough cases of obviously conventional means of marking various attitudes to make us chary of claiming universality lightly. We saw earlier (p. 192) that in Mandarin 'impatience' can be expressed by using a restricted high range, but even if the label is grossly imprecise the same range in English has nothing to do with patience or impatience or anything within that general area. In any case we should expect this kind of variety, having regard to the different parts that the different sound features play at different levels. If pitch is an essential part of word-shape, as in tone languages, the part that pitch can play in indicating attitude must be limited by the necessity for keeping words distinct: it can still play this role but some of the options open to a purely intonation language are closed to the tone language. Or if breathy voice is part of word-shape, as in various Indian languages, the possibility of using it for expressive purposes will be much less than in English, where it is never part of word-shape.

Neither sound nor any other single component of the linguistic complex is solely responsible for the meanings which language is all about: each plays its part and it is only after completing the whole process of matching the known possibilities of the language and of the situation and of the culture with the incoming signal and settling for the best possible fit that communication can be said to have taken place. But sound plays a respectable part in the process by the possibility that it has of giving shape to words and word formatives, and marking their boundaries; of shaping higher level sequences like Phrase, Clause, Subject, Predicate and marking their boundaries; and still higher-level sequences of these elements in sentences or groups of sentences; and it has means for going beyond this to the conventional expression of the speaker's attitudes and feelings. Go beyond these highly controllable aspects of sound in speech to the uncontrollable ones of individual voice quality and sex and age, and it is clear that the amount of information carried by sound is both enormous and enormously complex. Some of it we know about but there is a great deal more to be learned both about what sounds are – phonetics – and what they do – phonology.

9. Present and Future

What use is Phonetics? It is a common enough question and the immediate (and often least welcome) answer is that like any other branch of study it advances our knowledge of what things are and how they work in a certain limited area. If the advancement of knowledge is a sufficient reason for the existence of any discipline, then it is sufficient for phonetics. But if the questioner is thinking of more concrete uses, they are not lacking and it may be of interest to give some account of these and of what we may expect to come from future researches.

Language analysis

There are still hundreds upon hundreds of unwritten languages in the world and it is very desirable that they should be given written form, to the advantage of the users of the language and the linguist. Quite certainly the most satisfactory method of reducing languages to writing is based on sound. We could, as is more or less the case with Chinese, contemplate giving a separate written character to every word of the language but this is not an economical solution; the large number of different characters which it would be necessary to learn in order to be able to cope with even a restricted vocabulary would make prohibitive demands on the learner. In those languages which have a simple syllabic structure and therefore a relatively small number of different syllables it might be profitable to produce a syllabary, giving to each separate syllable a separate character, so that a four-syllabled word would be represented by four successive characters; this is already a sound-based system. Or we might divide the syllable into two parts, an initial and a final, for example /str-/ in English *strong* would be represented by one symbol and /-ɒŋ/ by another.

This would work in languages which do not have too many initials and finals. But it would not be at all economical for a language like English which has literally thousands of different syllables and hundreds of initials and finals, so for English we would arrive at an alphabetic system, also sound-based. An alphabetic system is a system based upon the identification of phonemes, each phoneme being given a separate letter-shape to represent it. A word is then represented by a sequence of letters representing the phonemes, plus some representation of any other essential feature of word-shape, e.g. stress or tone. The representation of stress or tone may be in line with the representation of phonemes, or it may be handled differently; for example stress could be shown as we have shown it here by ['] before the appropriate syllable or an accent above the appropriate letter – so *be'fore* or *befóre* – or we could capitalize the vowel letter – *befOre*. If, as in English, the phonemic shape, as represented by letters, is sufficient identification for practical purposes, stress marking can be omitted. Similarly with tone: it may be represented by either marks like our tone mark, e.g. 'mà' or 'ˋma' for a falling tone and 'mā' or 'ˉma' for high level, etc. or it may be done by adding a letter-shape with only a tonal value, so 'maf' meaning 'ma with falling tone' and 'mal' meaning 'ma with level tone', and the like. In Chinese some form of tone marking is essential because there are too many words which would be homophonous without it, but in a language like Xhosa there are very few words which are not sufficiently distinguished by their phonemic shape, even though each syllable has its own tone, and therefore Xhosa orthography is viable without tone marking, as English is without stress marks.

Then it is desirable that words and word formatives should

always have the same shape in writing, so that conditioned variations like /ʌn-, ʌŋ-, ʌm-/ in *unseen*, *unkind*, *unpleasant* will retain an invariant form; it is also desirable that related words with differing pronunciations like *photograph*, *photography* or *nation*, *national*, should be shown to be related by their spelling; and if the writing is to serve a whole language community, provision must be made for differences of phoneme systems and of phoneme occurrence among accents; it is right that *horse* and *hoarse* and *caught* and *court* should be spelt differently in English because many accents differentiate them in speech.

So alphabetic writing of a language is by no means identical with a phonemic transcription, but it is nevertheless dependent in the first place upon an adequate phonemic analysis of the language and without it no satisfactory orthography of this kind can be developed. Similarly, any scheme for spelling reform in those languages, like English and Irish, whose orthography is to a greater or lesser extent at variance with pronunciation, must take account of the phonemes whilst bearing in mind the special demands of an orthography mentioned above. It would probably save a good deal of time and effort and frustration among children learning to read such languages and the teachers teaching them if anomalies such as *pear*, *dear* and *seat*, *head* and *though*, *bough*, *enough*, *cough* could be eliminated. But it is quite unlikely to happen for English in the immediate future, beyond the sort of tinkering represented by American spellings such as the respectable *humor* and the less respectable *nite*, *sox*. Too many of us have learned to handle the present orthography and therefore have a vested interest in it for there to be any widespread support for schemes of spelling reform such as that of the Simplified Spelling Society in this country.

In more general terms, the deeper analysis of particular aspects of one language and the wider analysis of more and more languages can bring great profit by providing a clearer understanding of the way in which the human brain works. For example, investigations into the development of speech in children seem to show that distinctions between different sounds are acquired in a dichotomous way by successive splits of formerly unitary items. So the basic syllable /pɑ/ splits in two at the earliest stage into an opposition /pɑ ∼ mɑ/ or /pɑ ∼ ɑ/ or /pɑ ∼ tɑ/. Then comes /pɑ ∼ pu ∼ tɑ ∼ tu/ or /pɑ ∼ pi ∼ tɑ ∼ ti/, where the single vowel is split, and so on until over a period of years the child can handle all the oppositions that the language uses. If this type of development is universal it is a strong indication of a very basic binary principle at work in the brain. Furthermore it seems possible that people whose speech is impaired by brain damage or deterioration lose the oppositions of sound in the reverse order from that in which a child acquires them, the last learned being the first to go. If this is proved, it will be important to our understanding of how information is stored in the brain.

If, in investigating different languages, we can show that all the sound distinctions they exhibit can be referred to a limited number of distinctive features (p. 204 ff.) it will explain a great deal about our ability to derive subtle and complex systems from basically simple beginnings. And when we show that the complicated output of a speaker is referable to a relatively small number of interacting categories (such as pitch range, choice of tone group, tempo, voice quality, etc.) and if we can then show that this is not merely a 'Hocus-pocus' procedure on the part of the analyst but validated by the way in which a listener copes with what he hears, we shall be a good way towards understanding the way in which the brain processes all kinds of incoming signals.

Language teaching

Back on the practical level, the progressively deepening study of all aspects of languages makes more efficient and successful foreign-language teaching possible, and this is true of the pronunciation aspect. It is still very widely believed that the *only* way to acquire a good pronunciation of a foreign language is to go and live amongst native speakers – this is however not true. In the first place, we must all have come across examples of foreign speakers who have lived for years and years in a particular community and never acquired an even approximately native pronunciation. And secondly, there are plenty of foreign speakers who, on their first visit to England, already have an extremely competent pronunciation because they have been well taught. Very few people can be brought to perfection in this respect, but good teaching can effect an improvement to at least respectability of pronunciation, and it seems a waste, if we are interested in speaking a foreign language, to be doing it less well than we might.

The basis of good pronunciation teaching is a knowledge of the systems and structures of both languages. If the native language has a five-vowel system /i $\sim$ ɛ $\sim$ ɑ $\sim$ ɔ $\sim$ u/ and the target language a seven-vowel one /i $\sim$ e $\sim$ ɛ $\sim$ ɑ $\sim$ ɔ $\sim$ o $\sim$ u/ we not only know that there is going to be difficulty in establishing two extra phonemes for the target language but we also know where the trouble is likely to be, namely, in distinguishing /e/ from /i/ on the one hand and /ɛ/ on the other, and similarly /o/ from /ɔ/ and /u/, and we can set about devising material for helping. Equally, if we know that initial consonants always come singly in the structure of the native syllable, and in clusters of up to three, as in English, in the target language, we can see why it is that the learner says /esteɪ/ or /seɪ/ for *stay*. But knowing about systems and structures is only the background: we also need a good knowledge of the realizations of the different phonemes in both languages. For example, in teaching the difference between *beat* and *bead* /biːt, biːd/ to a French speaker we have to be aware that in French there is no difference in the lengths of the two vowels (whereas in English the difference is considerable), that /t/ and /d/ are both realized with dental articulation in French but alveolar in English and that the difference between /t/ and /d/ is largely a voiceless/voiced opposition in French, but in English a mainly fortis/lenis one. An awareness of all the discrepancies of these kinds and a knowledge of how they are produced articulatorily and perceived auditorily will make it easier to give effective instructions to the learner about what to do and what to listen for. Similarly with longer structures: it is necessary to know that Spanish and French have rhythms based on the individual syllable whereas English rhythm is based on the stressed syllable, and the implications of this for syllable lengths in the three languages. We need to know that English tone groups have a tripartite structure of pre-head, head and nucleus whereas French has only head and nucleus, and that both the choices and the realizations at the head and nucleus positions are different in the two.

Most of all phonetics can give the teacher the ability to make quick decisions about sounds by training his auditory memory, strengthening his capacity to relate what he hears to how it was produced and developing in him the capacity to give well-based instructions which will help the learner. The learner himself does not need to know a lot of phonetic theory, but a certain amount plus a lot of pertinent practice under close supervision will help him to put aside the strait-jacket of his native speech habits and slip into those of the target language. This sounds easy, but it is far from easy in fact and requires a great deal of patience and resolution.

Speech therapy

Infinitely more patience and resolution are required when the learner, instead of being a normal hearing person, is a congenitally deaf child who cannot develop his own native speech spontaneously because he cannot hear either himself or others. Teaching such children to speak by concentrating on articulation and on what they can perceive through their other senses is tremendously devoted, laborious and difficult work. To help the deaf to speak so that they can be understood by their hearing fellows, even if the quality of their speech is poor, is to give them a priceless gift, which the normal person takes very much for granted. The difficulty of the task both for teacher and child is a measure of the enormous importance of hearing to communication.

When the acoustic spectrograph was first developed it was hoped that it would prove to be a powerful aid in the teaching of the deaf, by providing a visual record of the patient's efforts, so that he could gradually match these to the visual patterns provided by the teacher and thus have a visual check on the sounds coming from his mouth, a mouth-to-eye feedback instead of the normal mouth-to-ear one. But it is exceedingly difficult even for a hearing person, with all the stored knowledge he has gained from using and hearing speech, to interpret spectrograph patterns, and all the more so for the congenitally deaf who have never used or heard it, and the spectrograph has therefore not been of great help.

Other types of speech defect can be very serious, notably those due to massive brain damage, but at least hearing is not impaired and can be used in the rehabilitation process, provided that the damage is not too widespread. The types of speech defects which can best be handled by entirely phonetic methods are purely articulatory defects like [ɬ] (the voiceless alveolar lateral fricative) for /s/, and [ʋ] or [ʁ] (labiodental or uvular frictionless continuants) for /r/. These can be treated much like the foreigner's failures in realization, by simple articulatory instruction and training in discrimination.

Of the same order but greater difficulty is the problem of the cleft-palate patient. This congenital defect consists of a failure of the two sides of the palate to knit together along the median line during antenatal development, and consequent inability of the patient to prevent air passing into the nasal cavity through the cleft in the palate. Nothing can be done about this until the cleft is repaired, but once this has been accomplished by the very skilful surgical techniques now available it is still necessary to teach the patient how to use the soft palate in its valvular role of preventing air from escaping through the nose. Whether the cleft has been in the front or back of the palate, the patient will not have learnt to control soft-palate movement since, even if it was intact, it could never prevent air passing through the cleft. In addition, if the soft palate itself was cleft the surgical repair may not have been able to provide entirely normal muscular function in the soft palate, so that exercises must, and can, be provided to develop control over its raising and lowering. Also the patient may have developed substitute articulations for those made ineffective by the cleft, e.g. substituting [?] for other plosives or pharyngal for other fricatives, and these must be replaced by normal articulations. This often proves to be a lengthy and difficult task, which is why surgeons prefer to repair the cleft very early, before the child has learned to speak, so that it can learn normal soft-palate function from the beginning.

More difficult still are laryngectomy cases, when patients have had to have the larynx removed because of disease. This entails not only the absence of the vocal cords, so that normal voice is impossible, but also absence of a usable breath stream, since the windpipe is closed at the top to prevent food, etc. from passing down the air passages into the lungs, and the patient breathes through a tracheotomy tube in the neck. There are two solutions to this problem: first, a buzzer, which may be kept permanently in the mouth or applied externally to the throat and to which the cavities resonate as they do to vocal cord vibration. This produces continuously voiced speech because the buzzing is continuous, and it is on a monotone and rather weak; also no fricative or plosive sounds are possible, for obvious reasons, though the movements of the vocal organs will produce the transitions normally associated with such sounds. The second solution, œsophageal speech, depends on the possibility of drawing air into the œsophagus or food-passage and expelling it to produce vibration of the sphincter at the top of the œsophagus: in other words, a controlled belch. This rather rough vibration is used to cause resonance in the cavities. However, the amount of air available from the œsophagus is very small compared with that from the lungs and its use is best limited to the non-friction sounds like vowels, nasals, laterals, frictionless continuants, which are entirely dependent on resonance. For the plosives and fricatives it is best to use the pharynx-air mechanism, which is still available, and therefore make all these sounds ejective. This preserves the precious œsophageal air for those sounds which cannot be made otherwise. A word like *strike* will then have all its consonants made ejectively and only the diphthong /aɪ/ with œsophageal air. The fortis/lenis pairs /p, b/, /s, z/ etc. can be distinguished by differences of energy in air pressure and articulation. Once the speaker has learned to handle the two air mechanisms and coordinate them well his speech is very intelligible, though it is difficult to regulate the sphincter vibrations to give controlled pitch patterns.

Communications

Research into the properties of speech, particularly into the relation between acoustic structure and perception in a given language framework, is contributing continuously to improvement in communication systems. It is no accident that the Bell Telephone Co. in the United States and the Post Office in this country, as well as many other organizations concerned with communication links, undertake research of this kind, since the development of more efficient and economical apparatus depends upon a knowledge of what frequencies and amplitudes it is essential to transmit and what may be omitted without making the result unacceptable to the listener; and the evaluation of telephone systems, radio links, recording apparatus and the like is ultimately based on what the ear hears.

Sophisticated methods have been developed to assess differences in efficiency in the transmission characteristics of such systems; known, rather oddly, as *articulation tests* – they test recognition rather than articulation in the sense in which we use the word – they provide a reasonably accurate means of comparison between one system and another and also of establishing norms of hearing from which degrees of deafness can be judged; this has obvious practical advantages in determining what compensation is appropriate in cases of deafness caused by war or occupational hazard. Combined with experimentation designed to specify the performance of the normal and deafened ear at different frequencies in the speech spectrum they have contributed to our knowledge of both degree and type of deafness, and this has made possible the development of hearing-aids better adapted to the particular needs of the user. Looking at the producer rather than the receiver of speech, this also affords us a rational method of assessing a speaker's efficiency over a given link, in cases where such efficiency is important, as for instance with air-traffic controllers: intelligibility in these circumstances is probably conditioned more by the clarity of the speaker than by variations in efficiency of the hearer, and any shortcomings on the speaker's part may lead to danger. This can be countered either by removal of the demonstrably indistinct speaker or by improving his performance.

Our knowledge of the auditory and acoustic aspects of speech has progressed far enough for it to be possible now to produce reasonable synthesis of speech by rule; that is, we can store rules in a computer so that when we subsequently feed it a sequence of phonemes it will operate a speech-synthesizing machine, according only to our rules, to produce electronically the changing frequencies and intensities which will enable the message to be understood. We are therefore within measurable distance of a speech typewriter which would give high grade speech simply from typing out the words of the message.

The future

In the past hundred years or so we have learned a very great deal about the production, transmission and reception of speech, but there are many areas in which we would like to know a lot more, both in order to satisfy our legitimate human curiosity and because practical advantages invariably accrue sooner or later from increased understanding. Some of these areas are discussed below.

Lung action

We are still fairly ignorant about details of the connection between the action of the lungs and that of the articulators. We need to know more about the contribution of the relevant muscles to the breath impulses which we produce in speech, how the breathing apparatus contributes to stress and loudness, what is its relation to vocal cord vibrations of different kinds, what variations of pressure and air flow are associated with different sounds or syllables or rhythm groups. Is there, for instance, a difference in the action of the lungs in the marking of junctures such as *grey tape* and *great ape* or *more ice* and *more rice* which would enable us to explain in a more general way than at present the many different allophones which signal the junctures; are the allophones conditioned by a variation in pressure at word boundaries, which would account in one step for all the detailed differences between initial /t/ and final /t/, initial /r/ and final /r/ etc. etc.? And what differences are there in the action of the lungs in different languages? What is the connection, if any, between lung action and rhythm in languages with a staccato, syllable-based rhythm like French and Spanish and Hindi, and those with a broader, stress-based rhythm like English and German and Russian? Instruments such as the pneumotachograph, for measuring speed of respiration, and techniques such as electromyography, the detection of electrical activity in muscles, are already available for researches of this kind, and there is no reason why, with further refinement in instrumentation and techniques, the answers to all the above questions should not be forthcoming quite soon.

Vocal cord function

Part of the difficulty in learning more about how the vocal cords work is the matter of getting at them for observation purposes. We can do this by means of laryngoscopy, but this involves introducing a mirror into the oro-pharynx and this may interfere with the working of the vocal cords. Even discounting this, the view of the vocal cords from above does not show clearly everything that we would like to know, though, backed by high-speed photography, it has taught us a good deal of what we know about the movements of the vocal cords in various states of the glottis. But there is still more that we would like to know about the differences in vocal cord vibration in different types of voice: breathy, creaky, hoarse, various whispers and combinations of some of these. The control of rate of vibration in pitch changes and the relation between this and breath pressure are also imperfectly understood. And it would be good to know just how the vocal cords and the breath stream interact to set up the complex harmonic structure of the vibrations which are differentially amplified by resonance in the upper tract and on which the recognition of individual voices must presumably depend, at least in part. It seems likely that before long we may be able to get an answer to this last question, i.e. what is the relative contribution of vocal cord vibration and resonance in the upper cavities to our ability to recognize people by voice?

The laryngograph is an electrical device which enables the state of opening or closure of the vocal cords to be deduced from a record of the way a current passes from one side of the larynx to the other. A trace of this record can then be reconverted into sound and this will represent the result of vocal cord action with no resonance effect from the upper tract – as if we could cut off everything above the larynx and hear only the vocal cords vibrating. The laryngograph also has the virtue that it does not interfere with articulation at all, unlike laryngoscopy, and that it is noiseless, unlike the high-speed camera, which means that it can be combined with recordings of the sounds produced. It should be possible to get a great deal of the information we seek by relating the traces given by the machine to the corresponding sounds and their acoustic structure; we may ultimately achieve an integrated classification of voice qualities, both normal and pathological, something at present lacking.

Voice production

It may seem surprising that there is very little precise information available about what is a 'good' voice and what a 'bad' and how this kind of aesthetic judgement relates to the actions of the vocal organs and to the acoustic structure of the sound produced. It is probably necessary in the first place to set up an auditory scheme, perhaps like the cardinal vowel system, which would account for the different quality of different voices. Given that, we could then investigate the articulatory and acoustic features which differentiate them and arrive at some estimate of the contribution of various factors to our auditorily based judgements. Factors which suggest themselves are breath control, vocal cord action, cavity size and shape, vigour of articulation, and, acoustically, the nature of the periodic vibrations of the fundamental, formant intensity and bandwidth, and the contribution of the higher formants which seem to play so small a part in primary recognition of differences of vowel quality in a strictly linguistic function. And since we cannot by any means assume that every language community will have the same views about what is good or bad, effective or ineffective, we would need to extend the research to different languages.

This would make it possible to say just what it is that differentiates one person's speech from another's when they have the same accent and are apparently, so far as we can express it within our present framework, saying 'the same thing'. It has certainly been necessary in the past to concentrate largely on what is *common* to different speakers, since it is the common element which primarily serves communication, and indeed we still do not know all that there is to be known about these common, conventional features; but to pay attention to the aesthetic and the idiosyncratic may not only enlarge our understanding in those areas, it may also give more power to our methods of classifying and explaining the whole of speech.

Pitch

Quite apart from the desirability of knowing more about the control of vocal cord vibration and its frequency, there is still a great deal to be found out about the way pitch functions in languages. We know something of the workings of many tone languages, we know a lot about the intonation of English and something about other intonation languages, but we know very little, for instance, about how tone and intonation interact in tone languages and what categories of, for example, range and pattern shape must be set up to deal with the complex pitch patterns actually found in such languages. It seems likely that the more complex the tonal system is, the less pitch can be used for intonation purposes: if Cantonese has six tones, one of which must be applied distinctively to each syllable, there will presumably be less possibility of other types of pitch variation than there would be in Mandarin, with only four tones. But this supposition needs far more testing than it has had.

Most work on tone and intonation has been carried out by ear and this is right, since what matters is relative not absolute pitch, but if the system is established in that way there is then no bar to investigating what pitches and ranges of pitch in absolute, musical terms correspond to the functional patterns. Knowledge of this kind would be helpful in the further development of speech synthesis by rule, and it is only when such synthesis is developed to the point where it is totally accepted as speech that we can be satisfied that we at last know the relation between the linguistic message and its acoustic shape.

Where every worker on intonation is particularly unhappy at the present time is in the domain of meaning. This is not strictly a phonetic problem, and the phonetician may be satisfied simply to say that a rise and a fall in pitch on *No* do mean something different (without saying what), and therefore they are distinct terms in the system, and leave it at that. But one cannot help feeling dissatisfaction at being unable to define such differences of meaning in a coherent way, and one of the great advances in this field in the future will be the elucidation of meaning as carried by intonation. It may have to await the appearance of a new general theory of meaning, which is in any case badly needed, but we must have it before we can for instance teach the intonation of a foreign language in anything but a rather vague and unsatisfactory way.

Articulation

What we most need to develop here is a scheme for describing articulation and accounting for its dynamics. It is easy to fall into the trap of thinking that there are certain extreme positions which correspond to vowels and consonants, and that we hold one of these positions for a certain time and then move smartly to the next and so on. But it has been realized for a long time that articulation is continuous, and cineradiography has made it quite plain that the organs of speech are never still during the course of an utterance. Yet we continue to describe sound sequences in a way that suggests a series of jerks from one static position to another, and this is not helped by the traditional type of articulatory diagram used in this as in other books, showing a fixed position of the articulators and labelled [k] or [s] or whatever. Now there is some truth in these diagrams, they do represent a position that has to be gone through or approximated during an utterance, but what we badly need is more information about how a series of articulatory movements affect each other, and how a movement or movements of one articulator relates to time: for example, in *did* and *kick* what difference do the different starting and end points make to the vowel articulation we recognize as [ɪ] between them? And whilst we know that the tongue will never be still from beginning to end of either word, is there some slowing down of movement corresponding to the closed phase of [d] and [k] or the openest phase of [ɪ]? There is some indication that differences of articulation linked to differences in what precedes and/or follows can be accounted for as deviations from an ideal position and the actual articulatory movements calculated from that position, but we need to study actual records of dynamic articulation a great deal more before we are in any position of certainty. The development of cineradiography to the point where one person could be exposed for long periods to the X-rays without danger of tissue damage would undoubtedly help here: we have been hampered by the limited amount of material we can get from one speaker, and we really need a considerable amount of controlled material if we are to be able to make the necessary measurements and draw conclusions.

If we were able to substantiate the hypothesis suggested above, that an ideal position might serve as a base for calculating actual positions in different surroundings, it might be a valuable clue to the way in which the brain controls articulation. Articulatory movements are of an incredible complexity, but perhaps this results not from an equally complex series of commands from the brain but rather from a succession of relatively simple commands for the articulators to move to certain positions – only the effects of one command are overtaken by the effects of the next and therefore modify it to cause the complexity. In concrete terms, the brain may always command the tongue to do the same thing for [ɪ], but previous and subsequent commands to produce [d-d] or [k-k] will affect the actual movements achieved. We hope to approach this control problem from the other end in the future and investigate the control mechanism in the brain and the nervous system direct, but that is not possible at present and we must get what clues we can from the articulatory and acoustic ends. Changes of acoustic patterns have already been helpful, both in establishing the fact of continuous articulatory change, and in suggesting what articulatory movements to look for. Detailed exploration of connection between cavity shape and the acoustic output is already making progress, but it will not be completely understood until our methods of specifying the very complicated, changing shapes of the cavities are further refined.

A different subject which will certainly repay investigation is the different *bases of articulation* of different languages, that is, general differences in tension, in tongue shape, in pressure of the articulators, in lip and cheek and jaw posture and movement, which run through the whole articulatory process. Comparing English and French, for example, in English the lips and jaw move little, in French they move much more, with vigorous lip-rounding and spreading: the cheeks are relaxed in English but tensed in French: the tongue-tip is tenser in English and more used than in French, where the blade is dominant, and so on. We know a good deal more about the detailed articulatory movements in a language than we know about the general articulatory background on which they are superimposed, and with greater knowledge we might be able to explain in these terms a great many differences in sound between languages, which at present puzzle us. And the basis of articulation has already been shown to be important in foreign-language teaching: better results are achieved when the learner gets the basis of articulation right rather than trying for the foreign sound sequences from the basis of his own language.

We could also probably shed some light on this subject by

studying mimicry. We do not know at all how it is that some people are able to mimic others to the point where they really sound like them, but it seems likely that it has something to do with basis of articulation as well as with accent, voice quality, rhythm and the like, since one can get all these latter things right and still not sound very like the other person. This probably accounts, too, for the fact that a mimic not knowing a word of a foreign language can nevertheless give the impression of speaking that language with a stream of nonsense, and we might learn something fundamental about the nature of articulation if we were to investigate these abilities. It might help in this direction to look at the speech of those identical twins or other (generally) close relatives whose pronunciation is uncommonly similar and confusible, to determine whether there is a common basis of articulation – as opposed to the other factors mentioned above – which sets them off from the rest.

Nasality is another topic which we certainly do not know all about. Clearly it is connected with air passing into the nasal cavity and perhaps for most of us that is all. But there are disturbing cases where a cleft-palate patient has had the cleft repaired and apparently learned to operate the soft palate correctly, and yet retained a high degree of nasality. Is there some other articulatory factor which can produce the same impression as air passing into the nose, some particular shape of the pharynx perhaps? It would be a great service to many cleft-palate patients disappointed by the results of their operation and post-operative training if we could find this factor and devise methods for its elimination.

All in all, despite the fact that articulation has been studied for longer and more intensely than any other aspect of pronunciation there is still a lot that we do not know and that it would be of great interest to find out; not only because it would bring new information but because it would force us to enlarge and give greater generality to our framework of reference in articulatory matters. The study of articulation has been given a fillip by the interest of acoustic phoneticians in the relation between their acoustic findings and the ways in which the acoustic patterns are produced; a good deal of what we are learning at the moment comes from this source and will no doubt continue to do so in the future.

Child speech and aphasia

The study of how children gradually acquire the pronunciation features and systems and structures which are the common property of their language group, and the ways in which pronunciation is impaired by functional damage to the brain can both tell us more than we have yet learned from them about the way in which pronunciation is controlled by the brain. We already know a good deal about the stages a child goes through in differentiating the necessary terms in the phoneme system but we know comparatively little about his acquisition of other systems such as stress, intonation, rhythm, whose development may not be at all parallel to the acquisition of phonemes; and research here might go far towards explaining why it is that such systems seem to be more basic than the phoneme system in so far as they are much more difficult to replace by foreign systems in learning other languages. If our first experiences of communication turned out to be closely linked to intonation it would not be surprising that this should cling to us very tenaciously. In progressive deterioration of speech capacity we should also get some idea of what is shallower in its roots in the brain and what deeper.

We know that the average adult speaker of a language makes use of multiple cues in recognizing a particular linguistic distinction, for example, that breath effort, pitch, length and vowel quality all point together towards the place of stress in English. Experiments have shown that adults use all these cues in differing degree to identify the placing of stress, but we do not know that this is true for children or for aphasics, and we have no right to suppose it is so without investigation. Just as the child develops systems gradually and just as the aphasic may lose them gradually, so too the ability to make use of several cues to the same linguistic distinction may well be something that is gradually acquired or lost, and if we find a consistent order of acquisition or loss we shall understand more about the development of recognition and perception in human beings and the relatively deep or shallow nature of a certain feature, such as length, in its contribution to a particular distinction like stress.

Experimentation in these fields is not easy and probably a good deal of what we find will come from observing the uncontrolled speech of children and aphasics, but controlled listening experiments have been carried out with quite young children and there is no reason to suppose that these cannot be deepened and extended. However, articulation is another matter, and though it would be of great interest to know how articulatory control develops throughout childhood to its final form, it is difficult to see how this can be investigated directly at the moment. No doubt harmless methods will be devised, but for the time being we must rely on auditory and acoustic analysis, and informed deduction from these, as to the likely articulators. The child is father of the man in speech too, and child speech may well hold the keys to many of the problems of articulation control and of recognition which we find in adult behaviour.

Universals and typology

As has already been pointed out (p. 209), it is possible to envisage the establishment of an agreed set of distinctive features which could characterize the make-up of all the phonemic oppositions found in the world's languages, and that this universal set of features could be used to order languages on a scale of similarity and difference in their use and combination of the features. The search for language universals, those properties of language itself which all languages exhibit, is engaging a lot of attention at the moment. Universals are rooted in the innate capacity of the human being to acquire language in whatever community he is born into or adopted into in infancy, and their main importance is to throw light on that capacity. If it is a phonetic universal that utterances are specifiable as a succession of phonemes, and that phonemes are specifiable as bundles of simultaneously operating distinctive features, this tells us a good deal about linearity and simultaneity as essential properties of pronunciation and recognition in language as a whole. The more universals we can establish the more we shall know about the nature of language as a human activity, and from the point of view of pronunciation this can only come from an increased understanding of *all* the pronunciation features which contribute to meaning in many languages: features of pitch, of stress, of tempo, of tension, etc. about which we know too little to be able with any confidence to draw conclusions of universality. But deeper research in these areas over a wide range of languages will give us the material for decisions about what is and what is not a universal fact of language.

Similarly with typology; it is tempting and perfectly proper to try to classify languages as like or unlike in the matter of their pronunciation on the basis of what we do know – similarity of vowel or consonant systems, of stress or its lack, of tone or non-tone, of syllabic structure, etc. – but again we must realize that until we have more information about many aspects of pronunciation in many languages our typology will be incomplete. That is no reason for not attempting it and subsequently refining the typological framework as more and more information comes in, so bringing increasing order to the bewildering variety which languages exhibit, to make some sense again of the Tower of Babel.

Acoustic phonetics

The techniques which in the past twenty-five years have enabled such wide advances to be made in the understanding of the transmission and recognition of speech sounds will undoubtedly continue to be of outstanding importance in the research field in future. Firmly based on swift and accurate measurement and analysis of the sound wave, speech synthesis through increasingly sophisticated and flexible machines, more and more under computer control, will enable us to test the relevance and relative contribution to recognition of every aspect of the acoustic pattern. This process of testing an analysis by means of synthesis is already well established and can be applied to a much wider range of languages than has hitherto been possible. From it we shall learn not only the cues enabling us to recognize phonemic differences and the relative contribution to recognition of each cue, where most effort has been concentrated so far, but also the acoustic bases of intonation and tone distinctions, of voice-quality differences, of stress and rhythm, and of personal differences. The machines used to display the speech spectrum have hitherto been better adapted to doing this for the adult male voice than for women's and children's voices, and we need to tackle this to establish that the features which are important for recognition in men have equivalent importance for women and children.

From all of this will probably come the complete set of distinctive acoustic features used in all the languages of the world, but even more important in the long run will be the continuing light it sheds on the fundamental processes of sound perception. We already know that the same acoustic stimulus may be given a different linguistic interpretation in different surroundings, as for instance that a fixed vowel quality may be interpreted as /æ/ or /ʌ/ depending on the qualities of other vowels in the same utterance: if the other vowels suggest a Yorkshire speaker the interpretation is /æ/ e.g. in *cap*; if a Cockney speaker, it is taken to represent /ʌ/, so *cup*. It remains to be seen whether this difference can be accounted for in terms of distinctive acoustic features, there being the same *relation* between the features characterizing contrasting vowel qualities in the two accents, or whether something much more complex is going on, involving levels other than the acoustic, and in that case how much we rely on the acoustic features and how much on other factors.

Related to this is the discussion as to whether we perceive speech by reference to acoustic patterns or to articulation. There is some evidence that our perception of speech is more closely related to articulatory events than to acoustic ones; for example, the apparent double locus for /g/ mentioned on p. 118 suggests an acoustic discontinuity which is not at all parallel with the continuous articulatory differences among /g/ allophones conditioned by neighbouring vowels (p. 137). Since we perceive /g/ in all these cases, may we not assume that we do so as a result of our own experience of articulation rather than direct interpretation of the acoustic signals? In other words, before actually interpreting what we hear do we subconsciously relate it to how we would produce it? There does not seem to be any absolute need to accept this idea; the human brain is perfectly capable of interpreting quite different things as the same for functional purposes, but this does not mean that the theory is false. The production and the reception of speech must be quite closely linked; it is hardly possible that they can be completely separate brain functions since they share so much. But it will need a good deal more work in both acoustics and articulation before we are able to say with any certainty whether we have to filter the acoustic signal through our articulatory experience before we can come to a decision as to its linguistic relevance.

Since we cannot at present investigate the contribution of the brain to hearing by direct inspection or experiment we have to rely largely on using the hearer's response to known acoustic stimuli in order to deduce what is going on. This makes it difficult to determine, for instance, just how much of hearing resides in the ear and how much in the brain. We know that the ear is capable of a certain amount of analysis of the incoming signal, but how the results of that analysis are passed to the brain is less well understood, and how the brain operates further on what the ear sends up to it is largely unknown territory. It has been possible to deduce from monaural and binaural experiments that the brain performs an integrating function for different signals arriving at the two ears and being passed largely to the opposite hemispheres of the brain, but that the action of the two hemispheres is to some extent independent for hearing, since a masking noise introduced into one ear must be much more powerful to mask a sound introduced to the other ear, than if the sound to be masked and the masking sound are both at the same ear. The brain's integrating function is also displayed by our ability to judge the direction from which a sound comes by comparing in some way the slightly different signals at the two ears. We shall have to find out much more about the function of the brain and its relation to that of the inner ear by experiments of this kind before we are able to look more directly into the neurophysiological operations of the brain in speech.

Better understanding of all these fundamental processes will bring practical benefits. Once we know how little of the total acoustic signal can be transmitted without unacceptable loss of quality, it should be possible for instance to make more use of a telephone cable either by passing more messages through it at the same time or by improving the quality of what is passed. Telephone speech at present uses a band of frequencies some 3,000 cps wide; if all the requisite information could be packed into a band 300 cps wide by omitting what is not essential, then ten simultaneous messages of comparable quality could be passed through the same cable instead of just one. Another possibility would be the incorporation of an analysis-synthesis system into the telephone link; such systems already exist and consist essentially of an automatic analyser of the speech at one end and a speech synthesizer at the other. If the key features can be identified in the analysis, then information could be passed through to the synthesizer in a simple coded form and the resulting sound at the receiving end would be a reconstruction rather than a transmission of the original. Such systems at present have defects due to the difficulties of automatic analysis: it is not easy to build a machine to give accurate running information on the changing spectrum, but so much has already been done that perfecting analysis-synthesis systems can only be a matter of time.

A speech recognizer, that is a machine of the kind imagined on p. 173, which could reduce an input of ordinary speech to a written text, is almost certainly out of the question for a long time, and if it ever comes it will not be based solely on recognition from acoustic signals. It will need a capacity to store and retrieve and match information on the acoustic and phonological and grammatical and vocabulary levels, at least, which would rival the brain's own capacity for speech. Recognizers have been built which will distinguish on an acoustic basis a small number of items, like the digits 1–9, but only if they are said nice and slowly by one voice – speed up or change the voice and the machine cannot cope. So at the moment the speech recognizer is a dream.

Phonetics and psychiatry

When we laugh or cry we give vocal information about our state of mind. Does our pronunciation give other indications of mental states and could these indications be used diagnostically to identify the presence and nature of mental and other disorders? If so, this would be of very great interest to the psychiatrist, and it is mainly psychiatrists who have hitherto worked on this aspect of speech. Stammering is an obvious example of a vocal indication of emotional disturbance, and it has been claimed that epileptics and stutterers characteristically use an abnormally restricted pitch range in speech, so there obviously are cases where pronunciation can be diagnostic.

To establish a general framework which would be of use in this area, close collaboration between the psychiatrist and the phonetician is essential; there have been notable cases of such collaboration already but much more is needed. The phonetician must be able to provide a classification which will handle not only the linguistically relevant sounds in which he has been primarily interested but also vocal features which have often been considered outside his scope, such as sniffs, grunts, giggles, various kinds of voice interruption, sighs, etc. As a matter of fact, in view of recent work, this does not present great difficulties, but a great deal of analysis will have to be undertaken to make a statistical treatment possible. We need to know what the normal is before we can say anything about the abnormal and it is very unlikely that the phonetic indications of abnormality will often be unique, as they are for the stammerer; it is much more probable that they will consist of features which everyone uses in speech but with different frequency. So we shall need to find out what can be considered normal in, e.g. pitch range or length and frequency of pause or the use of different voice qualities, and this can only be done on a statistical basis, so that it will be necessary to listen to a lot of both normal and abnormal cases before we have enough material to draw reliable conclusions. Such detailed analysis is very time-consuming but the results might be very worthwhile for both partners in the enterprise. The psychiatrist would gain a more precise tool for recognizing and classifying the disturbances he is concerned with (he has after all been using speech for a long time in arriving at his diagnoses, though in an intuitive way); and the phonetician would increase his knowledge of sound features in general and also benefit from detailed statistical information which has often been lacking. We can guess that at least part of our impression of a given speaker's personality is derived from, say, the frequency with which he uses a wide or a narrow pitch range, or a breathy voice quality, but this will remain no more than a guess until it has been placed on a firm statistical footing, or perhaps disproved by the same means.

Phonetics and society

Language is an instrument of society, used for purposes of social cooperation and social intercourse. It must of its nature be tightly linked at many points to the structure of the community in which it operates, and it must therefore be capable to some extent at least of serving as an index of groups and attitudes within that community. So far as pronunciation is concerned, we are aware that it characterizes geographical areas in the form of regional accents and perhaps classes within those areas by modification of the accent, but we really have very little knowledge about even these apparently obvious connections and no general theory to enable us to give a coherent account of the relation between differences of pronunciation and differences of social grouping and social attitudes.

Studies of regional pronunciations have been of two kinds: a survey of differences over a larger or smaller area, and a study of the pronunciation of a particular place as exemplified by the speech of one or a small number of native speakers, usually old, so that the older form of the accent shall not die out unrecorded. The broader survey is liable to concentrate on difference of pronunciation in a necessarily limited number of words and to fail to make it plain whether these differences are systemic or not; the narrow one cannot guarantee that the characteristics it finds are necessarily typical of the place as a whole, with all the speakers of different age groups and social positions that it contains. What we need, therefore, to fill in large gaps in the picture are area surveys designed to study the systems and not merely the realizations found at different places; and at the same time some attempt to characterize in a broader way the situation regarding pronunciation in a particular place.

Urban accents have been largely neglected in favour of rural ones, yet it is surely of interest to know just what the situation is in the cities and towns where the bulk of the population lives, and to know just what amount of variety there is, ranging from the most characteristic form of the accent to very modified forms. And the picture would certainly not be complete without some attempt to relate pronunciations to age and social or economic status, and to note what, if any, changes take place with changes in age and status. By selecting key features of pronunciation both systemic and non-systemic, and following them through the social and age range, we would get a soundly based view of the social implications of accent, which we all know to exist and to be important in British life, perhaps more than elsewhere. Linked with this is the question of accent and prestige: within a particular accent, does one form of pronunciation carry greater prestige than others, and what social factors is this linked to? And more generally what is the attitude of speakers of all social backgrounds and all accents to their own and other accents? Is the prestige of RP declining amongst younger speakers? There is some reason to think so, but all this needs putting on a firm, statistical basis so that we have something more than each individual's impression to go on. And incidentally there is plenty of time for all this work. It is sometimes thought that regional accents are on the point of dying out, of being levelled into one common accent, but this is to misconceive the whole position. Accents change, no doubt, but they do so slowly and they do not necessarily move towards the same centre. The fear – and it generally is a fear rather than a joyous prospect – that local accents are being eliminated usually stems from a belief that RP is likely to take them over through being heard more often than other accents on radio, television and film. There is at present no firm evidence that this is happening or likely to happen, so we can settle down to gathering the sort of evidence which would throw light on the situation, without feeling the hot breath of imminent disappearance on our necks.

A connection has often been made between pronunciation and occupation, but again on a rather impressionistic basis. We are all aware of the existence of something called the 'clerical voice', even if we only hear it in low comedy; the salesman may be characterized as 'a fast talker'; politicians often use the same features of pronunciation, at any rate in their public utterances; barristers similarly. There is certainly something in it, but how much? This is a question which can again only be answered by looking for evidence, and we can be sure that we will *not* find that every single politician or every single barrister has even one feature in common with all his fellows which marks him off from the rest of us. The situation will be much less cut and dried than that and we will need to develop methods which enable us to deal with gradations of occupational marking by pronunciation.

These are questions of social role, but each of us plays a variety of roles and again these differences are often marked by pronunciation. We adapt ourselves to social situations in our manner of speech as well as in our matter; our pronunciation is not the same in a relaxed, friendly conversation as in an interview for a job or in saying prayers or in making a speech. It may be appropriate to pronounce *I don't know* as [ədə'nəʊ] in informal conditions or as [adəʊ'nəʊ] or [aɪ'dəʊnt'nəʊ] or even [aɪ 'duː nɒt 'nəʊ] as formality increases (and notice too that the last pronunciation quoted is much more likely to be heard from an American than a British speaker, which is itself of considerable significance). Stylistic variations of this kind have been commented upon from time to time *ad hoc*, but no systematic investigation has yet been carried out even for one person's speech.

It has also been suggested that the pronunciations of men and women differ within the same accent and the same social group. The reason advanced is that in Britain at any rate women are more sensitive to 'correctness' in speech and that their pronunciation is therefore somewhat different from men's in the direction of what they take to be more desirable. Again there is probably something in this idea, and just how much there is in it could be established by investigation. This has raised the question of correctness in pronunciation, and that is probably the best topic on which to end this book.

Most people, when they talk about pronunciation, talk about it purely in terms of correctness, of what is 'right' and what is 'wrong', what 'good' and what 'bad'. The only kind of question a phonetician ever gets asked by his non-phonetic friends is 'Which is best, /iːðə/ or /aɪðə/?' and this is difficult because the correct (and quite unacceptable) answer is 'It all depends.' In fact, the answer can only be a social one: what is correct depends upon what group you are talking about and what the preponderant pronunciation in that group is. So in most American or N. English groups the pronunciation /iːðə/ for *either* is correct in the sense that it is by far the most common one. In RP on the other hand /aɪðə/ is correct for the same reason. It is this social form of correctness which is operating when people change their pronunciation according to their environment, why a Yorkshireman who comes South starts to pronounce *glass* as /glɑːs/ instead of /glæs/ or an Englishman in the United States may pronounce *fertile* to rhyme with *turtle* or *lever* to rhyme with *never*. It is a process of adaptation to or identification with a particular social group and it seems clear that some people adapt more quickly and more completely than others in pronunciation, and no doubt in other linguistic and extra-linguistic ways. It would be very interesting if we could work out an adaptability scale, ranging in theory from total independence from environment at one end to complete adaptation at the other; if we were then able to relate an individual's adaptability quotient for pronunciation to other factors such as personality traits or social attitudes it might provide a useful tool for investigating such matters.

Before we dismiss the notion of correctness as purely an aspect of social adaptation we must take into account that when someone asks 'Is this or that correct?' he usually has at the back of his mind the idea of prestige. One pronunciation carries more kudos with it than another, and there may be a certain amount of one-upmanship involved in using, say, the pronunciation /aɪðə/ for *either* in a group where it is predominantly /iːðə/. The disentangling of these two strands, adaptation and prestige, in the idea of correctness, presents a complicated problem, and solving it would require the cooperation of the phonetician, the psychologist and the sociologist, but if it were solved we should understand more deeply the way in which not only pronunciation but language as a whole is used and the way in which its users regard it. Britain provides a particularly rich field for this kind of research because pronunciation and social class are intimately linked. It is often said that in, for example, Germany or indeed the United States, very much less prestige attaches to one or several types of pronunciation, and that a speaker is not placeable socially by his pronunciation to the same extent as in Britain. Before this can be stated definitely we will have to undertake the same sort of research in other countries to elicit typical patterns of attitude and of relations between accent and social groups.

From the point of view of social justice it is very sad that one pronunciation should confer social advantage or prestige and that another should bear a stigma. It would be much more equitable if we could all pronounce in our native way with no feelings of guilt or smugness, of underdog or overdog. However, language does not itself shape society, rather the reverse, and in language, particularly in pronunciation and the attitudes it evokes, we may see a faithful reflection of the society in which we live. If it is true, as we surmised earlier, that younger speakers pay less attention to correctness and prestige in pronunciation this may well be a sign, and a welcome one, of change in our social attitudes.

Further Reading

Chapter 1

For other reviews of the part played by sound in language see:

Bloch, B. and Trager, G. L., *Outline of Linguistic Analysis*, Baltimore: Waverley Press, 1942

Bloomfield, L., *Language*, London: Allen & Unwin; New York: Holt, Rinehart & Winston, 1935 (Chapter 2)

Chomsky, N. and Halle, M., *The Sound Pattern of English*, New York: Harper & Row, 1968 (Chapter 1)

Firth, J. R., Introduction to *Studies in Linguistic Analysis*, Oxford: Blackwell, 1957

Halliday, M. A. K., McIntosh, A. and Strevens, P. D., *The Linguistic Sciences and Language Teaching*, London: Longmans, 1964 (Chapter 3)

Sapir, E., *Language: An Introduction to the Study of Speech*, New York: Harcourt, Brace & World, 1921 (Chapters 1 and 3)

Chapter 2

More detail on the vocal organs and their functioning can be found in G. W. Gray and C. M. Wise, *The Bases of Speech*, New York: Harper & Row, 1959 (Chapter 3); K. L. Pike, *Phonetics, A Critical Analysis of Phonetic Theory and a Technique for the Practical Description of Sounds*, Michigan University Press, 1943, is excellent on the theory of sound production and description. D. Abercrombie, *Elements of General Phonetics*, Edinburgh University Press; Chicago: Aldine, 1967 (Chapters 2, 3 and 4) gives a good account of how speech sounds are produced. See also *The Principles of the International Phonetic Association*, London: International Phonetic Association, 1949, for phonetic symbols and specimens of phonetic transcription, and Abercrombie (op.

cit., Chapter 7) for a good discussion of impressionistic and systematic notation.

Chapter 3

A very helpful introduction to the acoustics of speech is P. B. Denes and E. N. Pinson, *The Speech Chain*, New York: Bell Telephone Laboratories, 1963. So too is P. Ladefoged, *Elements of Acoustic Phonetics*, Edinburgh University Press; Chicago University Press, 1962. A more detailed treatment is M. Joos, *Acoustic Phonetics*, Baltimore: Linguistic Society of America, 1948. For the locus theory of consonant transitions, see A. M. Liberman, P. Delattre and F. S. Cooper, 'The Role of Selected Stimulus-Variables in the Perception of the Unvoiced Stop Consonants', *American Journal of Psychology 65*, 1952. See also Chapter 8 of *Manual of Phonetics* (ed. B. Malmberg), Amsterdam: Mouton, 1968, 'Analysis and Synthesis of Speech Processes' by G. Fant for discussion of this and other topics, a useful collection of spectrographic reference material, and relations between production features and acoustic patterns.

Chapter 4

Denes and Pinson (cited under Chapter 3 above) give a good simple account of the ear's functioning. The standard work on hearing is H. Fletcher, *Speech and Hearing in Communication*, New York: Van Nostrand; London: Macmillan, 1953. For the Cardinal Vowel system see D. Jones, *Outline of English Phonetics*, Cambridge: Heffer, 1956 (Chapter 8). On pitch, loudness, length and their acoustic correlates, see D. B. Fry, 'Prosodic Phenomena', Chapter 12 of *Manual of Phonetics* (see Chapter 3 above). The articulatory theory of hearing is presented in A. M. Liberman and others: 'A Motor Theory of Speech Perception', *Proceedings of the Speech Communication Seminar*, Stockholm, 1963, and discussed by Fant in the chapter above (under Chapter 3).

Chapter 5

On the sounds of English see the reference above (Chapter 4) to D. Jones, and particularly A. C. Gimson, *An Introduction to the Pronunciation of English*, London: Arnold, 1962. Also E. Kolb, *Phonological Atlas of the Northern Region*, Bern: Francke, 1966, for certain regional variants, and similarly the continuing publication of the Survey of English Dialects, Leeds: Leeds University, Arnold, 1962 and following.

Chapter 6

On phonemes see D. Jones, *The Phoneme: Its Nature and Use*, Cambridge: Heffer, 1962, and Bloomfield's *Language*, Chapters 5, 6 and 7 (details under Chapter 1 above). K. L. Pike, *Phonemics: A Technique for Reducing Languages to Writing*, University of Michigan Press, 1947, gives an operational view of the phoneme. On linguistic aspects of pitch, loudness and length see the reference to Fry under Chapter 4 above. On distinctive features see Chapter 13, 'Phonology in Relation to Phonetics', by R. Jakobson and M. Halle in *Manual of Phonetics* (Chapter 3 above) and particularly Chapter 7 of Chomsky and Halle, *The Sound Pattern of English* (Chapter 1 above). For an American analysis of English vowels see H. A. Gleason, *An Introduction to Descriptive Linguistics*, New York: Holt, Rinehart & Winston, 1961. The view that the phoneme is an unnecessary complication can be found in Section 4 of N. Chomsky, *Topics in the Theory of Generative Grammar*, The Hague: Mouton, 1966.

Chapter 7

Two excellent accounts of phoneme systems are in N. S. Trubetzkoy, *Principles of Phonology*, University of California Press, 1969 and C. F. Hockett, *A Manual of Phonology*, Indiana University Press, 1955. On tonal systems see K. L. Pike, *Tone Languages*, Michigan University Press, 1958. On intonation and related phenomena see particularly the fine account given in D. Crystal, *Prosodic Systems and Intonation in English*, New York and London: Cambridge University Press, 1969.

Chapter 8

On assimilation and elision see Gimson, Chapter 11 and Abercrombie, Chapter 8 (references in Chapters 5 and 2 above). Tonal assimilation is treated in Pike's *Tone Languages*, Chapter 11 (see Chapter 7 above). For juncture see I. Lehiste, *Acoustic-Phonetic Study of Internal Open Juncture*, Michigan University Press, 1959. On the relation of intonation to grammar and meaning in general see Crystal, Chapters 6 and 7 (Chapter 7 above).

List of Works Consulted

Abercrombie, D. *Problems and Principles*, London: Longmans, 1956

'Syllable quantity and enclitics in English', in *In Honour of Daniel Jones*, ed. D. Abercrombie *et al.*, London: Longmans, 1964, pp. 216–22

'A phonetician's view of verse', *Linguistics 6*, pp. 5–13

Elements of General Phonetics, Edinburgh University Press; Chicago: Aldine, 1967

Armstrong, L. E. *The Phonetics of French*, London: G. Bell & Sons, 1932

The Phonetic and Tonal Structure of Kikuyu, Oxford University Press, 1940

and Pe Maung Tin. *A Burmese Phonetic Reader*, University of London Press, 1925

Baldwin, J. R. *Alternative Analyses of the Structure of Consonant Clusters in Modern Russian, and Their Implications for Phonological Transcription*, London University M.A. thesis, 1966 (unpublished)

Beach, D. M. *The Phonetics of the Hottentot Language*, Cambridge: Heffer, 1938

Berry, J. *The Pronunciation of Ewe*, Cambridge: Heffer, 1951

The Pronunciation of Ga, Cambridge: Heffer, 1951

Bloch, B. 'Studies in colloquial Japanese, II: syntax', *Language 22*, pp. 200–48

and Trager, G. L. *Outline of Linguistic Analysis*, Special Publication of the Linguistic Society of America, Baltimore, 1942

Bloomfield, L. *Language*, New York: Holt, Rinehart & Winston, 1933; London: Allen & Unwin, 1935

Bolinger, D. L. 'Intonation – levels v. configurations', *Word 5*, pp. 248–54

'Intersections of stress and intonation', *Word 11*, pp. 195–203

Boyanus, S. C. *A Manual of Russian Pronunciation*, 3rd ed., London: Lund Humphries, 1946

Catford, J. C. 'Vowel systems of Scots dialects', *Transactions of the Philological Society*, 1957, pp. 107–17

  'Phonation types: the classification of some laryngeal components of speech production', in *In Honour of Daniel Jones*, ed. D. Abercrombie *et al.*, London: Longmans, 1964, pp. 26–37

  'The articulatory possibilities of man', in *Manual of Phonetics*, ed. B. Malmberg, Amsterdam: North Holland Publishing Co., 1968, pp. 309–33

Chomsky, N. *Topics in the Theory of Generative Grammar*, The Hague: Mouton, 1966

  and Halle, M. *The Sound Pattern of English*, New York: Harper & Row, 1968

Classe, A. *The Rhythm of English Prose*, Oxford University Press, 1939

Coustenoble, H. N. *La Phonétique du provençal moderne en terre d'Arles*, Hertford: Stephen Austin, 1945

  and Armstrong, L. E. *Studies in French Intonation*, Cambridge: G. Bell & Sons, 1934

Crosby, K. H. and Ward, I. C. *An Introduction to the Study of Mende*, Cambridge: Heffer, 1944

Crystal, D. *Prosodic Systems and Intonation in English*, Cambridge University Press, 1969

Delattre, P. C. *Comparing the Phonetic Features of English, French, German and Spanish*, London: Harrap, 1965

  and Liberman, A. M. and Cooper, F. S. 'Acoustic loci and transitional cues for consonants', *Journal of the Acoustical Society of America*, 27, pp. 769–73

Denes, P. B. 'The effect of duration on the perception of voicing', *Journal of the Acoustical Society of America* 27, pp. 761–4

  and Pinson, E. N. *The Speech Chain*, New York: Bell Telephone Laboratories, 1963

Ewing, I. R. and A. W. G. *Speech and the Deaf Child*, Manchester University Press, 1954

Fant, G. *Acoustic theory of speech production*, The Hague: Mouton, 1960

'Analysis and synthesis of speech processes', in *Manual of Phonetics*, ed. B. Malmberg, Amsterdam: North Holland Publishing Co., 1968, pp. 173–277

Fischer-Jörgensen, E. 'Acoustic analysis of stop consonants', in *Miscellanea Phonetica*, 2, London: I.P.A., 1954, pp. 42–59

Fletcher, H. *Speech and Hearing in Communication*, New York: Van Nostrand; London: Macmillan, 1953

Fry, D. B. 'Duration and intensity as physical correlates of linguistic stress', *Journal of the Acoustical Society of America*, 27, pp. 765–8

'Prodosic phenomena', in *Manual of Phonetics*, ed. B. Malmberg, Amsterdam: North Holland Publishing Co., 1968, pp. 365–410

Gairdner, W. H. T. *The Phonetics of Arabic*, Oxford University Press, 1924

Gimson, A. C. *An Introduction to the Pronunciation of English*, London: Arnold, 1962

Gleason, H. A., Jr. *An Introduction to Descriptive Linguistics*, 2nd revised ed., New York: Holt, Rinehart & Winston, 1961

Gray, G. W. and Wise, C. M. *The Bases of Speech*, 3rd ed., New York: Harper & Row, 1959

Halle, M. *The Sound Pattern of Russian*, The Hague: Mouton, 1959

Hughes, G. W. and Radler, J. P. A. 'Acoustic properties of stop consonants', *Journal of the Acoustical Society of America*, 29, pp. 107–16

Halliday, M. A. K. 'The tones of English', *Archivum Linguisticum*, 15, pp. 1–28

'Intonation in English grammar', in *Transactions of the Philological Society, 1964*, pp. 143–69

MacIntosh, A. and Strevens, P. D. *The Linguistic Sciences and Language Teaching*, London: Longmans, 1964

Heffner, R. M. S. *General Phonetics*, University of Wisconsin Press, 1960

Hockett, C. F. *A Manual of Phonology*, Indiana University Press, 1955

A Course in Modern Linguistics, New York: Macmillan, 1958

Honikman, B. 'Articulatory settings', in *In Honour of Daniel Jones*, ed. D. Abercrombie *et al.*, London: Longmans, 1964, pp. 73–84

Hughes, G. W. and Halle, M. 'Spectral properties of fricative consonants', *Journal of the Acoustical Society of America*, 28, pp.
303–10

International Phonetic Association, The Principles of the, University
College London, 1949

Jakobson, R. *Child Language, Aphasia and Phonological Universals*,
The Hague: Mouton, 1968

and Halle, M. 'Phonology in relation to phonetics', in *Manual of
Phonetics*, ed. B. Malmberg, Amsterdam: North Holland Publishing Co., 1968, pp. 411–49

Fant, G. and Halle, M. *Preliminaries to Speech Analysis*, 2nd ed.,
Cambridge, Mass; M.I.T. Press, 1952

Jassem, W. *The Intonation of Conversational English*, Warsaw, 1952
'Stress in modern English', in *Bulletin of the Polish Linguistic
Society*, 11, pp. 21–49

Jespersen, O. *Modersmålets Phonetik*, 3rd ed., Copenhagen: Munks-
gaard, 1934

Jones, D. *The Tones of Sechuana Nouns* (International Institute of
African Languages and Cultures, Memorandum VI), London, 1928

An Outline of English Phonetics, 8th ed., Cambridge: Heffer, 1956

The Pronunciation of English, 4th ed., Cambridge University Press,
1956

The Phoneme; Its Nature and Use, 2nd ed., Cambridge: Heffer, 1962

and Ward, D. *The Phonetics of Russian*, Cambridge University Press,
1969

Jones, S. *A Welsh Phonetic Reader*, University of London Press, 1926

Joos, M. *Acoustic Phonetics* (Language monograph no. 23), Baltimore:
Linguistic Society of America, 1948

Karlgren, B. *Sound and Symbol in Chinese*, Oxford University Press,
1923

Kenyon, J. S. *American Pronunciation*, 10th ed., University of
Michigan Press, 1950

Kingdon, R. *Groundwork of English Intonation*, London: Longmans,
1958

Kolb, E. *Phonological Atlas of the Northern Region*, Bern: Francke, 1966

Kurath, H. and McDavid, R. I. Jr. *The Pronunciation of English in the
Atlantic States*, University of Michigan Press, 1961

Ladefoged, P. *Elements of Acoustic Phonetics*, University of Chicago Press, University of Edinburgh Press, 1962

  A Phonetic Study of West African Languages , Cambridge University Press, 1968

  Draper, M. H. and Whitteridge, D. 'Syllables and stress', in *Miscellanea Phonetica III*, London: International Phonetic Association, 1958, pp. 1–14

Langacker, R. W. *Language and Its Structure*, New York: Harcourt, Brace & World, 1967

Le–Van–Ly, M. *Le Parler vietnamien*, Paris: Huong Ahn, 1948

Lee, W. R. *An English Intonation Reader*, London: Macmillan, 1960

Lehiste, I. *Acoustic-phonetic Study of Internal Open Juncture*, Ann Arbor: University of Michigan Press, 1959

Liberman, A. M. 'Some results of research on speech perception', *Journal of the Acoustical Society of America*, 29, pp. 117–23

  Delattre, P. C. and Gerstman, L. J. 'The role of selected stimulus-variables in the perception of unvoiced stop consonants', *American Journal of Psychology*, 65, pp. 497–516

  Delattre, P. C., Cooper, F. S. and Gerstman, L. J. 'The role of consonant-vowel transitions in the perception of the stop and nasal consonants', *Psychological Monographs no. 379*, 1954

  Cooper, F. S., Harris, K. S. and Macneilage, P. F. 'A motor theory of speech perception', in *Proceedings of the Speech Communication Seminar*, Vol. II, Stockholm, 1963

Lieberman, P. *Intonation, Perception and Language*, Massachusetts Institute of Technology Press, 1967

Luchsinger, R. and Arnold, G. E. *Voice – Speech – Language*, London: Constable, 1956

Malmberg, B. *Phonetics*, London: Constable, 1963

Martens, C. and P. *Phonetik der deutschen Sprache*, Munich: Max Hueber, 1961

Martinet, A. *La Phonologie du mot en danois*, Paris: Klincksieck, 1937

Meinhof, C. and von Warmelo, N. J. *Introduction to the Phonology of the Bantu Languages*, Berlin: Reimer, Vohsen, 1932

Mitchell, T. F. *An Introduction to Egyptian Colloquial Arabic*, Oxford University Press, 1956

Moulton, W. G. *The Sounds of English and German*, University of Chicago Press, 1962

Obrecht, D. H. *Effects of the 2nd formant on the perception of velarization consonants in Arabic*, The Hague: Mouton, 1968

O'Connor, J. D. and Trim, J. L. M. 'Vowel, consonant and syllable – a phonological definition', *Word*, 9, pp. 103–22

and Arnold, G. F. *Intonation of Colloquial English*, London: Longmans, 1961

Palmer, H. E. *English Intonation with Systematic Exercises*, Cambridge: Heffer 1922

Patniowska, M. *Essentials of Polish Grammar*, Glasgow: Ksiaznica Polska, 1944

Peterson, G. E. 'The speech communication process', in *Manual of Phonetics*, ed. B. Malmberg, Amsterdam: North Holland Publishing Co., 1968, pp.155–72

Pike, K. L. *Phonetics: a Critical Analysis of Phonetic Theory and a Technique for the Practical Description of Sounds*, University of Michigan Press, 1944

The Intonation of American English, University of Michigan Press, 1945

Tone Languages: a Technique for Determining the Number of Pitch Contrasts in a Language, with Studies in Tonemic Substitution and Fusion, University of Michigan Press, 1948

Potter, R. K., Kopp, G. A. and Green, H. C. *Visible Speech*, New York: Van Nostrand, 1947

Pring, J. T. *A Grammar of Modern Greek*, University of London Press, 1950.

Pulgram, E. *Introduction to the Spectrography of Speech*, The Hague: Mouton, 1959

Samareh, Y. *The Phonological Structure of Syllable and Word in Tehrani Persian*, London University Ph.D. thesis (unpublished)

Sapir, E. *Language; an Introduction to the Study of Speech*, New York: Harcourt, Brace & World, 1921

Schubiger, M. *The Role of Intonation in Spoken English*, Cambridge: Heffer, 1935

English Intonation, its Form and Function, Tübingen: Niemeyer, 1958

Scott, N. C. 'A study in the phonetics of Fijian', *Bulletin of the School of Oriental and African Studies, XII*, pp. 737–52

Sharp, A. E. 'The analysis of stress and juncture in English', *Transactions of the Philological Society*, 1960, pp. 104–35

Sigurd, B. *Phonotactic structures in Swedish*, London: Lund Humphries, 1965

'Phonotactic aspects of the linguistic expression', in *Manual of Phonetics*, ed. B. Malmberg, Amsterdam: North Holland Publishing Co., 1968, pp. 450–63

Sivertsen, E. *Cockney Phonology*, Oslo University Press, 1960

Smith, S. *Stödet i dansk Rigssprog*, Copenhagen: Kaifer, 1944

Stetson, R. H. *Motor Phonetics*, 2nd ed., Amsterdam: Nijhoff, 1951

Strevens, P. D. 'Spectra of fricative noise in human speech', *Language and Speech, 3*, pp. 32–49

Studies in Linguistic Analysis (Special volume of the Philological Society), Oxford: Blackwell, 1957

Survey of English Dialects. Leeds: Arnold, 1962

Introduction, H. Orton, 1962

The basic material:

1. *The six Northern counties and the Isle of Man*. Eds. H. Orton and W. J. Halliday, Part 1, 1962

2. *The West Midland Counties*. Eds. H. Orton and M. V. Barry. Part 1, 1969

3. *The East Midland Counties and East Anglia*. Eds. H. Orton and P. Tilling, Part 1, 1969

4. *The Southern Counties*. Eds. H. Orton and M. F. Wakelin, Part 1, 1967, Part 3, 1968

Thalbitzer, W. *A Phonetical Study of the Eskimo Language*, Copenhagen, 1904

Tomás, T. N. *Manual de pronunciación española*, 3rd ed., Madrid: Hernando, 1926

Trim, J. L. M. 'Major and minor tone-groups in English', *Maître Phonetique, 112*, pp. 26–9

'Tonetic stress marks for German', in *In Honour of Daniel Jones*, ed. D. Abercrombie *et al.*, London: Longmans, 1964, pp. 374–83

Trubetzkoy, N. S. *Principles of Phonology*, transl. C. A. M. Baltaxe, University of California Press, 1969

Tucker, A. N. *The Comparative Phonetics of the Suto-Chuana Group of Bantu Languages*, London, 1929

Uldall, E. T. 'Dimensions of meaning in intonation', in *In Honour of Daniel Jones*, ed. D. Abercrombie *et al.*, London: Longmans, 1964, pp. 271–9

Uldall, H. J. *A Danish Phonetic Reader*, University of London Press, 1933

Van Riper, C. and Irwin, J. V. *Voice and Articulation*, Englewood Cliffs, N. J.: Prentice Hall, 1958

Ward, I. C. *The Phonetic and Tonal Structure of Efik*, Cambridge: Heffer, 1933

   An Introduction to the Ibo Language, Cambridge: Heffer, 1936

   The Phonetics of English, 4th ed., Cambridge: Heffer, 1948

Westerman, D. and Ward, I. C. *Practical Phonetics for Students of West African Languages*, Oxford University Press, 1933

Wiik, K. *Finnish and English Vowels*, Turku, 1965

Žinkin, N. I. *Mechanisms of Speech*, The Hague: Mouton, 1968

Index